1001 ways to be a
better gardener

1001 ways to be a
better gardener

Pippa Greenwood

MITCHELL BEAZLEY

1001 ways to be a better gardener

Pippa Greenwood

First published in Great Britain in 2008
by Mitchell Beazley, an imprint of
Octopus Publishing Group Limited,
2–4 Heron Quays, London E14 4JP.
An Hachette Livre UK Company

www.octopusbooks.co.uk

ISBN 978 1 84533 367 6

A CIP catalogue record for this book is available from
the British Library.

Set in Grotesque

Colour reproduction in Singapore by Bright Arts Ltd.
Printed and bound in China by Toppan Printing Company Ltd.

Commissioning Editor: Helen Griffin
Art Director: Tim Foster
Art Editor: Victoria Burley
Project Editor: Ruth Patrick
Copy Editor: Candida Frith-Macdonald
Special Photography: Torie Chugg
Picture Research: Mel Watson
Picture Research Manager: Giulia Hetherington
Production Manager: Peter Hunt

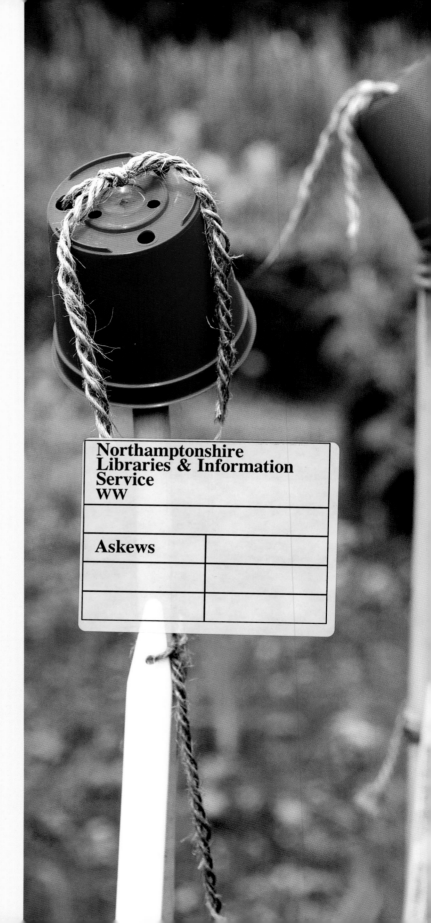

Contents

Foreword

There is nothing like a garden to bring enjoyment, and to allow you to relax and feel pride and fulfilment in your achievements. The combination of fresh air, beautiful plants, and some gentle or sometimes not quite so gentle exercise is enough to bring a smile to your face. Grow some vegetables, fruit, and herbs then you too can enjoy that further feeling of satisfaction and happiness that a garden can bring.

Gardening has the potential to be all these wonderful things, but throw in too many hiccups, and the positive benefits run the risk of being outweighed by the problems. Gardening is like any hobby and passion; it is not always straightforward. Whether you are new to gardening or have gardened for years, there are still things that you can learn. That goes for each and every one of us, including those of us who earn a living by broadcasting, lecturing, and writing about gardening! If you can learn from other peoples' experiences and know-how, you can get some useful advice on making gardening easier, quicker, and of course, more successful.

In *1001 Ways to be a Better Gardener*, I hope you will find plenty to interest and inspire you, and hopefully also to feel the truly infectious nature of gardening encourage you to try new things. There is nothing like talking to other gardeners about the problems they have taken on, their successes and failures, and the hints and tips they have to offer. This book is packed full of tips I would like to pass on to you, as other gardeners have passed their observations on to me. Have fun!

Introduction

If you have just started tackling your garden, there are bound to be a whole host of questions and queries, problems, and even minor panics that crop up as you go about your gardening.

If you are an old, experienced hand at gardening then there are still likely to be things you are tackling for the first time or perhaps simply things that you could do more efficiently or more successfully.

1001 Ways to be a Better Gardener should prove useful and interesting if you have a love (even if it is still in the bud stage) for your garden and you want to take on more and more different aspects of gardening. If you are also keen to find easier, quicker, greener, or less expensive ways to perform any aspect of gardening without having to compromise the end result, then this is the book for you.

It is not a chapter and verse tome which contains an encyclopedic-style reference to every aspect of gardening and every plant, but by having a read of the relevant section in the appropriate chapter you will find suggestions to help you on your way to a better-looking garden, fewer problems, and, perhaps most importantly, a garden that really starts to take its hold over you and provides you with more and more fun.

To me, that is what it should be about, as a garden may need some thought and quite a lot of time to be spent on it, but it should also provide you with a perfect surround to your home, and if you wish, a plentiful supply of fresh home-grown vegetables and fruit… and a constant supply

of really invigorating, muscle-toning exercise, much better for you than the sweat-filled atmosphere of most gyms and fitness centres!

Each chapter covers either a different aspect of gardening or the garden itself, so it should be easy to find the information you need before you take on any new area of your garden, or any unfamiliar garden task. If you have taken on a new garden and hope to alter it dramatically or construct it from scratch then there are also some tips and suggestions for making that initial planning and decision-making process a little easier. For those who have only just been bitten by the gardening bug, there are chapters on just about every aspect of your garden and its contents – including furniture and patios, fresh-grown food, and pumps for your pond.

You will also find top ten style lists for specific plant recommendations to help you to select the plants that will do best in the situation you have to offer. There is no need to regard these as the only plants worth having, but they are my recommendations for each particular situation. Similar lists for specific gardening techniques such as various propagation techniques are also included as a guide.

Whatever your knowledge of gardening and whatever the style of your garden (or the garden you aspire to) you will always find parts of it more fun and easier to look after than others. With the aid of this book, you will start to find those less-appealing parts of your plot and your regime less of a challenge and more of a pleasure.

Getting started

Perhaps you have just taken on a new garden, become a garden owner for the first time, or found yourself with a garden that's different in its opportunities and conditions than any you have managed before. Maybe you find yourself needing some "inside information". Have you finally decided to get to grips with the garden that's been lurking outside your back door for the last few years? You know it well, but sorting it out and getting it into shape is also likely to make you feel as if you need some support. Whatever your starting point, you can save yourself a lot of time and effort if you take charge from the beginning.

Taming a new garden
A new garden should be something that gives you a lot of pleasure, but it can also be hard work. There may be moments when you wonder who is in charge, and indeed if you will ever manage to take control. With a bit of forward planning and plenty of thought along

the way, you can make your initial attack a meaningful one, and pave the way for plenty of great things in the future.

Start by getting to know all your garden's advantages, tricky bits, and problem areas. It's like getting to know someone – you need a while to work out what they are like. Next, arm yourself with some great tools. Finally, give yourself lots of time to work and play in the garden, and use it as a place to relax and feel at home. It's all yours!

This chapter shows you how to:

❀ Exploit your garden's areas of sun and shade and its level changes.

❀ Find your soil's pH and texture, and discover local plants that will thrive.

❀ Discover how to improve your soil.

❀ Get equipped with the tools you need.

❀ Make some instant transformations.

❀ Assess fences and structures.

Assessing your garden

It is essential that you take a long, hard look at your garden, ideally in all weathers and at various times of year. Once you have formed an accurate picture of all it has to offer, you will be much better equipped to make the right choices and decisions later on.

Apparently empty areas may contain dormant bulbs.

Don't rush

❀ The age-old suggestion that when you move into a new garden you should wait for a full year before you do anything makes a lot of sense. A full four seasons allows time for everything hidden to appear: for bulbs and herbaceous plants to emerge, and for the uninspiring shrub in the corner to show you just how great it looks when the time of year is right for its display of blooms, autumn foliage colour, or stunning berries.

❀ While you give the garden time to reveal its treasures, make sure that you do keep on top of the weeding – this is something that definitely won't get better if left. Make sure all weeds are cleared, cut back, or dug out before they have a chance to set seed.

Consider any slope

There are advantages and disadvantages to having a garden on a slope. You will get more benefits and fewer problems from a slope if you deal with it carefully, rather than just pretending that it is not there, so try and determine the change in level and build it in to any rough plans you make.

Shade from buildings and trees

It is essential that you are fully aware of any harder-to-fill areas, and exactly how shady the shaded places are. Shade cast by nearby buildings, high hedges, or trees will influence what grows well and what looks miserable, so check how far the shade is cast, and how dense it is: some trees cast very dense shade, others more dappled.

Timber terraces

If you go for timber retaining walls on terraces, choose wood that's certified from a renewable source by the Forestry Stewardship Council (FSC). Check that softwood is pressure-treated to prolong its life.

Changing a slope

Terraces are one traditional way of gardening on a slope, although you will need to do a lot of earth-moving and build a series of retaining walls to keep the soil in place on each level. The initial input of time, money, and effort will be high, but terracing should make maintaining the garden a lot quicker and easier later on.

Living with a slope

If you are going to retain a steep slope, access to plants is likely to be difficult and maintaining them very time consuming. Make sure you choose plants that do not need a lot of maintenance. Ground cover plants will also help cover the soil surface rapidly, and so reduce the need for weeding.

Keeping soil in place on a slope

If the soil on a slope has been disturbed, perhaps as a result of extensive weeding or planting activities, it will be easily washed off during heavy rain. Covering the area with plenty of plants will help, but initially laying a woven, weed-suppressing fabric or netting on the soil surface will help to keep the soil where it needs to be, at least until the plants' roots spread. A thick layer of mulch helps to disguise ugly netting, fabric, or mesh, and benefits the plants (see page 19).

The damp and often shady conditions at the base of a slope will be perfect for hostas.

Watch the sunshine

Find out the aspect of your garden and the approximate amount of sun that each area receives at various times of day, and as the seasons change. Make notes or sketch the sunny and shaded areas on a rough plan of the garden, ideally grading them to indicate the depth of the shade and how long it lasts. This will make it easier to remember what you saw.

Meadow annuals need your sunniest spot.

Planting at the foot of a slope

The area at the base of a slope tends to become wet, especially during the autumn and winter months and if a large part of the garden is sloping. You can create a good-looking scheme and help remove some of the water by choosing moisture-loving plants for this area, such as hostas, astilbes, or shrubby dogwoods (Cornus).

Get help with trees

If you're concerned about the health, safety, or even simply the effect a large tree is having on your garden, employ a reputable tree surgeon to look at the tree in situ and advise you what the options are. It may be possible to reduce shading by crown reduction (reducing the size of the tree's crown or branch structure), crown lifting (removing some of the lowermost branches), or crown thinning (thinning out the crown or branch structure).

A tree's impact zone

Trees have a big influence on the soil beneath them, often making it very dry, especially during late spring and summer. Mark out the approximate area affected by tree roots – as a rough guide, the roots spread to 1m (3ft) or so past the outermost spread of the branches.

Understanding your soil

Before you even begin to think about designing new planting schemes, you need to find out what kind of soil you have as this will determine the plants that will thrive. You need to know your soil's acidity and texture, and then take advantage of what you've got.

Soil pH

The pH of the soil describes its acidity or alkalinity, so it's important that you know what your soil pH is. It will be one of the factors that determines which plants do well, which just about cope, and which look positively miserable.

Get testing

❀ It is worth buying an inexpensive soil pH-testing kit so that you can be sure exactly what the pH is, and find any variations within your garden. They are easy to use, so don't be put off at the thought of going scientific.

Be nosey

One good way to work out roughly what sort of soil you have is to take a good look over the neighbours' fences. There may be some local variations in soil conditions, but the soil type should be generally similar, so if you neighbour grows lime-hating plants which all look great, there's a good chance that the soil is acidic. Make a note of what is struggling to survive, and what is looking good.

If it grows next door, it will grow for you.

Mix the indicator, soil, and water.

❀ If you have a large garden, a small, electronic kit may be best. It will allow you to do as many tests as you need, repeating them after treatment if necessary.

❀ Make sure that you test the soil itself, not a mulch or matter that has been dug into the soil. Scrape off the mulch and check soil from a few centimetres below the surface.

❀ Do several tests, even in a small garden. There may be localized areas of alkalinity – perhaps due to the liming of a vegetable plot, weathering of concrete and mortar, or buried builders' rubble.

Take advantage of what you have

It is always better to try to work with what is there and improve it than to make dramatic changes. If you have an alkaline soil, for example, acid-loving plants will simply not thrive, often showing severe nutrient deficiency symptoms.

The colour shows the pH of the soil.

❀ If pH test results are given numerically, remember that pH7 is neutral: lower figures are acidic, and higher figures are alkaline. Remember that the smaller numbers relate to the shorter word (ie. acid) – hardly scientific, but it works.

Soil texture

Texture has a huge impact on how soil performs because this determines how well it retains moisture and nutrients. Sandy soils lose both quickly, but warm up fast in spring; clay soils are moist and fertile, but stay cold for longer over winter.

Handling the soil will tell you a lot about its potential.

Assessing soil texture

Finding the texture of your soil needs no more equipment than your bare hands. When the soil is moist, but not wet, take a handful and squeeze it: very sandy soils will not hold together, clay soils will form a solid, sticky lump, often leaving a considerable residue on your hand, and loamy soils will form a ball that crumbles if pressed.

If you really want rhododendrons and don't have acid soil, raised beds may be the only answer.

Raising the soil pH

If your soil is acidic or neutral, then you can often raise the pH significantly by using lime, or by mulching with and incorporating alkaline matter, such as mushroom compost.

Reducing the soil pH

❀ Making the soil less alkaline is not easy, but you can try using powdered sulphur. Incorporating and mulching with acidic matter, such as composted bracken, will have some effect too.

❀ In many cases, the pH will not stay at the desired and adequately low level for lime-hating or acid-loving plants, so it may be better to create a large, raised bed and fill it with imported acidic soil. You should then be able to grow these plants much more successfully and with less effort over the coming years.

Plants that indicate acidic soil

1 *Calluna*
2 *Camellia*
3 *Daboecia*
4 *Enkianthus*
5 *Eucryphia*
6 *Fothergilla*
7 *Gaultheria*
8 *Hamamelis*
9 *Kalmia*
10 *Lithodora*
11 *Magnolia*
12 *Rhododendron*
13 *Vaccinium*

Most magnolias do well in slightly acidic soil.

17

Improving your soil

Once you have discovered what kind of soil you have in your garden, you want your plants to have the best possible chance, and the easiest way to start helping them is through the soil. There are many ways that you can give your soil a boost.

Organic matter helps to improve the texture of all soils.

Digging in organic matter

Both light and heavy soils will benefit from organic matter. It helps to improve aeration in a heavy, clay-type soil and to improve moisture retention in a light, sandy one. You cannot really add too much, so get digging and see how it helps.

Improving drainage and aeration

Horticultural grit or gravel is extremely useful on a heavy soil, helping to improve drainage and aeration. Purchasing grit will be a lot less expensive if you buy in bulk, as opposed to the dinky bags you find in garden centres, but you must get horticultural grade grit; many of the similar materials used by builders contain salts or other contaminants, which can seriously damage plants and soils. To have the desired effect, you need to fork in grit to a depth of at least 30cm (12in).

Improve the soil before you plant

It is far easier to incorporate organic matter into an empty piece of ground, rather than trying to work it in around plant roots. Adding plenty as a mulch on the soil surface around established plants will help, since earthworms and other creatures will gradually do the work for you. Mulches should always go onto a moist soil; they help to lock moisture in the soil.

Avoid squashing down wet soil

When working on heavy soil, always try to wait until it is not too wet, otherwise you may do more damage by compacting the already heavy, airless texture. If you have to work when conditions are not ideal, lay planks or boards over the soil surface. This provides a surface on which you can stand and helps to spread your weight over a larger area, reducing the risk of compaction.

Old planks are part of the basic toolkit on a clay soil and will help prevent compaction.

Recycle and create compost

Start a compost heap or bin (or two) as soon as possible because garden compost is the perfect soil conditioner. In the meantime you can use well-rotted farmyard manure, leafmould, composted bark, grass clippings, or even proprietary bagged compost.

Large, hot compost heaps work fast, but all work eventually.

Spring bulbs push up easily through mulches.

Beware of woodchip

If material supplied as shredded bark contains too high a level of wood chip then there is a risk that the soil may suffer: wood or sawdust uses up nitrogen from the soil as it is broken down, and plants may then suffer nitrogen deficiency. Mixing in plenty of nitrogen-rich matter, such as manure, may help to balance this loss.

Choosing a manure

If your soil is heavy, choose manures carefully: the stickiest sorts, such as pig manure, tend to make the soil even heavier. Using garden compost or leafmould in conjunction with a heavier manure will help to counteract the problem.

Slow feeding

While any mulching material keeps the soil moist and suppresses weeds, organic mulches also feed the soil. Garden compost, composted bark, cocoa shells, leaf mould, and manure improve structure and nutrient levels. Mulches are best applied on moist soil in late autumn or early spring.

Using bark

Composted bark can be used to condition soil, but it is essential that it is well composted. Ideally, it should be used not alone but together with other materials since it may contain levels of tannins that can inhibit healthy plant growth. This is more likely to cause problems with bedding plants than with shrubs and climbers.

Perennial plantings benefit enormously from mulches of almost any kind.

Tools you can trust

Good quality tools are what you need, whatever the size of your garden, and whatever your level of gardening expertise. It is worth stocking up with fewer, better tools that will do an excellent job over many years, than a lot of poor quality ones.

Do you really need it?

You don't need a huge number of fancy, complicated tools to get started in your garden. Make a vow not to buy gimmicky tools: there is a lot of junk for sale out there.

Top tools

Fork

Hoe

Pair of secateurs

Pronged hand cultivator

Spade

Trowel

Watering can

If possible:

Gardening line

Hosepipe and outside tap

Lawnmower

Onion hoe

Spring-tined rake

Wheelbarrow

The essential toolkit is neither bank-breaking nor space-hungry.

In a larger garden, you will need a decent shed to store your tools.

Check what it feels like

Always handle garden tools before you buy; they vary immensely. Check that the length of the shaft or handle feels comfortable and that the tool is not too heavy. Also ensure that the handle grip is comfortable – there are various different styles available.

Your digging tools can make or break your back.

Forks for clay

If you garden on heavy clay soil, you should use a fork for digging most of the time. This is less likely to exacerbate the poor drainage characteristics of clay than a spade, so make a really good quality (and heavy duty) fork your first priority.

The price is right

With garden tools, you really do get what you pay for, both in terms of their design (and therefore how easy to use they are) and also in terms of how long they last. If money is short, start with just the very bare essentials and add to your collection slowly, as necessary, but go for quality. The only piece of equipment I would recommend buying from the lower end of the range is a wheelbarrow: the very basic galvanized barrows from builders' merchants are extremely tough (in fact almost indestructible), and often cost a fraction of what you would pay for a slightly more attractive, up-market model.

Choosing a wheelbarrow

❀ Whatever price you pay for a barrow, it is essential to get one with a pneumatic tyre because it'll be so much easier to push than one with solid tyres. Although repairing punctures is not my favourite job, at least it can be done and does not take too long.

❀ If you can, try pushing a wheelbarrow before you buy it. Your barrow needs to feel balanced and comfortable on the move, and it must be easy to hold with the stabilizer legs off the ground. Choose carefully.

Make digging easier

If you intend to dig a lot with a spade, look out for one with a tread on the head – a small flange running along the length of the top of the head. Small as it is, this tread really helps to prevent your boots from slipping off when you drive the spade in to the ground.

Scaled down tools

❀ If you are not very tall or prefer a lighter tool, you could choose a so-called border fork or border spade.

❀ If you are smaller still, there are some very good quality children's tools, the larger ones of which can perfectly well be used by a small adult.

Try each tool till one suits

A sturdy can with a removable rose will give years of useful service.

A seriously useful watering can

❀ When choosing a watering can, make sure you would be happy carrying it full of water. If you are reasonably strong, a standard large can should be fine – in fact you might find some of the very pretty (but often less functional) types quite infuriating.

❀ Galvanized watering cans are considerably more expensive than plastic types, but are virtually indestructible and are well worth the money.

❀ Avoid watering cans without removable roses; they are extremely difficult to clean when the rose gets clogged, and only allow you to water in one way. A rose that you can rotate and remove gives two degrees of sprinkling and a solid surge of water.

Instant transformations

It is well worth indulging in an instant transformation or two – a quick-fix solution that will produce immediate results. It can make your garden look so much better and encourages you to carry on in the bleaker moments too!

Clematis can cover a multitude of sins in a garden.

Disguise a heap of rubble

If there is the odd pile of rubble in your garden and you are not yet ready to hire a skip to remove it, don't be tempted to bury it because its effect will come to light in the future. In the short-term, plant an inexpensive, fast-growing climber next to it, and allow it to scramble over the heap. Try a clematis or a rose, but make sure you do not plant any acid-loving plants nearby if the rubble includes concrete.

Start by tidying up

It is very easy to accumulate things you do not need, or to put off removing dead plants and broken flower pots. But one hour, or sometimes even just half an hour, spent with two containers – one for junk that is destined for the bin, and the other for compostable items – will make a huge difference to how the garden looks for relatively little effort.

Look at the paving

Paving often looks awful as slabs start to crack or the surface becomes discoloured. If you are sure you want to keep the paved area, then it is worth spending a bit of time on it. If it is possible to obtain replacement slabs, just lift and replace any damaged ones that are spoiling the area's overall appearance.

You may find you can turn marked slabs over.

Create storage

The idea of a shed that takes up valuable planting space may not appeal at first, but it is worth getting one if you possibly can. It can be used to keep tools and equipment dry and safe, store seeds and bulbs before planting, and be the perfect storage place for all those things that are currently stacked and dotted about looking messy.

A packed shed keeps the garden tidy.

Age replacement paving

Brand new slabs may be of exactly the same type as the original, but because they are totally un-weathered they will look radically different. Use the trick that is often used on new pots, and paint the surface with either liquid manure or natural yogurt. This encourages algae and mosses, and should not make the surface slippery unless you use huge quantities.

Re-lay paving

Sometimes slabs have simply suffered subsidence. Use a spade inserted beneath the edge of the slab to lever it up carefully, taking care not to damage the edges. A small amount of hardcore or dry, sharp sand placed beneath the slab should then allow you to raise or level as necessary, and replace the slab quickly and easily.

Renovating gravelled areas

If there are a lot of weeds coming up through a gravelled surface, it may well be because no landscape fabric was used when the path or gravelled area was first constructed. If this is the case, it is best to start from scratch completely (*see* page 165) but do not be tempted to use a solid plastic sheet; rain will not be able to drain away and waterlogging will soon become a problem.

Protect adjacent plants when cleaning with chemicals or pressure hoses.

Clean up paving

Sometimes the surface of a patio or steps may have simply become discoloured, and pressure washing or scrubbing using a proprietary cleaner may be sufficient to transform the area. But before you tackle the whole surface, check that the treatment won't cause further damage: pressure washing can damage a slightly loose surface, and some cleaning agents can cause discolouration themselves, so do a test-slab first in a less prominent area.

Topping up gravel

If gravelled areas have become thin, try to ensure that any replacement material you buy to top it up matches the original stone. If you cannot achieve this, then make sure you mix in the new stones as evenly as possible over the whole surface. This will give a different but acceptable appearance without starting from scratch.

Gravel should be at least 3cm (1in) deep.

Plant in paving gaps

If you want to ring the changes, you can remove damaged or discoloured slabs completely. Dig out the material beneath the slab and replace it with good top soil to a depth of at least 15cm (6in) and you'll have a great planting hole for a small plant.

Replace slabs beyond the most-used routes with plants.

Damaged edges

Paved areas, including paths, may have become damaged around the edges, especially if the area has been well used. It is essential to repair them promptly; they'll not only be safer but also look a lot more attractive. Take out broken bricks, pavers, or slabs, and replace them. If you cannot match them, consider a new edge all along the path, or perhaps replace several slabs in a regular pattern so that it looks intentional.

Plants for paving

Precisely what you plant is up to you, but drought-tolerant plants, such as the thymes, sages (*Salvia*), and sempervivums, usually do well. For gaps towards the edge of a paved area, you could always choose a small shrub, or perhaps even a climber that will grow to cover an adjacent wall.

Sempervivums will produce offsets and soon fill a planting pocket.

Pots of bright flowers can hide or distract from any defects.

"Pretty up" with pots

Broken or damaged steps or paths that are still perfectly safe will look a lot better if you add a few small pots, prettily planted, at the edges. Change the contents of the pots each season for a year-long display. Make sure that the paths or steps are wide enough to take this reduction in their useable space without becoming cramped.

Tackle the jungle effect

Seriously overgrown climbers could pose a threat to your house foundations, but more likely are simply obstructing pathways and blocking light. Before you grab the secateurs or saw, check your plant's needs, because pruning methods do vary considerably.

Great plants for edging paths and patios

1 *Arenaria*
2 *Armeria maritima*
3 *Aubrieta*
4 *Dianthus deltoides*
5 *Draba*
6 *Erinus alpinus*
7 *Helianthemum*
8 *Iberis sempervirens*
9 *Salvia officinalis*
10 *Saxifraga*
11 *Sempervivum*
12 *Thymus*

Plants creeping over paving edges hide minor uneveness or damage.

Timing pruning

It is always best to avoid pruning a plant towards the end of the summer; this may stimulate new growth which will not have the chance to toughen or harden up properly before the onset of frosty weather. It is generally best to cut back either when the plant is dormant or earlier in the year, when any new growth produced will be able to harden off.

Take your time

If in doubt about just how far you can go with serious pruning of an overgrown shrub or climber, it is best to err on the side of caution. The work can be spread out over two or maybe even three years.

How to prune overgrown shrubs

❀ Different plants need tackling in different ways, so try to identify exactly what the plant is. But whatever you are renovating, there are basic guidelines that you should always follow, the first job being to prune out dead, diseased, and dying growth.

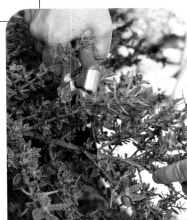

Most plants do fine if you don't cut back beyond leafy parts.

Renovate and feed

It may seem illogical to feed overgrown plants that have had to be cut back, but they do benefit. Feeding an old shrub that has been heavily pruned helps encourage new, productive growth. Feeding does not mean the plant will put on excessive new growth, provided you do not apply excessive quantities of feed.

❀ Look at the plant with a critical eye to decide whether it needs general thinning out or whether the crown needs opening out. Whatever you are pruning out, always ensure your secateurs, saw, or loppers are in good condition and very sharp – crushed stems often become infected and show die-back. Choose a vigorous-looking, outward-facing bud or shoot and cut back to this, creating a sloping cut just above the bud but not right on top of it.

Sort out boundaries and structures

Your garden will both look and feel better with well-kept boundaries that suit its overall style, giving privacy and security. Screening can also be used within the garden to hide washing lines, compost bins, or sheds that can all be a blot on your landscape.

Spruce up fences

A decrepit fence can make a whole garden look unkempt and allows unwanted visitors, such as other people's pets, to get in to your garden too easily. Replacing a fence may be a job you want to leave until later; in the meantime, once you have made sure that it is basically safe and secure, it will look a lot better if you paint it with timber treatment, using a coloured type if that suits your site.

A clean, uniform boundary gives a feeling of tidiness.

Make sure fences are where they should be

If you've just moved in to a new house, make sure that any queries about boundaries are sorted out promptly. Problems like this don't disappear, they tend to get more complicated instead.

Hide eyesores

Evergreen ivy (*Hedera*) is perfect for screens.

❀ Use fence posts to support a trellis and make a free-standing screen that allows quick and easy access for maintenance, pruning, and so on. While longer-term climbers are getting established, fill in gaps with quick-growing annuals, such as sweet peas (*Lathyrus*).

❀ To obscure taller, thinner eyesores, roll up chicken wire to create a column, anchor it firmly to the ground, and grow climbers up it.

❀ If the eyesore has a less-than-desirable odour – like a compost heap – include some perfumed plants in your screen or a nearby planter. Jasmine, roses, or honeysuckle (*Lonicera*) not only look good, but also act as great natural air fresheners.

Plant up boundaries

Unless the fence is in a seriously bad state, you can plant climbers to cover it. Choose fast-growing plants, such as *Clematis montana*, for a speedy effect. If you intend to remove the fence within a year or two, you can use annual climbers including sweet peas (*Lathyrus*), cup-and-saucer vine (*Cobaea*), or morning glory (*Ipomoea*) on wire mesh or a temporary frame. Alternatively, tackle the problem from the top down with trailing plants in hanging baskets.

Lysimachia and *Verbena* are a winning combination.

Shabby sheds

Sometimes a shed can be an eyesore, not because it is ugly in itself, but because it looks decrepit. A coat or two of wood treatment, perhaps in an exciting colour, can help to make it look better instantly. Make sure the treatment adheres well by cleaning off all algae, moss, and general dirt, and then allowing the wood to dry thoroughly before applying the wood treatment.

Coloured stains allow a shed to stand out or fade into the scenery.

Damaged roofs

❀ The roofing felt on sheds often deteriorates after a few years, leaving the shed without a fully waterproof roof, and making it look ugly. Replacing the felt on a reasonably sound shed will instantly make the whole thing look so much better.

❀ If it doesn't seem worth re-roofing a shed, make it look better for what is left of its life by growing a climber up and over its roof. A tatty shed covered with hundreds of flowers of a clematis or honeysuckle (*Lonicera*) can look really beautiful. Doing this may, however, speed up the deterioration of the shed, so it's best reserved for those that are definitely well past their sell-by dates.

Planting near the house draws the eye away from the edges.

Use distractions

If the edges of your garden are still looking lacklustre, despite your efforts at tidying them up, then get planting (*see* pages 38–39). In the meantime, make good use of seasonally filled containers to focus attention elsewhere. A good-looking pot or tub or two will help to draw your eye away from the less attractive areas of a garden, making the whole place seem more appealing. They also indicate just what the whole garden will look like when you've had time to get to grips with it.

Honeysuckle will smother a shed and remain green for most, or all, of the year.

Instant screening

You don't need permanent planting to make a screen or hedge: beautifully planted containers can be lined up to make an instant screen. This can be of almost any height, depending on what you plant in them, from lavender to laurel.

Flowerbeds & borders

Unless you want the ultimate minimalist look in your garden, it is likely that you will have at least one flowerbed or border, quite possibly several. The size, shape, and number of beds you have will of course be determined by the size and shape of your garden and the emphasis you want to put on flowers and other plants as opposed to the hard land-scaping element. Each may have a similar theme, or they may be quite different in character and content, but whatever their style, flowerbeds and borders are an integral part of most gardens, and something that can make or break them.

Creating the perfect scheme

There is an art to creating beautiful borders and ensuring that they develop as you want and look good for as much of the year as possible. Beds and borders that are devoid of colour and interest for all but a fraction of the year are a lost opportunity. It's easy to cobble together a flowerbed that looks good for a season or two, but harder to ensure that the space is used to its best effect as time goes on. I would certainly not want to suggest that you should steer clear of herbaceous borders unless you are an experienced and very knowledgeable gardener – far from it – but there is no doubt that this is one of those areas of the garden where a few timely tips can go a long way towards making that dream border a great-looking reality! Whatever your parameters, it is all about ensuring that your flowers really fulfil their potential.

This chapter shows you how to:

- ❀ Make a new border – choose a shape that fits in with your garden design and cut it into an existing lawn.
- ❀ Choose a variety of plants for a new border, thinking about shape, colour, and height.
- ❀ Plant up a new border or bed.
- ❀ Look after established beds – staking, protecting, feeding, and weeding.

How to make a new border

It is an exciting moment when you sit down to plan a new border, and that planning is vital to the border's long-term success. Take time to choose those really magical ingredients.

Smooth, broad curves are easier to plant and maintain.

Keep it simple

An unusually or intricately shaped border may appeal, but is also likely to be a nightmare to keep in shape, especially if the border is next to a lawn, which has convoluted edges that need to be mown. Smooth, flowing outlines are an easier option, and usually end up being changed less frequently as a result – go for the classic, timeless look.

Think ahead

Try to imagine what a new flowerbed will look like before you begin creating it. You may not yet know exactly what plants you will have in it, but think about its shape and dimensions and how it will affect or interact with the rest of the garden. Remember that a flowerbed or border is likely to be visible from several different places, including the ground floor and upper windows of your house. Make sure that you create your border in a position that can be enjoyed from wherever it is seen.

Marking curves

❀ Get a bit of help with the border edge. Ideally use a peg and line to help you mark out circular curves, marking the grass with landscaper's paint in an aerosol. If you have only one to do and want to economize, use plenty of dry horticultural sand to mark out the edge. You can either drizzle this on to the turf by hand or make a dispenser by cutting the base off a plastic bottle. Tie the end of the line to the bottle and invert it. Pour the dry sand in, and it will flow out when you remove the lid, allowing you to mark the turf as you move the bottle.

❀ A garden hose laid in the desired shape of the edge of the border will work, but there is a risk of accidentally creating a lop-sided or uneven curve.

A solid edge is a good investment, saving hours of work later.

Keep it neat and easy

Lawn grass will try to grow into the flowerbed. Sink a barrier to a depth of 5cm (2in) around the edge, protruding above the grass roots, but not so high that you cannot mow right up to the edge. This should prevent the grass creeping in and hugely reduce the time you spend tidying the edges.

A path in a large bed can be practical and a pleasure.

Size matters

The size of your bed or border depends on what you want and the size of the garden. But consider its future maintenance and any way to make this simpler, quicker, or easier. Bigger borders may look better because they hold more plants, but if they are too deep it may be difficult to reach central areas, especially once it is full of plants. Stepping stones or a path through the middle make access easier.

Recycling turf

❀ Removed turf needs to be lifted with its roots, so that it can be used as patching material for any sparse bits in the rest of the lawn, or to repair broken lawn edges. If you don't need it for this, turf composts brilliantly, so add it to the compost heap.

❀ If there is a lot of turf, you can make your own miniature loam heap. Stack the turf grass side down in an out-of-the-way spot; as long as it does not become too dry, it will rot down into super loam.

Get straight lines straight

A straight-edged border that has not got really straight edges looks awful. Even when plants are growing in it and partially hiding a wobbly line, the problem is still obvious. Don't try to cut the edge by eye, use either two pegs and a line or a long steel rule or plank, and then make sure you cut precisely along the line.

Take care to undercut deeply enough to remove all roots.

Cutting the edge

The best tool for cutting the edges of a border in an existing lawn is a half-moon edging iron, which makes it relatively easy to cut accurately and neatly. Alternatively, a good, sharp spade will work pretty well, but it is essential that you keep the blade at a right angle to the lawn as you cut.

A half-moon edger has a completely flat blade.

Cutting out the turf

Once you have created the shape of the edge, you will need to remove all the turf from within the outline. It is much easier (and makes for a much neater end result) if you stand inside the new border area and cut out towards the edge. Cutting inwards from the edge is likely to crush that nice, neat vertical cut. It is also best to remove a relatively small ring of turf first, then as you get in to the central area of the border you can move a lot at a time.

Choosing plants for a new border

Start by deciding when you want the border to look its best. If you are creating a border to look good for as much of the year as possible, you need a wide range of plants whose main performance times or seasons of appeal span many months.

Use a mix of plant types

If you want a border that will be interesting at all levels, use a mix of shrubs and perennials. To achieve a gloriously solid mass of colour, you may also want to top up with disposable bedding plants whose flowering times fit in with your specific need. Once you've got your core of permanent plants in place, visit garden centres for seasonal interest plants at the time you need them. These easy-come, easy-go plants give maximum impact in quick time when other plants flag.

You will see your garden differently when sitting or standing: use plant heights to suit both angles.

Mix and match

Considering the heights and spread of the plants is important. Make sure you don't choose plants that are all of a very similar height; you will be able to enjoy more of the display they offer if some are taller than others.

Follow your heart, but use your head

Choosing plants is a very personal business, but remember to check on their fundamental requirements before you take them home. Unless you can provide the right amount of sun or shade, soil texture, moisture levels, and soil pH, they'll find it impossible to thrive.

Read the label

Plants in small pots always look easy to cope with in the nursery or garden centre, but remember that while many herbaceous plants do look rather similar early or very late in the season, they have hugely different potential heights and spreads. The information given on the plant label or the header-board in the garden centre is something you really need to take note of.

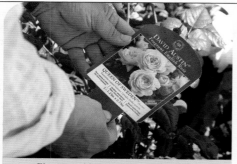

Illustrated labels are useful to tell you what a plant does when.

Out of reach

When you are choosing plants for an island bed, especially one that is quite large, make sure that the plants in the centre are relatively low maintenance because they will be harder to reach, and so maintenance could be difficult.

The centre of the border is ideal for low-maintenance evergreens and those spiky plants that you wouldn't want too close to the edge.

Think about shape

Everyone probably has a favourite plant shape – you may love dreaming spires of delphiniums or sprawling mounds of catmint (*Nepeta*) – but one shape repeated endlessly quickly looks dull. Vertical spikes of flowers bring a border of solid, sturdy shapes to life, while cascading plants can soften and knit blocks together. And don't automatically send all the tall plants to the back: some, such as *Verbena bonariensis*, are gauzy enough to put at the front.

Leaf shades and shapes last most of the year.

Look at leaves

There is a lot more to a plant than just its flowers; many herbaceous plants have stunning foliage too. Make an effort to incorporate some good foliage plants in your design because the leaves offer interest far longer than many of the flowers.

Vertical plants can act like exclamation marks, giving punch to borders of lower, more solid shapes.

When to buy your plants

If you need widely spread seasons of interest, you can still buy the plants you need in the main buying seasons (spring and, to a lesser extent, autumn for herbaceous plants). If you want to ensure you have some seriously showy plants throughout much of the year, make sure you visit a good garden centre at regular intervals. You can be sure that the real seasonal show-stoppers with the most flamboyant displays will be in a prominent position each time you visit.

Shades of blue and purple give a
soothing, harmonious garden.

Colour harmonies

I'm a great believer that colour combinations are a very personal
thing and that you should have what you like, not what someone else
says. However, if you need a bit of a suggestion to get you started,
remember that generally hotter colours go better with other hot
colours, and cool with cool. You could go for a border with a very
limited or even single colour theme, or perhaps, with a longer border,
grade colours from the hot to the cool.

Buy fresh

If possible, find out when the garden centre has its
main deliveries and go on that day. You'll get the pick
of the plants before they have had a chance to become
dry or damaged!

Learn by example

If you find choosing plants that go well together difficult, try
visiting plenty of well-planned and beautifully planted gardens.
This will not only provide you with a gorgeous day out, but also
inspire you and provide plenty of great planting ideas.

Safe passage

If the flowerbed is
next to a path, avoid
plants with prickly
or spiky foliage and
anything known to
cause skin reactions,
such as the euphorbias
or rue (*Ruta*).

Use movement

Plants of various heights add a dimension to a flower border, but your
creation will look even more delightful if you can include plants that
introduce movement as well. Use tall plants with flexible stems, such as
Verbena bonariensis, and your border will positively dance in the breeze.

Please yourself

Colour combinations can be daunting, especially to those
who are not artistically inclined. Remember, you are
creating your own beds and borders. You and the others
who live in the house and admire the garden are the only
people whose opinions really matter!

Be choosy

Avoid garden plant outlets where
the plants are not looked after well.
Dead or drought-stricken plants or
a lot of weed growth on the compost
are all tell-tale signs.

Neat edges

If the border is adjacent to a lawn, make sure that you choose some plants to go around the edges of the border that are not inclined to spread too much and which have a fairly upright habit. Plants that flop over the grass will make mowing difficult, and will soon cause the grass that they shade out to deteriorate. Plant a little way back from the edge to allow some room to spread.

Planting time

It's easy to get carried away when suddenly you find yourself with a great new planting space, but if you're too hasty you may regret it later on. Make sure you prepare the soil for the new border before you start planting.

Reduce weed seeds

If the bed is in an area where there were a lot of annual weeds, remove them. Then, having dug the soil over, leave the bed empty for at least three weeks before you even think about putting in any plants. During these weeks, numerous weed seeds previously lying dormant in the soil will germinate (especially rapidly because the soil has been dug over) and you can regularly hoe off the growth. If you do this throughout the first few weeks following the creation of the bed, you should be able to clear most of the dormant weed seeds before you plant, making future maintenance much easier.

Repeated hoeing to kill weeds as they germinate reduces them dramatically.

Feed the soil

The soil may be impoverished, so incorporate plenty of well-rotted manure or garden compost to improve its texture and fertility. Fork this in well throughout the entire bed.

The easiest time to improve the soil is before you put plants in it.

Remove roots

The new, well-fed, and manured bed you're about to create is an ideal place for any pernicious weeds, such as dandelions, docks, or bindweed, to survive and thrive. This means you must fork the area over really thoroughly, carefully removing as many intact weeds and their roots as you can. It's crucial that you clear all the roots and other plant fragments, because many have the ability to form an entire new plant if they are left in the soil.

Check the pH

If you are unsure about the soil's pH, this is a good time to carry out a pH test (*see* page 16) to determine what exactly it is before you start to add anything. Most herbaceous plants perform perfectly well on all but the most extreme soil types, but it is still a good idea to check. If you intend to plant any shrubs in the border, knowing the pH will really help you to work out what to grow.

Open up the soil

Soil, especially the soil in an area beneath a well-used lawn, often becomes seriously compacted. Fork over to at least a spade's depth, preferably more, breaking up any hard layers or "pans" that have developed. If the top soil is thin, do make sure you do not bring any subsoil to the surface!

Using fertilizer

To make sure that fertility is really good, you could also use some proprietary fertilizers, but if you have very fertile soil or have just incorporated lots of manure or compost then a general feed should not be necessary initially. Instead, wait until the plants have started to grow strongly.

How many of each?

❀ If the space you have to plant up is very small, then a single plant of each type may be all you need. If you want a bolder effect, restrict yourself to plants that stay small and go for several of each type.

❀ Plant in odd numbers, say three or five of the same plant, rather than even numbers; this will help the border to look more natural.

Odd numbers of plants give the appearance of a more naturally formed border.

Leave each plant in a bucket of water while you dig its planting hole.

Working on clay

If your garden soil is heavy clay, try to do major digging or bed creation when the weather and soil is not too wet, or else the soil will become seriously compacted (*see* page 18). Do as much of the digging as possible with a fork, rather than a spade; a spade is more likely to cause smearing or compaction of the soil at the edges of the bed.

Pre-soaking plants

Once you have got the plants home and just before you start to plant, give them a thorough watering if their compost is at all dry. Standing them in water ensures that the entire root ball is thoroughly moistened when they go into the soil.

If you have a paper plan, marking it on the ground with sand or landscaper's paint will make things easier.

Prior arrangement

Before you start to plant, arrange the pots of plants in the positions in which you intend to plant them. It is much easier to change your mind at this stage than it will be once they are in the ground. If you have not yet managed to get all the plants you need, use an empty pot to represent each missing plant.

When to plant

❀ I recommend planting in autumn or early spring so that the plants have a chance to get their roots into their new surroundings and start to establish before the weather gets too hot or the soil too dry.

❀ If the weather is already getting warm, plant on as cool a day as possible or failing that, in the early evening so that at least the plants are not subjected to the hottest part of the day straight away.

The size and condition of the hole are the key to success.

Prepare holes well

❀ Make sure that each plant has a planting hole a bit larger than the plant's rootball.

❀ If the weather is dry, fill each hole with water just before you put the plant in to the hole. A bit of localized watering works wonders for its establishment and reduces water wastage.

Last minute moves

Keep each plant in its pot until you are ready to put it in. If you remove them from the pots in advance of planting, their roots are more likely to get dry, especially if you unexpectedly take longer than you had anticipated.

Hold your position

Leaving the plants in position while you start to plant makes planting quicker and easier. It also makes it easier for you to ensure that each one goes in exactly the right position in relation to its neighbour.

Don't dig too deep

Don't be tempted to plant at anything other than the depth the plant was at in its pot. Planting too deep may cause rotting and death, and too shallow makes a plant more prone to drought.

Be a tease

Once you have taken the plant out of its pot you will be able to check the roots. If the roots are very congested in the pot, gently tease out a few of the outer roots before the plant goes in the hole. This will help to ensure that the roots spread through their new surroundings more rapidly.

Matted roots may stay that way after planting.

Keep cool

If the weather is already quite warm and the plants have a lot of leaf growth, they could suffer quite badly, particularly in the first few days after planting. Erect some temporary shelter to give them a bit of light relief.

See off the competition

Once all the plants are in position, top off all the soil surface with a bulky mulch such as cocoa shell or bark. This will reduce weed growth dramatically, saving you time and reducing any competition between your plants and the weeds, and will help to keep the soil relatively moist. Top up the mulch as soon as it starts to thin out, first pulling out any weeds that have appeared.

A good layer of mulch is invaluable for keeping competition out and moisture in.

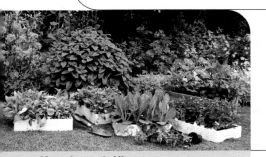

Have fun with fillers in a young border: they may spark new ideas.

Keep the labels

It is worth keeping a record of exactly what you planted, but I can't stand seeing plant labels in flowerbeds. If you're like me (but also too busy to staple them all in to a special folder!) then simply put all the labels into a jar or an envelope labelled with the area of the garden they are from, so you have a record.

Fill the gaps

A newly planted bed of herbaceous plants will have a lot of gaps in it for the first few years. If you don't like all that gappiness, use seasonal bedding and bulbs, and perhaps some hardy annuals, to create colour that won't affect the border in the longer term but will look great while the bed develops.

Use landscape fabric

Planting through holes in a landscape fabric can serve all sorts of purposes. On a slope, it can help keep the soil in place (*see* page 15). In other places fabrics can suppress weeds, reducing maintenance. They also prevent decorative materials, such as bark or pea shingle, working their way into the soil.

Looking after established beds

Once a flowerbed starts to grow and develop, it will soon begin to look great. All this movement does, however, mean that you will need to keep an eye on the plants, and supply the TLC they deserve!

Plants will quickly conceal any frames that they grow through.

Stop the flop

Many herbaceous plants, and indeed many annuals that you may be using as temporary display plants, are a little too tall for their own good and have a tendency to flop. This not only spoils the way they look, but may damage adjacent plants (including the lawn) and makes them more prone to slug attack. A bit of hidden support is worth its weight in gold.

Get it in early

It always pays to insert plant supports as early as possible. If you put in supports once there is quite a bit of foliage on the plant, the job takes longer as you try to avoid damaging the plant, which is always inevitable, and the support tends to be less well hidden. As soon as the plant is appearing above ground and you can gauge fairly accurately just how wide it will spread, you should start staking.

Stop supports rooting

With heavier plants or where you actually want the support to be an integral part of the look you create, supports such as freshly cut willow or hazel stems fit the bill perfectly. These only pose one problem, and that's if they left are in the soil for more than a month or two they may root and quickly develop quite extensive root systems. Wrap layers of parcel tape tightly around the entire length of the wood that will be in contact with the ground before you insert the stem into the soil; this should prevent it from taking root.

Natural materials make virtually invisible stakes.

Subtle staking

Most plants look better if the support that they need is hidden away. Twiggy sticks, cut to a length to suit the individual plant, but generally about 45cm (18in) tall with the lowermost 10–15cm (4–6in) driven in to the soil, work well.

Make your own supports

If you plan in advance there should be no need to buy special "pea sticks" for plants; just save prunings when cutting back shrubs, trees, and hedges.

Proprietary supports

There is a whole host of supports available from garden centres and mail-order catalogues, and it is well worth shopping around for good deals. Choose supports in sizes and colours to suit the plants you are growing, and if they are metal make sure that they are either galvanized or plastic coated.

Use any soft material for ties: the softer the stem, the softer the tie should be.

Tall stems

Some plants, such as hollyhocks (*Alcea*) and delphiniums, may not need general support, but their tall and sometimes slightly fragile flower spikes may need it, especially if the plant is in a particularly windy spot. A single bamboo cane usually does the trick, but take care not to damage the crown of the plant as you insert it into the soil. Tie the plant in using a figure of eight to allow room for expansion and reduce the risk of the stem being damaged.

A figure-of-eight tie allows movement.

What to use for plant ties

You can use a variety of materials to tie plant stems to supports: soft garden twine, raffia, proprietary plastic ties, foam-covered wire, open wire circles, or even a short section taken from the leg of a pair of stockings or tights.

Keep plants under wraps

Flower buds, flowers, and soft foliage are especially vulnerable to frost damage. Protect them by draping with horticultural fleece, old net curtains, or even newspapers; the edges must be properly anchored with metal pegs, hoops, or large stones and bricks to be effective. Fleece bags with drawstrings are now available, and make protecting larger tender plants or their flowers much easier, quicker, and more effective.

Be prepared for cold

Changes in temperature, when tender plants are subjected to frost, can do a lot of damage, especially if the arrival of frosts is sudden. Make sure that you have all you need for protection ready and waiting, and keep listening to the weather forecasts.

Keep on top of weeds

Hoeing is a great way to kill off annual weeds, but can do a lot of damage in a crowded flowerbed. Invest in a tiny hoe, such as one sold as an onion hoe and you will be able to hoe quite safely in tight spaces.

You will need all the tricks there are to keep hostas hole-free.

Slugs, snails, and other problems

❀ The soft, young foliage produced early in the year is a magnet for certain pests, in particular slugs and snails. Some plants, such as dicentras, seem to be damaged only rarely, but check all plants regularly so that you can collect and dispose of the pests.

❀ Mulching with cocoa shells seems to reduce slug and snail damage; barriers such as crushed shells, pine needles, or proprietary copper rings also help to keep the slugs and snails away from your plants.

❀ Later in the year, large, floppy foliage from herbaceous perennials makes a perfect place for slugs and snails to hide, so check beneath large leaves around the bases of the plants and collect any lurking pests.

❀ In any area of your garden, you can be sure that there will be a fair selection of pests and pathogens that could attack your beloved plants. *See* pages 218–23 for more tips on some of these problems.

Allow plants to toughen up

Although it may be tempting to keep fleece or other protection on plants, doing this means that the plants will not be able to harden off naturally. It may also become rather damp beneath some forms of frost protection, making pests and infections all the more likely to become a problem too. During mild weather, or at least during the warmer part of the day, remove or partially remove frost protection – but don't forget to get it back in place on time!

Water well

❀ Flowerbeds and borders will be likely to need some water, especially during the first few months after planting, while the plants get established. For watering *see* pages 176–78; most importantly, water thoroughly and less often (avoid frequent sprinklings), and water in the evening or early morning.

❀ Many herbaceous plants are prone to fungal infections that thrive on wet foliage. Try to get water direct to the roots, not on the leaves – this is less wasteful too.

❀ Both rainwater and "grey" water from baths or hand basins are fine for using on flowerbeds and borders. So collect all you can and make use of it!

Using a can is a slower but efficient way to water.

Deadhead to keep displays
tidy and make them last.

Faded flowers

❀ As flowers start to fade, make sure you regularly deadhead the plants. Removing these faded blooms helps to avoid the plant wasting energy producing seeds.

❀ Regular deadheading is the key to success, but if a lot of flowers have faded simultaneously and there are not many more to come, you can often save time by giving the plant a "haircut' with sharp scissors or, in the case of tougher plants, a pair of shears.

Feed with care

❀ If the soil has plenty of organic matter, it should be healthy and full of nutrients, but occasionally you may feel it is necessary to use fertilizers. These are generally best applied in spring or early summer – put them on too late in the season and they may encourage soft, new growth which will be hit by frosts.

❀ If spraying a foliar feed onto the leaves, or applying nutrients such as a magnesium solution to the leaves, do it on a dull day, or when the leaves and petals will have dried completely before the sun gets hot, to avoid scorch. Water drops focus the sun's rays, like tiny lenses.

Make a soil mound

It is normally bad to mound soil around plant stems and crowns but, in very cold weather, it can help to protect the plant from frost and reduce any loosening effect on the roots. On heavy soil or in wet conditions, mound up compost or composted bark. As soon as it warms up, scrape the material away from the stems.

Mound up soil ahead of
heavy frosts.

Autumn tidying

❀ At the end of the season you can tidy up beds and borders a bit – removing faded leaves helps to clean up residues of pest and pathogen problems from earlier in the year. Use sharp scissors or secateurs to ensure that you don't damage the crown of the plant as you remove infected foliage.

❀ It can be worth leaving some old leaves on herbaceous plants, because they often help to protect the crown from winter cold.

❀ Leave in place the seedheads of sedums and others that look good or provide useful food for the birds. They can be removed in the spring.

Brown, dried leaves should
be promptly removed.

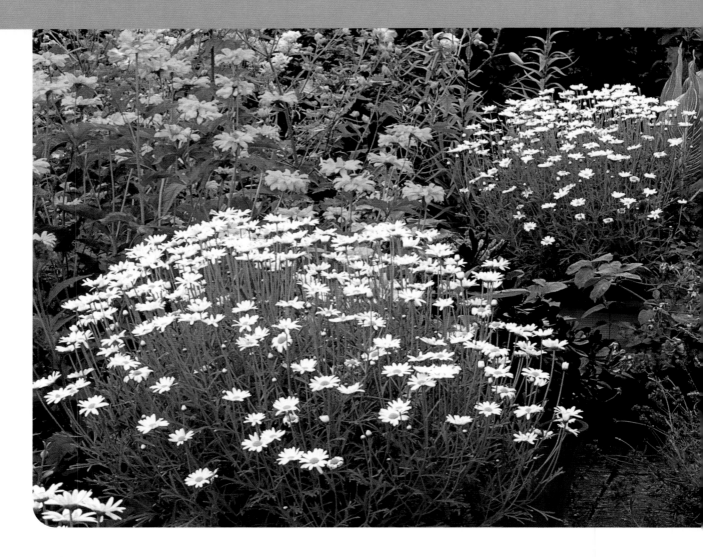

Creative containers

Containers are well worth the effort they take to create and maintain, and they allow you to have things that would perhaps not naturally suit your garden soil, such as the ever-popular camellias, rhododendrons, and azaleas. They would not be a wise choice if you garden on an alkaline or chalky soil, but if you are prepared to get some ericaceous compost, these once impossible plants become proud features. Containers can rapidly transform a garden; you just have to remember to water them!

Using containers to the full
For many years people thought of container gardening as inextricably linked with summer bedding, but more and more of us are now exploring its full potential. Not only summer bedding, but indeed any seasonal bedding will look great, and will look stunning if combined with seasonal bulbs. Longer term containers are well worth considering too, perhaps for shrubs or small trees under-planted with bedding and bulbs, so making a miniature garden in itself.

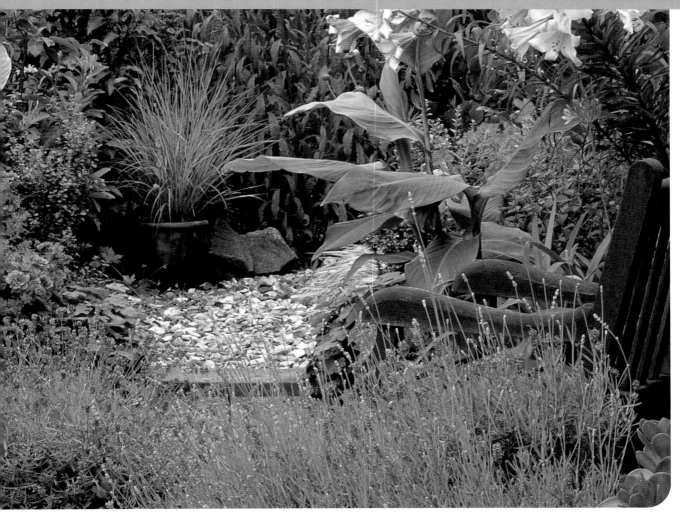

Then of course there are the vegetables and herbs – most of these are perfect candidates for life in a good sized pot or planter and will allow you to grow root vegetables or slug-prone crops whatever your soil and its population of problem creatures. You can create numerous mini-gardens, of a wide range of plants, pretty well regardless of your natural garden soil. If you choose attractive containers then these too can help to bring colour and interest to your garden, even when the plants themselves are not at their best.

This chapter shows you how to:
❀ Choose your containers – different plants have different needs.

❀ Choose your baskets and liners – which are best for which purpose?

❀ Plant up your containers – get the best compost and right plants for you.

❀ Cultivate crops in containers – which fruit, vegetables, and herbs thrive and how to care for them?

Choosing your containers

The size and type of containers you use can make the difference between your plants surviving and thriving: pots should be big enough for good root growth, and contain adequate compost to act as a reservoir for water and soil nutrients.

Frost-proof pots are fired at a higher temperature.

Frost-proof containers

Unless you're happy to move containers to a frost-free place over the colder months, look out for those described as frost-proof. The beautifully decorated, wonderfully coloured glazed pots that are usually sold at knock-down prices are rarely even frost resistant. Frost-proof terracotta emits a higher-pitched "ting" if flicked hard with a finger nail.

Think big

For ease of maintenance, choose larger pots and tubs. They hold a greater volume of compost, protecting plant roots from the effects extreme heat and extreme cold.

Avoiding a bog garden

Unless you want to produce a miniature pond or bog garden, it is essential that your container has plenty of drainage holes. Terracotta or stoneware pots often have one single, central hole, while containers made from artificial materials may have more. But whatever you choose they must be there, so don't get taken in by some of the gorgeous-looking but drainage-hole-free pots that are on sale!

Several holes help to ensure good drainage.

A straight-sided or outward-flaring pot makes potting-on possible.

Pots for long-term plants

Containers for plants such as small trees or shrubs, which may need moving into larger containers or open ground in a few years, need to be chosen very carefully. Use pots with upright sides or sides that flare outwards, never pot-bellied pots, because it is nigh-on impossible to remove a well-established plant from one of these, unless you're prepared to smash the container!

Making pots look attractively aged

If brand new terracotta, stone, or concrete pots just look too new and perfect, the trick of painting them with a solution of manure or live yoghurt really does work. Manure does not tend to smell as you might imagine, and is less likely to be licked off by passing cats! The pot should be dry when you start, to help the manure or yoghurt to adhere better.

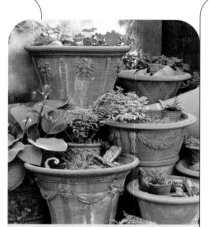

Pots will age faster if they are left in a damp place.

Protect roots from extreme temperatures

Thicker-walled containers, perhaps made from wood or double-skinned plastic, are the best for keeping roots insulated against temperature extremes. To give extra protection, you can line inside of the container with a sheet of bubble-wrap polythene, but ensure that the drainage holes are not covered.

A layer of bubble-wrap inside the pot makes great insulation.

Special care for acid-loving plants

Concrete containers are fine for most plants, but avoid them if you are planting an acid-loving plant, such as a camellia, pieris, or azalea (*Rhododendron*). The concrete may gradually weather and leach an alkaline solution into the compost, resulting in yellow-leafed, miserable plants. If you're desperate to use a concrete container for an acid-loving plant, line the inner surface with polythene, keeping the drainage holes clear.

Acid lovers are happy in ceramic or synthetic pots.

Top ten plants for year-round interest

1. *Arbutus unedo*
2. *Pieris* species and cultivars
3. *Laurus nobilis*
4. *Buxus*
5. *Euonymus fortunei*
6. *Trachycarpus fortunei*
7. Ericas and callunas
8. Hardy yucca
9. Hollies (*Ilex*), especially variegated forms
10. Dwarf conifers, like *Pinus mugo*

Customized wooden planters

Most garden wood treatment paints are also suitable for using on wooden containers to add colour or hide stains and blemishes, but always check the label. Make sure the paint has dried completely before you start to plant.

Choosing baskets and liners

Hanging baskets can transform the front of your house or a bare fence in your back garden, and are the perfect gardening answer when space is short. There are many different basket and liner options, so make sure you choose what works best for you.

Check the chains

When buying a hanging basket, choose one which has removable hanging chains. This makes it much easier when it comes to planting up: you can simply do the planting without having to work around the chains, and plants are less likely to get damaged too.

Look for wide planting holes

Planting around the sides and even the base of a hanging basket makes it look really impressive. To make this easier, choose a basket with widely spaced wires – they do vary a lot.

The wide spaces between the bars on this basket will allow plenty of planting around the sides.

How long will it last?

The longest-lasting baskets are those with plastic-coated mesh; choose carefully and it will blend in well. Baskets made from natural materials do have a certain rustic charm, but rarely last more than a year or two.

Metal and plastic baskets should give several years of service.

Holes in liners

If you want to do a lot of side and base-planting, you will need holes in the liner. If you use moss as a liner, it can be built up in layers leaving holes as you plant. Otherwise go for one which is easy to cut holes in, such as foam or compacted wool. Coconut fibre (coir) can be cut, but it is much tougher and cutting accurately is difficult.

The easiest liner to plant through is loose moss.

Time-saving liners

For speed of planting, choose a wool, foam, or pre-formed card liner. Cardboard liners often come with ready-made gaps for planting; certainly time-saving, but they do restrict what you do. Cardboard also has a tendency not to fit as snugly into the basket as you'd hope.

Measure your basket before buying a liner – it is easy to get it wrong by eye!

Once covered with moss, a plastic liner is hidden.

Recycled liners

As an alternative to coir or other artificial liners, you could also use a circle cut from an old jumper or cardigan. Ideally use real wool, which will rot down naturally in the compost heap afterwards. Whether you go for bold and brash or a more subtle, natural colour is up to you.

Home-grown moss

If you like moss, but are unhappy about it having been taken from the wild, you can use the stuff you rake out of your lawn, as long as it has not been treated with a moss-killing chemical. This works well, but is rarely as moisture-retentive as the moss sold especially for basket lining. Use a thick layer or an inner liner to keep moisture and compost in the basket.

Hiding an ugly liner

Double liners in baskets can be useful – a very sturdy but unattractive liner can have an outer, thinner layer of real moss added. And in the winter, two layers make for warmer, better protected plants and better displays.

The ultimate recycled liner

If you have a pond, drape several layers of blanket weed pulled from it over an upturned hanging basket. Allow each layer of the weed to dry before you add another layer, and keep adding until it is at least 5mm (¼in) thick. When dry it can be used as a good, natural-looking basket liner.

Home-grown moss can look every bit as good as sphagnum moss.

Planting up your containers

Now you have chosen your containers, it is time to plant them up, which is the exciting part. Spend time thinking about the kind of plants you want, their requirements, and colour schemes – and don't forget to water them when finished!

A large pot may be impossible to shift once planted up.

Mind your back

If you are using a big and heavy container, get it in exactly the place you want it before you add the compost and plants – this will save a lot of potential back ache. Once the container is full of plants and moist compost, it will weigh an awful lot more.

Keep out pests

To reduce the number of pests, such as slugs, entering through the drainage holes, cover the holes with fine, strong mesh before you add the drainage crocks to the bottom of the container. Doing this will also help to keep out some of the other rather less troublesome garden creatures, such as woodlice.

Keep drainage holes open

❀ Many different materials can be used for drainage – broken terracotta pots are not the only option. Try broken household china or large irregularly shaped stones or rocks. Just make sure you position them so that they do not block the holes too much themselves.

❀ If you need to keep the weight of the container to a minimum, use crunched up polystyrene plant trays or packaging from parcels to create a low-weight drainage layer. Make sure that it is removed when the pot is eventually emptied, and not left around the garden, because polystyrene is not biodegradable and may prove hazardous to the local wildlife.

Frost-damaged, broken pots make excellent crocks.

Water your empty pots

Unglazed terracotta absorbs a lot of water when new, often causing new plants to suffer from drought almost immediately. Water the empty pot thoroughly several times before you add the compost. Once wetted, it won't cause any problems.

Don't fill to the brim

Leave about 3cm (1in) unfilled at the top of the pot, otherwise it will overflow when you water it.

Gappy half barrels

Wooden containers, such as half barrels, may have the odd gap in them when new. Don't be tempted to line these with polythene in an attempt to keep the compost in, as this has a drying effect. Instead, wet the wood thoroughly before you plant; it should swell as it absorbs the water, closing the gaps.

Barrels become gappy when standing empty and dry, but when wet should rapidly swell up to seal tightly.

Choosing your compost

❀ Don't be tempted to use garden soil in containers. Although you may get away with it, it rarely keeps its structure well in a container, and the plants often end up suffering from root rots. It really is best to buy fresh, new compost every year. Don't risk re-using compost because doing this makes it much more likely that the plants will suffer diseases or vine weevil attack in the second year.

❀ For short-term containers, such as those filled with summer bedding plants, a standard, multipurpose, loam-free compost usually fits the bill. I always add the larger chunks left after sieving compost for seed sowing – bedding plants don't need such perfect conditions, and I reckon these chunks make for even better drainage.

❀ For longer-term containers, it is usually best to choose a loam-based compost like John Innes No 2. If you find this tends to get a bit airless, add up to 50 per cent multipurpose loam-free compost, plus some grit. The added weight of the loam also helps to prevent pots containing taller plants from toppling over.

Save compost in tall pots

If you've fallen for a long, tall container for your summer bedding, it's easy to save on compost. Place an upturned flowerpot over the drainage hole, so only the upper part of the container needs filling with compost; shallow-rooting and short-term plants don't need a lot of compost depth and won't suffer. If the pot is to stand in a windy spot, reduce the risk of toppling by filling the bottom half with stones, gravel, or an extra-deep layer of crocks instead.

Feed in advance

Make life easy by mixing in feed before planting.

To save time later on, you can add controlled-release fertilizer granules to the compost at planting time; these usually supply food for about six months. For summer bedding I still add regular applications of a high-potash liquid feed because this will ensure an even better display of flowers.

Improve moisture levels

Moisture-retaining granules seem to prevent plants suffering from water-stress for a while longer – great if you are out at work all day. Make sure you follow the instructions with regard to quantities, and don't be tempted to add more than suggested – otherwise, as the granules absorb water and expand you may end up with a volcano effect! I prefer to hydrate the crystals thoroughly and then add them to the compost. This makes it easier to get them evenly distributed; dry crystals tend to fall to the bottom more easily.

The granules grow 30 times larger once wet.

Choose plants carefully

Creating your own container display is great, and you can do exactly what you like in terms of colour combinations, but don't forget to check what each plant that you want to include will look like when it is fully grown and in flower. Consider height, spread, and brightness. If necessary, amend your line-up now rather than later.

Think about colour combinations

When planting for a single-season display, for example when you use seasonal summer bedding, it generally looks best to stick to just two or three types of plant, and also to a restricted colour range – unless, of course, you want to create an "Aaagh, where are my sunglasses" effect! If the plants will be in flower at different times, it is a different matter.

Because containers are much smaller than borders, keep combinations simple.

Pale colours and white make a serene combination.

Odd numbers cover up any variations

If you want to ensure that uneven plant growth is well hidden, use odd, rather than even, numbers for your larger, more high-profile plants. This way it should not look as if an attempt at symmetry has gone wrong!

Cooling colours

It can look great to have really bold colours, but if you are not careful you can end up with just too many. For a cooling effect in your plantings, use either plants with silver foliage or white flowers. These are calming on their own, but can also add some contrast and a bit of light relief to a very bright colour scheme. There's a wide range of likely contenders.

Plants on higher steps need to look good from below as well as above.

Looking good from all angles

When you are planting up a container, make sure that it looks good from all the angles it is likely to be seen from, not just from your view when you're doing the planting. A pot on the doorstep, for instance, needs to look good as you approach the door, from above, and from the doorway.

Starting the cascade effect

If you want to make trailing plants around the edges of the container start to perform that little bit sooner, angle the plants out slightly when you plant them. This way, they are leaning in the right direction from the start.

Remember where your plants will be sited

It is all very well falling for the plants you see in your garden centre, or those that are growing fantastically well in someone else's garden, but make sure that they will also perform well in the spot you have to fill. The amount of sunshine or shade the site receives is hugely important to a plant's success.

Will you water it enough?

If you know you may not be able to water the container quite as often as you should, it is no use going for the real moisture lovers like *Mimulus*, lobelias, and azaleas (*Rhododendron*). Instead choose plants known to be more drought tolerant, such as pelargoniums or herbaceous geraniums.

The pelargoniums that form the backbone of this display will tolerate fairly dry conditions.

Don't stint, pack them in!

Provided you make sure that there is some fresh compost between all the root-balls of adjacent plants, and between the root-balls and the container, you can really use as many short-term bedding plants as you can pack in. The normal rules for long-term planting do not apply here!

Planting for long displays

❀ Make any container look good for longer by under-planting with seasonal bulbs. Choose smallish varieties, such as miniature narcissi, iris, or perhaps crocus, to extend the season of interest. Make sure you plant them deeply enough, and avoid putting very dense-rooted plants like heathers directly on top of bulbs – they may not be able to make their way through the mat of roots. The roots of seasonal bedding plants should not be a problem.

❀ In longer-term containers, where bulbs could last for more than one season, you can also under-plant with seasonal bedding to provide even more colour and impact, but take care when planting these or else you may damage the roots beneath.

Many small bulbs are happy planted in layers.

Get plants off to a good start

Pinch out leggy shoots and fading flowers before planting in the container; it's easier than doing it once planted, when you're all too likely to dislodge the plant. Doing this will also allow the plants to concentrate on producing good, sturdy, bushy growth, and will help them to get established.

Make sure all the plants look their best at the start.

Keep moisture in and pests out

When the planting is complete, try dressing the compost surface with a layer of sharp grit. This serves two purposes: it helps to keep moisture in and decreases the risk of vine weevil adults laying their eggs.

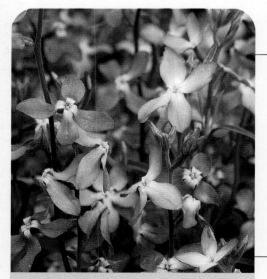

Night-scented stocks are compact enough for most containers.

Complete with some perfume

Bedding plants may look good, but not many are perfumed. Sprinkle seed of night-scented stock (*Matthiola bicornis*) into gaps in the compost to provide perfume during warm summer evenings.

Plant in advance

Try to plant containers of bedding a few weeks early. Provided they are kept in a sheltered and, if necessary, frost-free spot, the plants will establish better than if the container is put out in its final position immediately. Be prepared to wait.

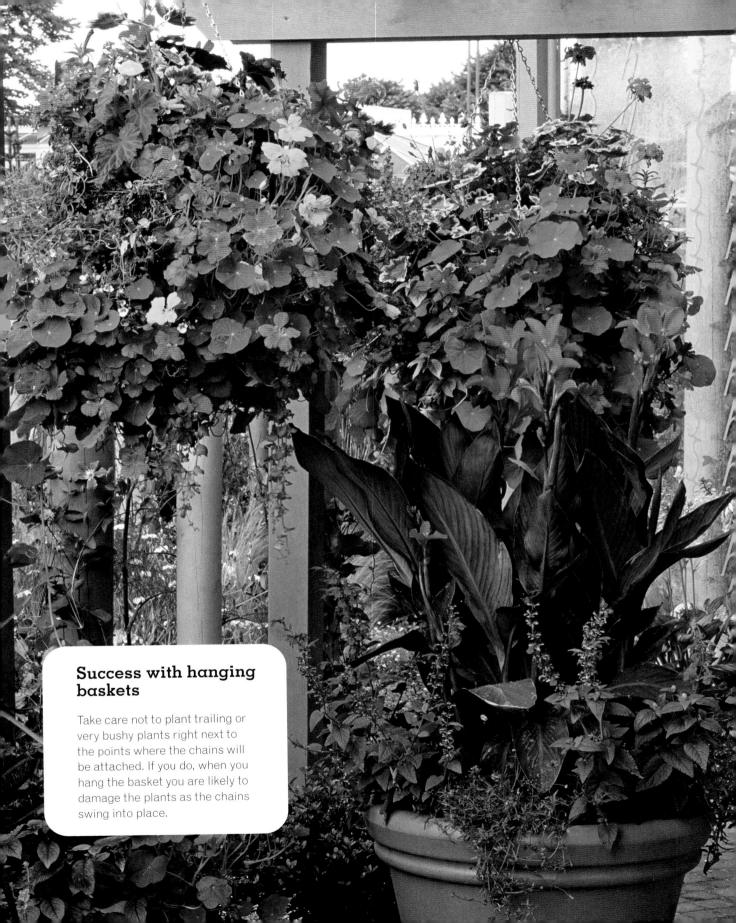

Success with hanging baskets

Take care not to plant trailing or very bushy plants right next to the points where the chains will be attached. If you do, when you hang the basket you are likely to damage the plants as the chains swing into place.

Cultivating crops in containers

Tasty tomatoes, succulent cucumbers, aromatic sage, and juicy apples are just four of the many edible crops you can grow in containers, providing you match the pot to the plant. Here's how to make the leap from pot to plate!

Any vessel with drainage holes that holds soil will be good for growing fruit and veg.

What can you use as a container?

You can use pretty much anything that's a suitable size with adequate drainage holes to contain your edibles. There are even plenty of good-quality, purpose-made fabric "planter bags", complete with drainage holes and handles for ease of use. The advantage of these bags is that you can fold them up over winter when they are not in use.

Big pots make a big difference

❀ By definition, cropping plants need to be productive. If your expectations are to be met, it's essential that they have a decent-sized container. Small containers are hard to keep moist, so avoid pots smaller than 30cm x 30cm (12in x 12in). Big is invariably best.

❀ Drought-tolerant plants, such as many of the Mediterranean herbs, cope happily in a smaller container, or several can be planted together.

Finding big pots

Recycle those huge flower pots that are used for sizeable shrubs and trees, either after you have planted them yourself, or if local landscapers and tree surgeons have any to spare. For those who do a lot of planting, big pots can become space-wasters, and they may be very happy to part with them.

Growing-bags are great

❀ Growing-bags can be bought in just about every garden centre or DIY outlet. They offer the lowest-cost option, and work especially well with crops such as tomatoes and capsicums.

❀ The compost in a growing-bag is often extremely compacted. Luckily the plastic of the bag tends to be tough, so make sure you thoroughly bash the bag to fluff up the contents before you start planting. This will also ensure that the compost is evenly distributed within the bag at the same time.

Before cutting or planting make sure you fluff up the compost.

How to use growing-bags

❀ Most standard-sized growing-bags will fit three tomato plants, but I find it much easier to restrict myself to two: it keeps the plants healthy, and I always get a heavier crop.

❀ Before cutting planting holes in the bag, make sure it is in exactly the spot you want it. Unless supported by a board, open growing-bags are impossible to move without losing compost.

❀ Make an H-shaped cut for each plant; rather than removing the two flaps of plastic this creates, fold each back on itself. This leaves a slightly protruding "lip" on the outer edge of the cut, which will help deflect a lot of water, decrease run-off, and make it much easier to get all the water into the compost.

❀ If you plan to support taller crops in bags, you need to put support structures in place before cutting holes and planting. Inserting them once the plants are in the growing-bags makes excessive root disturbance more likely.

❀ If you tend to over-water plants in containers, then it may be worth making a couple of holes in the base of the growing-bags to allow surplus water to drain off. Otherwise, with this type of container, you are essentially planting in an impervious plastic bag.

Pot feet really can make a difference.

Drainage means life or death

Drainage is important for any plant, so make sure that drainage holes in the base of a container do not become obstructed or clogged. This is easily prevented by using a layer of crocks in the bottom of the pot, or by raising the pot off the ground onto "pot feet", bricks, or even an old pallet to keep the holes clear of any debris.

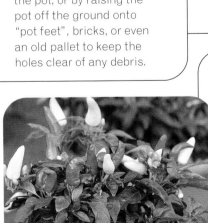

Chillies can be an attractive crop for the patio.

Suit the compost to the crop

❀ The choice of compost you use will depend on whether you are going to grow crops permanently or temporarily. Apples and other permanent crops will benefit from a loam- or soil-based compost, while crops such as annual vegetables grow perfectly well in a good-quality multipurpose compost.

❀ For lime-hating plants, such as blueberries, an ericaceous compost is vital. If they are grown in standard compost, they may develop lime-induced chlorosis, which is an iron and manganese deficiency that results in leaf yellowing between the leaf veins.

Top ten crops for containers

1. Chard 'Bright Lights'
2. Sweet or bell peppers
3. Chilli peppers
4. Aubergines
5. Outdoor tomatoes such as 'Tumbler' or 'Totem'
6. Dwarf French beans
7. Dwarf runner beans, such as 'Hestia'
8. Any herbs
9. Potatoes
10. Carrots

Given enough water and feed, almost any crop can be kept in a pot.

Which crops are suitable?

Just about any vegetable or fruit, including tree fruits, can be grown in a container. The only conditions are that the container must be large enough and filled with a suitable growing medium, and that you must be prepared to put in that bit of extra work required to produce successful crops in containers.

Add some manure

If you have access to well-rotted manure, add it to your compost. It will help to improve moisture retention and also provide a feed for the crops as they develop. I add about 30 per cent manure or garden compost to containers when growing vegetables.

Potted potatoes

❀ You can grow potatoes in a container and produce a very acceptable crop, I use a container with a minimum size of 45cm (18in) each way, and if you choose an attractive container it can even look good on a patio or terrace.

❀ There is no need to plant more than one or two potatoes in each pot of this size; more than this will not actually give much more of a crop, because the plants will compete too much with each other.

❀ It's often said that main-crop varieties work best in containers, but I have grown early and salad varieties in good-sized containers with great success – so grow what you actually like to eat!

❀ If you plant the tuber approximately 15–20cm (6–8in) below the rim of the container you can gradually build up the compost level in the same way that you would "earth up" a crop of potatoes growing in open ground. This will help to keep the plant cropping well, and greatly reduces the risk of light reaching the developing tubers, so causing them to turn green – and poisonous!

Make watering easier

Generally speaking, as far as the pots are concerned, big is always better. Large pots full of a lot of compost will be much easier to keep adequately watered, making your life easier and greatly increasing the chances of a healthy, heavy-cropping plant.

Tree fruits need the largest containers of all.

Thriving beans

❀ Runner beans will do well in a container, but as they are a really thirsty crop, keeping them well watered to produce a good crop can be difficult. Use as large a container as you can – the greater volume of compost means that it will dry out less readily – and line the inside walls with bubble wrap.

❀ Water in the evening to give the beans a chance to take up more water.

❀ Beans growing up a wigwam of bamboo canes creates an attractive bit of vertical gardening.

❀ The dwarf runner bean 'Hestia' is perfect for smaller pots; it does not even require a support, and has attractive red and white flowers.

❀ French beans are not only stringless, but are also much more tolerant of drier soil or compost than runner beans.

❀ Make successive sowings of dwarf French beans for an extended cropping period. The seeds can be sown direct; pests are less likely to eat the emerging seedlings.

❀ Get an extra early crop of dwarf French beans by sowing early and keeping the pot in the greenhouse. Once the danger of frost is passed, bring it outside.

Small containers are difficult to maintain.

Tips for tomatoes

❀ Tomatoes are the classic container vegetable, so simply choose any variety sold as being suitable for growing outdoors and get going.

❀ The "patio" varieties, which are generally particularly compact, are easier to keep happy in the confines of a smaller container.

❀ If you want attractive tomato plants for a hanging basket, then try the cascading varieties such as 'Tumbler' or 'Tumbling Tom'; the latter is available in red or yellow fruiting varieties. These also look good trailing over the edges of a container.

❀ Tomatoes are particularly intolerant of fluctuating temperatures, especially when the weather gets a bit cold. If planted out too early, the foliage often turns a miserable shade of purple! Always harden off the plants thoroughly and, unless you provide temporary protection, don't risk putting the containers out until early summer or even later.

Miniature or trailing tomatoes flourish in baskets.

❀ Choose a "bush" variety if you want to have a more compact tomato plant that does not need to have its sideshoots removed, and which only requires a bit of staking. "Cordon" or "indeterminate" types need more support.

Potted peppers

❀ Both sweet or bell peppers and chilli peppers can be grown in containers. If you want a decent crop, choose a well-protected and sheltered spot with plenty of sun.

❀ If you're growing hot chilli peppers and children also use the garden, position the pots well out of reach!

Try growing attractive peppers as a talking point, next to a sunny bench.

Aubergines

❀ I find that aubergines crop well in pots, but they do need a lot of natural light and plenty of warmth, so choose a site with care, and make it as sheltered and sunny as possible.

❀ The pretty purple flowers (and sometimes purple stems too) make aubergines an attractive patio plant, but remember most varieties have sharp thorns, so think carefully before you put the pots in position.

Carrots and parsnips

❀ Both these crops are best sown direct into the compost; the seedlings can then be thinned to the spacing indicated on the packet.

❀ If you want to avoid carrots becoming infested with the maggot-like larvae of the carrot fly, growing them in a container makes the task easy. Choose a container more than 45cm (18in) tall and the crop will be too high for there to be much chance of the carrot fly laying her eggs on it.

❀ Parsnip seed should germinate fairly reliably under suitable conditions in well-drained compost, but it is still worth "station-sowing the seed". This means sowing two or three seeds in each spot where you would like one parsnip to grow – you can always thin out any extras.

❀ Parsnip seeds are particularly slow to germinate, so why not sow a few lettuce seeds where you sow each batch of parsnip seeds? This makes it clear exactly where the parsnips were sown, and make good use of the pot until the parsnips start to grow. Once the seedlings begin to appear, simply use a sharp knife to cut the lettuce off just below the soil surface.

Beetroot

This is a crop I thoroughly recommend for pot growing, especially if, like me, you have a high population of slugs and snails in your garden. These pests are less of a problem in pots.

❀ It is best not to try to transplant beetroot; it rarely crops so well. Sow the seed direct into the container, then thin out the seedlings as you would if they were in open ground.

Try red-leaf beets like 'Bull's Blood'.

Marrows, courgettes, and squashes

❀ All these related, heavy-cropping plants can be grown in containers, but they all do far better when supplied with lots of moisture and food, so I definitely advise using the largest container you can get.

❀ These crops are both hungry and thirsty, so they definitely benefit from some well-rotted manure incorporated in the compost.

❀ Courgettes are the easiest to grow in a container; the plants are relatively compact, and the fruits are small enough not to need supporting. The others will need more attention and work.

❀ If you grow a squash in a container, remember that the plants generally produce plenty of wide-ranging, trailing stems. Try placing the container close to a hedge, trellis, or fence, which the plant can use as a support through which to scramble.

Courgette plants can spread out quite a bit, so give them some space.

Salad leaves and lettuces

❀ Lettuces and other cut-and-come-again salad leaf crops do very well in containers, and are so easy to harvest if you put the pot close to the house.

❀ Choose some varieties with coloured or interestingly shaped leaves, and the crop will have double value, being both decorative and tasty. Either grow single varieties, mix up the seed from a few of your favourites, or use one of the packets of mixed variety leaves.

❀ Reduce the risk of the lettuces running to seed by keeping pots at least partly shaded to help prevent the compost drying out.

Using containers can help keep off slugs.

Colourful chard

❀ To make a productive patio pot full of chard look particularly gorgeous, choose a very colourful variety, such as 'Bright Lights'.

❀ For some jazzy colour effects or serious colour co-ordination, you could grow the crop in a contrasting or matching coloured container.

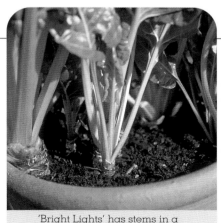
'Bright Lights' has stems in a range of eye-catching colours.

Plants per pot

This is approximately how many plants fit a 30cm (12in) pot:

1 plant: Aubergine, courgette, marrow, squash, pepper, tomato

1–2 plants: Potato

3 plants: Strawberry

4–5 plants: Runner bean and climbing or dwarf French bean

8–10 plants: Beetroot, chard

12 plants: Parsnip

35 plants: Carrot

Lettuce: depends on variety

Look for attractive crops

It is worth looking around for especially ornamental varieties of your favourite plants. For instance, you could have yellow, striped, or purple tomatoes, and why grow the standard grey-green sage when you could have it with purple, or purple, cream, and green variegated leaves?

Herbs

❀ Herbs make great pot plants and most look really attractive too, so combine their good looks with a stunning terracotta pot and, hey presto, you have something seriously ornamental, aromatic and tasty.

❀ Herbs need excellent drainage, so incorporate plenty of horticultural grit into the compost before planting; I add about 25 per cent by volume.

Terracotta suits herbs, both in terms of their looks and needs.

❀ If your garden soil is heavy and inclined to be moist, your herb growing may need to be restricted to pots. Make it even easier to get the most from what you grow by positioning the pots in a lovely, sunny spot that is easily accessible.

❀ Make a pot of herbs look all the more attractive by dressing the surface of the compost with a thick layer of attractive horticultural grit. This will also help to ensure good growth by reducing the risk of stagnant conditions around the plant crowns.

❀ Growing mint in a pot is the one absolutely foolproof way to ensure that it does not start taking over your garden, as it does when grown in open ground.

❀ Make a container of assorted herbs look especially attractive by including a few trailing or sprawling varieties of thyme planted close to the edge, where they can cascade downwards.

❀ If you want to keep a record of exactly which varieties of herb you have in the pot, remove the plastic labels when planting and slip each in to the compost close to its plant. This way you need not see the label, but you can retrieve the information easily.

Mint should be kept in a container to control it: you can plunge a pot into the ground if you want it in a bed.

Strawberries

❀ Strawberries are the favourite fruit for growing in containers, largely because they really seem to thrive, whether they are in a special strawberry planter, a window box, or just a good-sized pot.

❀ The advantage of growing strawberries in a pot is that because the plants are raised off the ground, the fruits are far less likely to be nibbled by hungry slugs and snails. This is the perfect way to grow them if you want undamaged fruits and don't like using slug controls.

❀ I find strawberry planters, with their flange-shaped holes, really difficult to plant up and maintain, though other peoples' efforts certainly look good. You can make your own tiered planter from three shallow terracotta pots of decreasing sizes. Fill each with compost, then stack them on top of each other, with the largest at the bottom. You can plant around the edges of the lower pots, and in the centre of the top one. A perfect strawberry mountain!

Give strawberries plenty of water and feed, and they'll guarantee a juicy crop.

Keep crops watered

Some flowering plants might cope with drought, but crops in pots need a good, regular supply of water. Drip irrigation systems can make all the difference, and most can be fed from water butts.

Tree fruit

❀ It is possible to grow tree fruit in containers, but you are not likely to get a heavy crop and, for me, the maintenance is a job I would prefer to avoid! if space is limited but you do have some open ground, it is easier and more productive to grow fruit trees in fan, espalier, step-over, or cordon forms.

❀ If you really want to use a pot, perhaps to move more tender trees under cover for winter, or to make a fig fruit better, the container must be large, ideally a full-sized half barrel, not one of the dinky sort about 45cm (18in) across.

❀ The compost needs to be loam-based, ideally John Innes No 3, but do add extra grit to keep the compost structure open and adequately drained.

You may want to keep trees near house walls and foundations in pots, but you will get smaller crops.

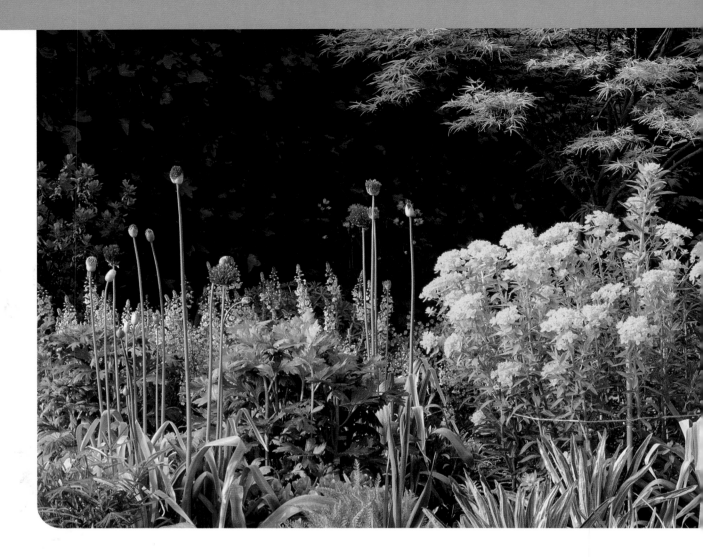

Trees & shrubs

Trees and shrubs form the "backbone" of a garden, providing structure and giving form for 12 months of the year. Trees and many shrubs too can be quite pricey, so it is all the more essential that you get the right ones.

Over the years trees will change their shape and size, and the effect they have on the garden will subtly change too. Being the largest plants in the garden, trees also tend to have the greatest influence on what other plants will grow and how they will flourish. Choosing the most suitable ones, and making sure that they grow and develop to create just the effect you had dreamed of can be one of the most important gardening tasks.

Choosing your trees
Choosing trees should be a pleasure, as they are plants that may be there for generations and will help to make your garden that perfect haven that it has the potential to be. This is probably the most significant purchase you will make –

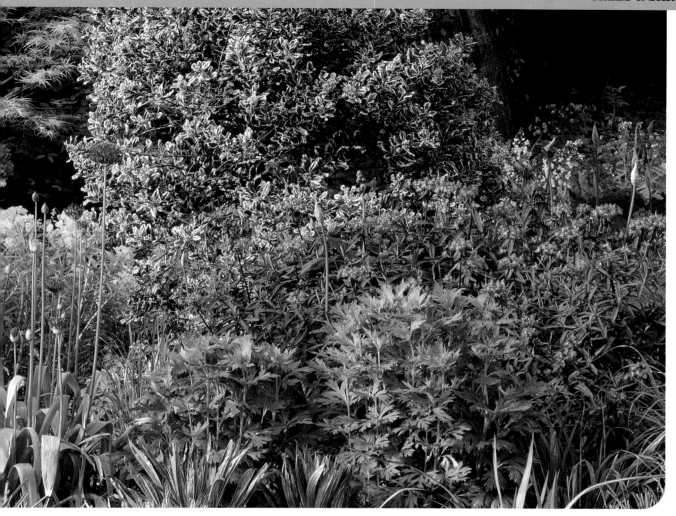

because they will have such a huge impact on your garden over the years. A tree has the potential to grow to many times the size it was when you bought it. So, when you decide you need some trees, make sure you do your research and try to avoid those impulse buys.

Every now and then established trees may need the help of an arborist or tree surgeon. This is an expense that you should try not to resent, because when properly looked after, those trees will give you untold pleasure in return.

This chapter shows you how to:

- ❀ Choose a new tree or shrub – getting the right species for the site.
- ❀ Tree and shrub maintenance: how to plant them, care for them, and prune them.
- ❀ Choose what to plant under the tree canopy.
- ❀ Deal with tender species.
- ❀ Buy, plant, and care for shrub roses.

Choosing a new tree or shrub

Trees and large shrubs often act as focal points within the garden's design, so you need to spend time researching before you buy. Make sure the species you have in mind will thrive in the conditions you can offer and that they won't grow too big.

Seeing trees in full leaf does make choosing easier.

Convenience plants

Container-grown trees and shrubs are popular because they are convenient. They can be bought and planted at any time of year, but there can be hidden drawbacks. Avoid buying them either during or just after extremely cold weather, when their roots may have been frozen in their pots, or during or after a long period of hot weather, when plants may have become stressed by drought.

Autumn is best

There is no doubt that autumn is the best time to plant trees and shrubs. This allows the plants time to acclimatize before facing the stresses of the following summer. More importantly, it also gives the roots time to move out into the soil while it is still relatively warm and moist.

Bare-root or balled?

Bare-root plants, lifted from open ground, are sold from late autumn to late winter or very early spring. The roots of root-balled plants are put into moist soil and wrapped. They are often very good value, but the roots must be kept moist. Both are planted while dormant and leafless to limit root damage and help them to establish.

Nurseries may prune roots to help plants establish.

See its true colours

If you would like to plant a tree or shrub with colourful autumn foliage, then autumn is the best time to buy. Autumn colour is influenced by several factors, including weather and soil conditions, but if you see the plant in its full autumn glory before you buy, then at least you'll know it has the potential to do great things.

Since acers can vary quite a bit, pick your plant when in leaf.

Paying for delivery

Although getting sizeable shrubs or trees delivered may add quite a bit to the cost of buying them, the cost of delivery may well be very worthwhile. If you have not got the right type of vehicle, you can end up damaging the stems, or having the top growth blown to bits in the wind!

Cutting down to size

It is important to choose a suitable size of tree for the space you are planting. If you fall in love with a tree that is likely too get too big, you could consider treating it as a short-term resident, perhaps planning to fell it after ten years or so. Alternatively, consider having it pruned and shaped regularly so that it retains its shape. Some trees respond better than others to this treatment, so do check before you buy.

Top ten trees for small gardens

1. *Acer negundo* 'Flamingo'
2. *Acer griseum*
3. *Acer palmatum*
4. *Acer pseudoplatanus* 'Brilliantissimum'
5. *Cercis siliquastrum*
6. *Koelruteria paniculata*
7. *Magnolia stellata*
8. Many *Prunus* species
9. *Pyrus salicifolia* 'Pendula'
10. *Robinia pseudoacacia* 'Frisia'

Acers are perfect for small spaces.

Be a choosy shopper

❀ To pick the healthiest plants, inspect stems for signs of die-back, pests, or infection, check that the leaves are in good condition, and look for plump, vigorous buds. Put back anything that does not look in perfect health.

❀ Avoid plants with moss, weeds, or lichens on the compost – it suggests they have been poorly cared for.

❀ Excessive pruning may have been done to remove die-back; the problem may not be there anymore, but the plant is weakened.

❀ Slip off the pot: compost that falls apart indicates recent re-potting or maybe root die-back; congested roots suggest a plant has been in its pot too long.

Bigger isn't better

The size of the tree or shrub you buy will affect its price. A big tree will make more impact when it's planted, but may also cost you ten times the price of a smaller one – and need more looking after than its smaller versions. Staking is rarely advised for average-sized new purchases, but it may be essential for a big tree, when the size of rootball cannot support the top growth. Watering needs are also greater, and the tree will establish more slowly, so think hard before buying big!

The growth below the surface is just as vital as what's above.

Planting time

Plant your trees and shrubs as soon as possible after you have bought them, so that there is less chance of their being damaged or suffering from drought. This is equally important when container-grown as you are unlikely to water as regularly as the nursery.

Look after container-grown plants

If you can't plant new pot-grown trees or shrubs straight away, water them well and stand them in a sheltered spot where they won't be knocked or blown over. If necessary, carefully tie taller plants to a support, or even lay them down so they're less likely to get damaged.

"Heel in" bare-root trees or shrubs

Bare-root plants need to be "heeled in" or temporarily planted to prevent their roots drying out. If you are sure that you can plant within 24 hours, cover the roots in damp hessian or rags overnight. Dig the planting hole before lifting them so that they can go straight in.

Heel in on a slant to avoid root disturbance.

Making a moat

If the site is dry or likely to become dry, scrape out the soil around the planting hole to create a slight depression and encircling bank that will funnel the water towards the roots. If this slight depression is maintained it should continue to direct water inwards for years to come.

The roots should grow out into a zone of planting mix.

Dig a big hole

Make sure that the hole you dig is bigger than the rootball of the plant. If possible, aim to make the planting hole at least 50 per cent bigger than the existing pot. This will give you plenty of space to spare in all directions, and allow you to add plenty of planting mix.

Planting on heavy soils

Dig as large a hole as possible, and mix grit and planting compost with the natural soil to reduce the contrast between it and the contents of the hole. This dramatically reduces "sump" problems. Sumps are the result of planting a container-grown plant in a smallish hole, in a heavy soil, with normal planting compost. The rootball and compost can act like a sponge, drawing in excess soil water when the soil gets wet, and drowning the plant.

Mound planting

On very heavy soils or those that are prone to waterlogging, it is best to plant trees and shrubs on a slight mound to reduce damage. Be careful not to leave any of the roots exposed, as that will have disastrous results. Hedges planted on a wet site will have a greater chance of thriving if planted higher than normal; plant them along a slight ridge, rather than trying to make a series of individual mounds.

Planting mixtures

A good mixture for planting consists of the soil that was dug out mixed with some well-rotted manure or garden compost, plus some general fertilizer. This should help to improve the soil texture and provide nutrients to get the tree or shrub started. Make sure that any fertilizers are mixed in very thoroughly and don't come into direct contact with the plant, and that you water the tree or shrub in well.

Using a cane across the hole is easier than judging depth by eye.

Extra care on dry soils

Fill the planting hole with water on a dry site, and allow the water to drain away before you plant. This should help the surrounding soil to become thoroughly moistened without wasting water.

Planting checklist

❀ If the roots are congested, teasing out the roots will really help the plant to establish quickly. Soaking the rootball in water for a couple of hours, or at most overnight, makes it easier to tease out the roots without damaging them.

❀ It is essential that you do not set plants too deeply or you will run the risk of stem bases rotting and the roots not getting all the oxygen they need.

❀ Plants from a reputable garden centre or nursery should be potted at the correct depth, but there's no harm in checking – just the roots should be below ground, not part of the stem or any of the trunk above the roots.

❀ To ensure you plant at the right depth, place a cane across the hole and use this as a guide for the positioning of the rootball.

❀ As you add the planting mix, periodically check the planting depth; it is a lot easier to adjust it at this stage.

❀ Firm the mix around the roots as you fill to prevent "subsidence" and ensure that the roots make close contact with the soil.

❀ As soon as the plant is in, water thoroughly, topping up the soil carefully if the level drops.

Care after planting

Once a tree or shrub is in the ground, you can't just walk off and completely forget it. Huge numbers of potentially lovely (and often rather pricey) plants are lost every year because they're not give enough aftercare.

When to stake

❀ You need only stake large trees, which are vulnerable to windrock before their roots become established and can support their own top growth.

❀ If you do need to stake, drive in a short stake at an angle. This encourages better root development and a stronger trunk than longer or upright stakes.

❀ Take great care not to damage the roots when you are driving the stake into position. Ideally you should have hammered the stake into the ground before the plant goes in the hole.

Water deep down

If you are worried about drought after planting, why not bury a piece of pipe at an angle (a length of downpipe will do) next to the roots of the new plant? Keep the pipe in position as you back-fill the hole, and leave the top end protruding just above the soil surface. You can pour water straight down the pipe, avoiding wastage and ensuring that the water goes straight to the roots quickly and effectively.

Deep watering will draw roots downward.

Rabbit damage

If there is any chance of rabbit damage take precautions immediately, using at least one spiral tree guard or erecting a rabbit-proof cylinder around the base of the plant. For multi-stemmed trees or shrubs, you may need to use a wire mesh to protect the base of the plant, or perhaps try several spiral guards.

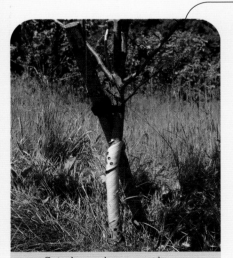
Spiral guards may not be attractive, but they work.

Tie time

When choosing a tree tie, look for one that is easy to adjust, which avoids constriction as the trunk expands. It must also have a "buffer" or spacer block on it; this should be placed between the tree's trunk and the stake to prevent chafing when the tree sways.

Check ties regularly and loosen as the trunk thickens.

Mulching last

✿ When planting is complete, apply a mulch 8cm (3¼in) deep to cover the entire root area, and ideally a little further. This will help both to decrease competition from weeds and to reduce moisture loss from the soil by evaporation.

✿ Do make sure that the mulch is not in contact with the tree's trunk or the shrub's stems because this may cause rotting and stress, possibly even death.

✿ Don't be tempted to use an impermeable material, such as sheet plastic, beneath the mulch. This might stop weeds from growing, but it will also dramatically reduce the amount of oxygen and moisture that can get through to the plant's roots.

Woven plastic covered with bark is very effective.

Under the mulch

There are plenty of weed-suppressing fabrics on the market now. These will allow moisture and air to get where they need to go, and can be used on the soil surface and then concealed beneath a layer of more attractive mulching material.

Weather damage

Occasionally, even a perfectly hardy tree or shrub may suffer damage from cold or wind shortly after planting. If there is any risk of this happening, drape horticultural fleece over it, or use a fleece drawstring bag large enough to keep the whole top growth snug. Regular drench-watering is a must during windy weather as well as in dry spells.

What can go wrong?

✿ Woody plants can suffer from replant disorder, in which a perfectly healthy new plant deteriorates rapidly when planted in the same spot from which a closely related plant has been removed. This is especially common with roses, apples, and pears, and can occur even when the plant looks in perfect health. The precise cause is uncertain – it may be nutritional, or due to the build up of soil bacteria or fungi – so never give it a chance to happen.

✿ Roots of woody plants can be surprisingly springy and may tend to curl back into their compacted or restricted shape. Make sure you re-spread them out carefully before backfilling the planting hole.

Banana fertilizer

If you eat lots of bananas you can make good use of the skins, which have a particularly high potassium content. When roughly chopped and added to the planting hole, they will improve the organic content and provide extra potassium as they break down, which will encourage both wood ripening and an excellent flowering display.

Pruning trees and shrubs

Always check the pruning needs of your trees and shrubs, either on the label or in a reference book, before you attack them with any sort of pruning tool. If in doubt, wait – too often plants are spoiled by unnecessary or excessive pruning.

Neat cuts without long stubs are the key to good pruning.

Cut at an angle

Make pruning cuts at an angle, so that rain is encouraged to roll off the surface rather than remain on it. Cut close to the bud, but not so close that the bud itself could be damaged.

Pruning directions

Always cut back to a good-looking, healthy bud facing in the direction you want any new growth to go. This is almost always going to be an outward-facing bud.

Keep tools sharp

Sharp pruning tools are vital; it is easy to create a horrendous, crushed mess with badly designed or blunt secateurs. The damaged stems not only look awful, but are also more prone to infection by fungi that cause die-back.

Pruning for health

❀ Remove weak and spindly wood, pruning back to an outward-facing bud. This should help to promote the development of healthy new growth.

❀ Dead wood can and should be removed promptly, regardless of the time of year, but it is easier to spot what is dead or dying when the plant is in leaf.

Always remove sickly or dead growth quickly.

❀ If you are pruning out dead or dying parts of a stem, make sure you cut well past any signs of the problem, into completely healthy growth, and then clean the pruning tool before using it again.

Pruning for flowers

When pruning to encourage new flowering stems, or to rejuvenate a neglected shrubs as a rule you can remove up to one in five of the old stems, pruning back to within about 5–7.5cm (2–3in) of ground level.

Checks and balances

When pruning, take your time and stand back from time to time to check that you are achieving a well-balanced look and removing stems evenly over the entire plant.

Ten common shrubs pruned in spring

1. *Buddleja davidii*	**6.** *Forsythia*
2. *Caryopteris*	**7.** *Hydrangea*
3. *Ceratostigma*	**8.** Shrubby lavateras
4. *Cotinus*	**9.** *Perovskia*
5. Hardy fuchsias	**10.** Spireas

Fuchsias flower on new growth.

Removing branches

If you cut a whole limb from a tree in one go, the bark underneath may be torn, unless you "under-cut" it first. Use a sharp saw to make a cut into the bottom of the limb about 30cm (12in) from the trunk, cutting about quarter of the way through. Next, saw down through the branch about 2cm (¾in) further away from the trunk until you can lift the branch away. Now make another undercut 3–5cm (1–2in) from the trunk, then saw down from the top of the limb, joining the two cuts. Make sure you do not damage the swollen "collar" at the branch base where the wound heals. Finally neaten off the newly created cut.

A short stub is easy to remove cleanly.

A cut away from the collar will heal well.

Remove suckers

Some trees are notorious for producing suckers or unwanted growth from the base or at some distance from the trunk – watch out for this especially on *Rhus*, *Prunus*, robinias, lilacs (*Syringa*) and poplars (*Populus*). Suckers need to be dealt with promptly: cut or pull them off right up close to the root from which they came, but be warned you may need to do this regularly. The very action of removing them often stimulates more to grow!

Ten common shrubs pruned in summer/after flowering

1. *Buddleja alternifolia*

2. *Chaenomeles*

3. *Cotoneaster*

4. *Deutzia*

5. *Kolkwitzia*

6. *Magnolia x soulangeana*

7. *Philadelphus*

8. *Photinia*

9. *Prunus*

10. *Ribes*

Under and through the canopy

Make the best use of every scrap of space by underplanting shrubs and trees, and growing climbers through them. Obviously this increases competition for moisture and nutrients, but as long as you supply plenty of both, everything should grow really well.

A few bulbs tucked around a sapling can spread to form a whole colony under the mature tree.

What plants can you use?

It is best to use relatively small and shallow-rooted plants for underplanting because they will make fewer demands on the soil and everything it contains. Bedding plants, herbaceous perennials, and bulbs generally work fine.

Plant together

Minimize damage to the tree or shrub roots by getting your permanent underplanting, such as bulbs, in place when planting the tree or shrub. This makes the whole business easier, and means there is no possibility of any root damage.

Drifts of bulbs

Bulbs planted in drifts look wonderful beneath trees, and can really transform any part of your garden. Try to plant the bulbs in a fairly random, scattered effect so that they look natural. Straight lines or spacing that is too perfect really look peculiar and certainly spoil the effect.

Keeping to scale

If you want to plant beneath a shrub, you can still use bulbs to great effect. To keep everything in scale, stick to smaller types such as crocus, snowdrops (*Galanthus*), cyclamen or grape hyacinths (*Muscari*) or use miniature narcissi such as 'Tête a Tête'.

Making space

If there is no space beneath a shrub, why not do a bit of crown-lifting? Just remove the lowermost branches – provided you don't overdo it, the shrub should still look great but there will be space for a lovely drift of bedding, bulbs, or small herbaceous perennials.

Purple crocuses look natural under trees.

Best climbers for scaling shrubs

1. *Eccremocarpus scaber*
2. Morning glory (*Ipomoea*)
3. *Tropaeolum speciosum*
4. Sweet pea (*Lathyrus*)
5. Clematis (most)
6. *Cobaea scandens*
7. *Thunbergia alata*

Ascending colour

❁ If you want more colour and interest in a limited space, give a tree or shrub extra value by growing a climber through it. A climber will increase the seasons of interest and, provided you use one that is not too heavy and is at least in proportion with the shrub or tree, both should grow well together. Such mixing is really best done with fully established shrubs or trees, and any shrubs that are used as supports need to be quite large.

❁ Annual climbers can look great, particularly on relatively small shrubs, and will not pose significant competition.

❁ If you go for a clematis, unless it is for an extremely large shrub or preferably a tree, avoid the very vigorous *Clematis montana*; its rampant growth may prove just too much!

A clematis in a tree gives it a whole new look.

Protecting the roots

To ensure that both the tree and the climber do well, each needs an adequate root run. Therefore the climber needs to be planted at some distance from the trunk of the tree, not right up close to it. Make sure that there is plenty of bulky organic matter in the planting hole too, and pay extra attention over the first few years whilst establishment takes place.

Will they survive?

Choose plants that can either put up with the degree of shade cast by the tree or shrub, or which guarantee an adequate amount of time when the shade is not excessive. Underplantings and climbers are likely to need a bit of extra moisture and food, so keep the area well watered and mulched.

Supporting act

❁ To get the climber going in the right direction, run wire or rope from its base to the lowest branches; remove it once the climber is established.

❁ Thread the wire or rope through a length of old hosepipe where it goes over a branch, to prevent chafing.

Best climbers to grow into trees

1. Clematis
2. *Tropaeolum speciosum*
3. *Eccremocarpus scaber*
4. Honeysuckles (*Lonicera*)
5. Roses, including 'Rambling Rector', Albéric Barbier', 'Bobby James', 'Paul's Himalayan Musk', and, for large trees only, *Rosa filipes* 'Kiftsgate'

Honeysuckles in trees near seating give fragrance.

Tricks for tender species

If you've fallen for a tree or shrub that is a bit tender, do your utmost to provide it with what it needs, unless you are prepared to take the risk that it will be damaged or even killed when the weather is particularly cold.

A warm wall helps *Cytisus battandieri.*

Siting with care

Choose the planting site with extra care: consider how much protection is offered by nearby hedges, large shrubs, trees, boundaries, or heated buildings. Planting on a sheltered, sunny wall may make the difference between survival or die-back.

Tougher with time

Many marginally hardy plants are much hardier once established. Provide extra cold protection in the first few years, but often this won't be necessary after a few seasons.

Make a base camp

Create a seasonal shelter using galvanized chicken wire made into a tent over the shrub and filled with dry leaves, bracken, or straw. This works well on wall-shrubs because the cage or tent can be fixed to the wall or fence. Avoid using hay or other material that is inclined to hold moisture; this will encourage stem deterioration.

Wrap up warm

Cover potentially tender shrubs or small trees with a few layers of horticultural fleece, making sure that they are well anchored. Fleece drawstring bags are very useful for shrubs because they can simply be popped over them to provide a few degrees of frost protection.

Fleece bags are the most convenient protection.

Let them breathe

Never be tempted to wrap tender plants in plastic or other non-breathable material because condensation will build up, shortly followed by rotting and deterioration. Plastic can be used, but only in the very short term.

Wrap tree fern trunks with breathable fabric.

Tender tree ferns

Stems or bases of tender shrubs, such as tree ferns (*Dicksonia antarctica*), can be wrapped in hessian or old sacking held in place with twine.

Shrub roses

Roses are deservedly popular garden plants, but don't forget that most of them are well armed with thorns. Think about their proximity to paths or other places where they could regularly pose a danger to young children, or even you.

Shopping around for variety

The biggest range of roses is available from specialist growers and nurseries, so make sure you look through few a few catalogues or websites – the range is staggering.

Bare-root roses aren't expensive and establish well.

Buying bare-root

Most people agree that it is best to buy roses bare root, ready to be delivered and planted in the late autumn and winter. Most of the specialist nurseries supply them in this way.

With such a huge variety of roses, you cannot fail to find a favourite.

Planting depths

Roses generally have a clear graft-point where the rootstock has been grafted onto the chosen cultivar. When planting a rose, this swollen area should be at or only just below soil level; if it is buried too deeply you are much more likely to get unwanted sucker growth from it later on.

Know your roses

Roses differ in more than just their flower shape and colour. For example, musk roses are best where you need scent to carry on the air. If you live in a damp climate, rugosa types are the most resistant to fungal diseases, and are also surprisingly hardy. There are roses suitable for drier and wetter gardens too, so it is worth doing a bit of research. Good nurseries can advise if you tell them your conditions.

Special treatment for roses

Roses really do benefit from a specially formulated rose fertilizer, which has just the right balance of nutrients. These include potassium and magnesium, so helping to encourage flowering while preventing the foliage from yellowing as a result of magnesium deficiency.

Climbers & wall plants

Whatever your personal style may be, it is great to be able to garden not just on the horizontal, but also to include a little vertical gardening. Any garden has its fair share of vertical surfaces, and most of them will have the potential to become new planting spaces, so why not make use of them all? If you have always hankered after a larger garden than you have, or perhaps your gardening is restricted to a yard enclosed by fencing or walls, or maybe even a balcony, then making use of each and

every one of those potential planting sites that are on the vertical is even more important.

In this chapter I'm taking a closer look at how to ensure you succeed in making the best possible use of each and every surface, whatever its size, structure, shape, or aspect. Some of these surfaces are best suited to being covered with climbing plants, while others can be made beautiful using wall shrubs. It is well worth doing a little research into what is available before you go on a shopping spree.

Bringing height to your garden

Climbers and wall shrubs are not difficult to grow. Provided you plant properly in the right position and keep them in good shape, they can totally transform dull expanses of wall and fence. Many walls, especially those which are south or west facing, will offer you warmer and more sheltered growing conditions not available in other parts of your garden, and so need to be cherished and used to their very best advantage.

This chapter shows you how to:

- ❀ Support climbers with different kinds of structures.
- ❀ Choose climbers and wall shrubs – assess your needs and conditions to make the best choice.
- ❀ Plant climbers – tips and tricks for the best results.
- ❀ Prune and train climbers – at the best time of year.

How to support climbers

Some climbers are able to cling to surfaces and need no additional support, but most need a means to help them cover the surface. Generally speaking, the larger and woodier the stems of the established plant, the stronger the support will need to be.

Self-supporters

Self-clinging climbers include *Campsis grandiflora* (though some minor support may be needed), the ivies *Hedera helix* and *H. colchica*, *Hydrangea anomala* subsp. *petiolaris* (this needs support only until it starts to cling, which is usually within 18 months), *Parthenocissus henryana*, *P. quinquefolia*, and *P. tricuspidata* 'Veitchii', and *Pileostegia viburnoides* (which needs some support, but only initially).

Use a climbing hydrangea to cover a shaded wall.

Order of priority

If the climber you are planting is quite small, it may not be able to make much use of the support system initially, but always get the trellis or wires in place before you plant. It is simpler to work without the plant, and there is less chance of damaging it.

Anyone for trellis?

Trellis panels are a useful way to introduce a partial obscuring of a view or unsightly area whilst also providing a good surface up which to grow climbers. Choose light and medium weight climbers, which should be fine on trellis. Avoid the most vigorous ones such as Virginia creeper (*Parthenocissus quinquefolia*) or some types of clematis, and the heaviest, such as wisteria.

Thunbergia alata 'African Sunset' is suitable for trellis.

Leave a gap

A trellis panel on a wall should be fixed so that as much air as possible can circulate behind it. The easiest way to do this is to fix wooden battens about 5cm (2in) thick to the wall, and then attach the trellis to these battens.

Think about access

Walls or fences will need maintenance work at some stage. Make this easier by fixing the trellis so that it can be lowered if necessary. Fix horizontal battens to the wall and attach the trellis to the lower batten with hinges and the top batten with hooks and eyes.

Curves and panels fit together to make interesting outlines.

Any shape but square

Trellis comes in many different shapes and designs. If you thought it was always in squares and oblongs, take a look at what's available: there are sizes and shapes for just about every vertical surface imaginable.

Detachable panels

If you need to be able to remove the trellis from the wall completely, then you can still use the basic system of attaching it to battens. Use heavyweight hooks and eyes on both the top and bottom battens for attaching the trellis panel. It is certainly easier to repaint or treat trellis off the wall, and reduces the risk of damage to plants below.

Creating a supporting framework

❀ Heavier plants need something sturdier than trellis. If you have your eye on such a plant or if you simply don't like the look of trellis panels, then a system of wires is the answer. If you use suitable materials and do the job well this will support anything from the lightest to the heaviest climber.

❀ You can use any type of wire, but for the strongest and longest-lasting support system galvanized straining wire – available from garden centres – is best.

❀ Straining wires can be stretched between vine eyes, either horizontally or at any angle up to vertical to create a fan-shape. This provides the plants with room to grow and minimizes the build up of stagnant air behind the plant (which will encourage disease development). The wires need to be about 5cm (2in) from the surface of the wall.

❀ For the support to work it is essential that the wires are kept taut; if necessary, use a pair of pliers to tighten the wires, making sure that they are extremely taut when installed. Adjustable straining bolts will help to tension heavy wires. It really is worth buying good quality and rust-resistant fixings for this sort of job: go for galvanized or brass screws, and galvanized wire and vine-eyes.

The extra-long shafts of vine eyes hold the wires away from the surface of the wall.

Choosing climbers and wall shrubs

The general rules for choosing a healthy and worthwhile plant (see page 67) apply when it comes to selecting a climber or wall shrub. If you start with the best quality plant and look after it well, you should soon be rewarded with plenty of new growth.

Do your homework

With climbing plants, it is all the more important that you research before you buy. Make sure you get a climber whose growth approximates to your surface area: too vigorous or heavy a climber can be potentially disastrous.

Climbers for shady places

1. *Akebia quinata*
2. *Celastrus scandens*
3. *Clematis alpina*
4. *Clematis macropetala*
5. *Humulus lupulus*
6. *Hydrangea anomala* subsp. *petiolaris*
7. *Lonicera japonica* and varieties
8. *Lonicera periclymenum*
9. *Parthenocissus tricuspidata*
10. *Schisandra chinensis*

Honeysuckles have the bonus of superb scent.

Annual changes

You can concentrate on annuals if you want to have a regularly changing display. Try morning glory (*Ipomoea*), sweet pea (*Lathyrus odoratus*), or *Eccremocarpus scaber*.

Climbers for a sunny spot

1. *Actinidia kolomikta*
2. *Passiflora caerulea*
3. *Solanum crispum* 'Glasnevin'
4. *Trachelospermum asiaticum*
5. *Vitis* 'Brant'
6. *Wisteria*

Morning glories produce bright, trumpet like blooms throughout the summer.

Wisteria needs sunshine to perform to its full potential.

Make the most of shelter

Walls, especially those that are in a sheltered spot, often allow you to grow shrubs which might otherwise suffer in your garden. When deciding what to grow on these surfaces, remember that this is where you can choose something that will really benefit from the luxuriously protected conditions on offer.

Climbers favoured by birds, like Virginia creeper, are ideal on a fence or screen, but not near doors.

Climbers for perfume

1. *Clematis armandii*
2. *Clematis* 'Elizabeth' Montana Group
3. *Lonicera japonica*
4. *Lonicera periclymenum*
5. Roses
6. *Trachelospermum asiaticum*
7. *Wisteria*

Walls for wildlife

❀ Climbers and wall shrubs can provide great resources for wildlife, adding height and volume of plant cover.

❀ Scented flowering plants will attract insects: even humble ivy (*Hedera*) is a wonderful source of nectar in the winter months.

❀ Mature climbers may be used as roosting sites.

❀ Sturdy, leafy shrubs or climbers, such as Virginia creeper (*Parthenocissus quinquefolia*), provide a great roosting spot for local birds.

❀ Avoid climbers favoured by birds close to a doorway, or your doorstep will be constantly covered with their droppings. Plant a lighter or less leafy climber.

Evergreen *Clematis armandii* flowers in early spring, with a sweet perfume.

Planting climbers

The same basic planting techniques apply for climbers as for trees and shrubs (see pages 68–69). Remember that climbers often need to be gently untangled from their canes, planted at an angle and tied into new support systems in order to achieve a flying start.

Siting climbers near a wall

When planting against a wall, you need to take extra care because the site is likely to be less hospitable than one in a flowerbed. Dry soil is the main problem: the foundations of the house tend to have a drying effect, pulling in moisture from the surrounding soil throughout the year. The wall itself may act rather like a storage heater, absorbing heat and then releasing it later – great for those plants that need it, but perhaps a little too much for those that don't. The area close to a house wall also suffers from serious rain-shadow effects: the presence of the wall means rain cannot hit the soil from one direction, and the overhang of guttering and roof eaves creates further problems.

Planting distance from a wall

The planting hole should not be any less than 45cm (18in) from the house wall. At this distance, all the drying effects of the wall and foundations will be less of a problem.

A few canes and plenty of care should guide your climber to its support quickly.

How to avoid mildew

Plants growing in dry situations tend to be more susceptible to powdery mildew infection. To avoid this problem, do not choose mildew-prone plants, such as the honeysuckles (*Lonicera*) and many of the roses, for a potentially dry spot unless you are sure you will be able to keep them adequately supplied with moisture.

Mildew is often a sign that plants are dry at the roots.

Easy early training

Initially you may need to use a cane and some twine or wires to train the plant towards the wall and the support system. You can remove this once the plant is established, but it should ensure that it starts to move in the right direction from the start.

How far to plant near a fence

When climbers and wall shrubs are planted against a fence, you should still try to plant them about 45cm (18in) away. This will give the plants a chance to put on a bit of growth in the direction of the wall, and will make training easier.

Getting the climber at the right angle

Once the plant is in the hole, angle it at about 45 degrees, leaning it towards the wall to encourage it to start off in the right direction. Take extra care to ensure that the stems are not in contact with the soil surface.

Remove support before planting

Climbers are often very well wrapped up with mesh or attached to a framework when you buy them. It's easier to get this all off before you get the plant into the ground; often some fairly time-consuming and intricate work will be needed.

Adding nutrients to planting holes

Whatever the soil type, when planting close to a wall it is especially important to incorporate plenty of bulky organic matter into the surrounding soil and into the planting hole. Matter such as garden compost, well-rotted manure, or proprietary planting compost work well.

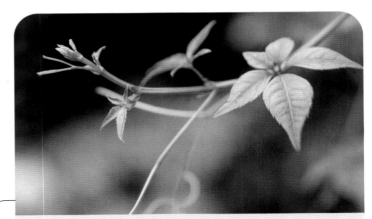

The young growth of climbers is soft, but older stems can be brittle, so tie shoots in carefully, ideally when young.

Dig deep for the healthiest clematis

Clematis benefit from deeper planting than other climbers. Plant them about 5cm (2in) deeper than they are in their pots; the stems are well adapted to growing up through some soil, and deeper planting means that they are less prone to damage by heat or soil dryness. It also seems to help reduce the risk of clematis wilt.

Spread out and tie in

Make sure that you spread out the existing growth as well as you can, because this should help to ensure that good coverage is made from the start. The young shoots will need to be attached to the support using foam-covered wire, soft twine, or proprietary ties . Any tying in needs to be done really carefully because the young shoots are likely to be very tender and easily damaged.

Long-term feeding

For the first couple of seasons, a climber planted with a well-prepared planting hole may not need any extra feeding beyond a small amount – about 50g (2oz) – of a balanced fertilizer sprinkled around the root area and then watered in. Once it is better established, any suitable slow-release feed should do perfectly. Apply this in the spring for the best results.

Early watering

Climbers are likely to need above average attention when it comes to watering, especially when they are still establishing. A weekly heavy drench is often needed: make sure it gets to the roots by carefully clearing away the mulch. After watering, carefully re-apply the mulch.

Cut back to healthy growth

Any stems that are dead or badly damaged are best cut out either before the plant goes in the ground or immediately after planting. If you have about five good, sturdy, and apparently healthy stems, you should get an excellent spread of growth.

Delicacies for slugs

Young clematis in particular are very prone to damage by slugs and snails. These eat away at the stems, effectively ringing them often in the space of just a few days. Large sections of the plant may be killed. Either apply slug-killing biocontrol, or put in place copper rings or other suitable barriers to prevent this happening. The damage is generally only very severe in the first year.

Deadhead for a longer display

Regular deadheading of flowering climbers and wall shrubs prevents the plants from wasting energy making seed and seedheads, allowing them to form new growth or flowers.

A snail is thwarted by a copper barrier.

Some remove just the rose flower, others cut to a full five-leaflet leaf; see what works for you.

Covering an arch or pergola

When training a new plant to grow over an arch, arbour, or pergola, it is best to tie the stems to the upright or else they will be inclined to flop outwards. Tie the main stems in evenly to achieve a uniform spread of growth. Check and tie in again repeatedly as the plant makes new growth.

Pruning and training

The exact pruning and training needs of climbers and shrubs vary, so make sure you know what's needed. In the first few years, aim for a good framework of balanced growth and the potential to cover the wall or shed, even if it is still too small to achieve it quite yet.

Immediately cut out old stems of climbing roses showing any die-back.

Remove sickly growth

Always aim to remove any dead, diseased, damaged, or dying growth, and do so promptly, even if it is not the suggested time for tackling your particular plant. If left in place it is likely to encourage die-back infections, such as coral spot or grey mould, which may then cause more stem die-back.

Pruning basics

When pruning, always use sharp secateurs and cut back to a vigorous-looking, plump bud. Choose a bud that is facing the direction that you need the stem to go – this way you will get quicker and more effective coverage, ideally without too many gaps.

Always make a slanting cut just above a bud.

Shorten lanky growth

If the new growth is rather sparse or excessively long, carefully cut back or shorten it; this will stimulate branching. Always cut back to a suitable sturdy bud or sideshoot.

Check flowering habits

Before you grab the pruning tools and attack an innocent shrub, remember that unnecessary and incorrect pruning can easily destroy all the flowering potential of some plants that year. Check what each plant needs in a reliable book, making sure you know whether it flowers on the current season's new growth or last season's old wood.

Tie in new shoots

Throughout the growing season, regularly inspect the climber and train in any new shoots that have developed. It is far easier to do this regularly when the stems you are manipulating are pliable, than trying to force (and possibly damage) a woodier stem to grow where you want it to.

Plants will recover

If you do have to prune at the "wrong" time of year, or if you simply make a mistake, there is rarely any need for panic. Getting it wrong generally only means the loss of one year's flowers.

Two-step pruning

If you need to prune a plant such as a *Pyracantha*, where you want to be able to enjoy both the berries and the flowers, try doing half the job after flowering. This gives you a chance to enjoy at least some berries, and after that you can complete the pruning.

Wait for winter

If you want to see what shape the pruning you are carrying out is creating, it is often easier to prune during the winter months when the branch structure is more readily visible.

Pruning when stems are bare gives a good idea of the plant's shape.

Flowering hormones stay in the tip of an upright stem; a horizontal stem spreads them evenly.

Lay low for more flowers

Training the stems of climbers, shrubs, or trees in to a more horizontal position helps to encourage more flowering and fruiting. This makes it a useful technique for plants whose main appeal is their display of bloom or berry.

Tie with care

When tying in stems of a climber, wall shrub, or other trained specimen, you can minimize the risk of branch or stem injury if you use foam-coated wires, or very flexible and stretchy ties. For larger stems, cover standard wire or cable with a length of old hose pipe to help spread the effect of the taut tie.

Bigger jobs need bigger tools

Even the best-quality, super-sharp secateurs that are your pride and joy may not be sufficient for larger pruning jobs. Be prepared to invest in a good quality pair of loppers or even a pruning saw, and leave the major pruning jobs at the greatest heights to the professionals.

Lawns & grass care

Most gardens have a lawn of some sort. Yours may be a beautifully manicured, perfect sward of lush green, or it may be a functional – and by extension, less than perfect – surface used by all the family. Whatever it is like and however big it is, the lawn often has such a central role that there is no ignoring it.

In many gardens a lawn is key to the whole design, so decide what percentage of the garden you want as lawn and its location, early on in the planning process.

Sometimes the existing lawn is so weedy that there seems no option but to start again. If this sounds familiar, all the tips you might need to create a new lawn from scratch are here.

Maintaining your new lawn
Once your new lawn is in place, you will need to maintain it and keep it in general good health or else it will soon start to look patchy and thin, and will also become more prone to attack from pests and pathogens, and infestations of

mosses and weeds. Lawn maintenance need not take up all your gardening time – in this chapter there are plenty of time-saving tips.

If your gardening time really is short but you desperately want a good-looking lawn, you may even decide to get someone else to do the time-consuming job of regular mowing during the high season. That way, you can have more garden time and the choice to do the lawn maintenance such as edging, feeding, and weeding yourself.

This chapter shows you how to:
❀ Make a new lawn from scratch, from seed or turf.
❀ Combat pests and diseases.
❀ Mow, water, and feed your lawn.
❀ Look after your lawn.
❀ Identify and solve lawn problems.
❀ Create a wildflower meadow.
❀ Naturalize bulbs into your lawn.

Making a new lawn from scratch

Making a new lawn is the perfect opportunity to start with a weed-free blank canvas and create a fine level sward. You can choose from hard-wearing to fine lawn seed mixes depending on how much wear and how much attention your lawn will receive.

A simple expanse of uniform green sets off plants – as well as being ideal to sit or play on.

What shape of lawn?

You may be tempted to create a really intricately shaped lawn, but remember that the simpler the shape, the easier it will be to mow – all those twists and curves that look so interesting on paper can make for a real nightmare.

Prepare the ground

Preparation is the key: it may seem like an endless process (and it does take a lot of time) but however much time and money you spend on the turf or the seed, it will all be wasted if you skimp on the preparation.

Choose the right spot

❀ Try to avoid putting your lawn in a shaded area. Lawn grasses are much less likely to succumb to pests or competition from weeds or and diseases if they are growing in a reasonably open, sunny, adequately drained (but not too dry) spot.

❀ If you do need to create a lawn in a shaded spot, it is essential to use a lawn seed mixture specifically for shady areas. This will contain varieties of grass much better able to cope with the conditions.

Turf or grass seed?

❀ Lawns from turf or from seed need a very similar amount of preparation work, and this is the time-consuming bit. Both will initially need extra care, especially watering.

❀ A turf lawn is much more expensive than one raised from seed.

❀ A new lawn from turf is generally ready for use much faster than one from seed.

Seed is ideal if you can wait that bit longer.

Reduce compaction

Compaction of the soil causes poor aeration and poor drainage in new lawns, which in turn causes poor grass growth and increases problems with moss and weeds, so try to break up any compacted areas before you start. Small areas can often be dealt with using a garden fork or a cultivator.

Fork over the ground thoroughly first.

Using power tools

If your soil is quite heavy, take care with powered cultivators; they can cause a "pan" or layer of compacted soil lower down in the soil, especially if used when the soil is wet. If necessary, delay using one of these until the soil has dried out.

Do some serious weeding

❀ Make sure you remove all pernicious weeds – those with fleshy root systems that are extremely difficult to control. Take time doing this because you need to get every tiny bit of root out: if you break the root of a weed, such as a dandelion, into pieces as you remove it, each piece left in the soil has the potential to become a new plant, so it is easy to make the problem worse!

❀ If you use a weedkiller, make sure that it is formulated to control the weeds that are there; not all products control the same range of weeds.

Remove stones

Fork out all large stones and other debris. It seems that each time you rake the area over more have a habit of appearing, but you will get there eventually. If you end up with lots of stones, don't bin them; save them for use as drainage material in the bottom of containers.

What type of grass?

Be honest about how much wear and tear – and how much maintenance – your lawn is likely to get. Fine grasses make the most elegant lawns, but take more looking after. With enough water and food, a bit of autumn care, and regular cutting, a tougher "utility lawn" can look really good.

Is your soil good enough?

If you're in any doubts as to the soil's fertility, use a balanced fertilizer before you sow or lay a lawn. This should make up for any shortfalls and get the grass growing and establishing well. Raking the fertilizer in helps to distribute it evenly and reduces the risk of it coming in to direct contact with the roots of the grass.

Tread to make sure the soil is evenly firm.

Treading the surface

Try to get the area as level as possible. Once you've achieved this, firm the soil by using a flat-footed walking movement over the entire surface. Any humps or hollows can then be filled in before you start to sow the seed or lay the turf.

A new lawn from seed

Early autumn is the best time to sow a new lawn. The soil is warm and seasonal weather will help the seed to germinate quickly. Late spring is also a good time, but the soil is colder and there will be a flush of new weeds competing with your seed.

How much seed?

❀ Measure the area accurately before you buy your grass seed, but don't forget to subtract the area taken up by any features such as paths or island beds.

❀ The seed box usually states the weight of seed needed per 1sq m (11sq ft) of soil. As a rough guide, a good handful of seed is approximately the right amount for this area.

❀ If you want to be more precise, mark out a trial area of one square metre (or yard) and weigh out the seed. Distribute the seed very evenly. Use this square to remind you what the correct sowing rate looks like when the seed is on the ground.

❀ If you can't do it by eye, mark out the area with 1m (3ft) long canes and weigh out the seed.

Don't breathe in

Even the freshest of grass seed from a great supplier tends to be very dusty and it is worth wearing a simple face mask when measuring it out and sowing it, especially if you are inclined to be dust sensitive.

Where to start

Always start sowing the seed at the far end of the area to be sown – this way you won't end up walking on the areas that you have just sown. Wear flat boots or wellies so you won't create any serious bumps and hollows as you progress.

Avoid thick and thin

Don't try to economize by sowing the seed too thinly. Sparse grass is more readily colonized by weeds, algae, and moss, and may make more work for you later on. But don't be tempted to sow the seed too densely; overcrowding will cause weaker growth.

Seeds should be well spaced, but not sparse.

Sowing in line

Make sure that straight edges are really neat and totally straight – lay a sheet of plastic or a lightweight board with a straight edge over the area that you don't want to sow, then sow the seed right onto the board or plastic. Lift it off carefully, and you should be left with a perfect line. Any grass seed on the plastic sheet or board can then easily be tipped off and re-used.

Raking settles the seeds into the soil.

Rake after sowing

You'll get far better germination rates if you lightly rake the soil after sowing the seed. This helps to cover the seed, protecting it from birds and helping to keep it moist.

Keep a record

I'm not a great filer of gardening information, but it is really worth keeping a note (or the old box) of the grass seed you used. If you ever want to extend the lawn or, more likely, simply patch it or over-seed it, you'll get a much better result if you match the grass seed mixture exactly.

Don't hand out a free lunch

Reduce bird damage to small areas of grass by netting until the grasses are growing away. Use scarers, such as buzz-lines or old CDs, suspended from canes on large areas.

Watering after sowing

Plenty of moisture is essential for the grass seed to germinate and the grass seedlings to establish well. Make sure the area is kept just moist at all times – if you're away and the weather is warm, get someone to do it for you! Use a watering can for small areas, or a medium-fine nozzle on a hose, so that you don't disturb the lightweight grass seed with aggressive watering.

Gentle watering leaves the seeds in position.

Be patient!

❀ Don't mow new lawn created from seed for several weeks after it is made; mowing too soon can cause serious damage. For the first cuts, leave the grass longer than you would do normally.

❀ Avoid weedkillers or heavy use of the lawn for the first year. The young grass takes time to knit together.

A mowing strip allows you to mow the edges easily.

At the edge

When a lawn is surrounded by flower beds, established plants often hang over the edge of the lawn, or even flop onto the surface. This causes shading which increases the chances of moss and weeds invading, and of the grasses failing because they do not have enough light. Edge the lawn, or at least the sides adjacent to flowerbeds, with a neat "mowing strip" consisting of a line of paving, and this problem is instantly avoided.

A new lawn from turf

Turf is best laid before the weather gets either too wet or too dry – early autumn or early spring is ideal and it is easiest to get it to establish properly and rapidly at this time. But turf can be laid at other times, as long as it is well watered and not frosted.

Rolls should be moist, green, and healthy.

Check the turf quality

Always examine a few rolls of turf before the whole lot is unloaded; you need to be sure that they are of the quality you expected. Reject any showing signs of deterioration, such as excessive yellowing, rotting grasses, or fungal growth, and any with weed infestations. It pays to check.

Ordering turf

❀ Measure the area you need accurately, then add a metre or two of extra turf to allow for the odd mis-measurement, or awkward ends of roll lengths.

❀ Try to order the turf so that it arrives on the day you are sure you can lay it – turf does deteriorate fairly rapidly.

Laying the turf

❀ Lay the first turf against a straight edge if your new lawn has one. This will make it easier to get subsequent turves in place.

❀ Lay the second turf while kneeling on the first one; this causes less damage than if you kneel on the bare soil.

❀ Kneeling on the newly lain lawn is going to cause dents unless you kneel on a wide plank or board. Doing this helps to distribute your weight more evenly, and so prevents dents.

❀ If you can, get someone to pass the turves to you. Otherwise, getting up and down repeatedly increases damage to the new lawn and makes it all much more time consuming.

❀ The edges of the turves will need to knit together, so place each turf with its edges flush with those of the neighbouring turves.

Use a plank for straight edges and to kneel on.

Butt up edges tightly for a solid surface.

Delays in turfing

❀ If you have to delay laying a lawn, then don't risk leaving it rolled up for more than a day or two; the grasses will soon yellow and fungal threads are likely to appear.

❀ If you need to delay for more than a couple of days, lay out a sheet of plastic and unroll the turves on to it, grass-side uppermost. Water well before using as promptly as possible.

Staggering joints while not wasting turf can be a bit of an art.

Stagger the joins

You are less likely to get unacceptable gaps in the surface of your new lawn if you stagger the joints in adjacent rows, laying them rather like bricks in a wall.

Marking a curve

❀ For a circular curve, use a peg and line with a funnel full of dry sand on the end. Drive the peg in to the soil, pull the string taut, fill the funnel with the sand and pull the funnel end round to draw a sand-curve.

❀ For other curves, you can use a hosepipe laid out on the grass to form the perimeter. Anchor it well in the ground with wire bent into U-shaped pins that will fix in place while you cut. Carefully check the shape before you start cutting.

No offcuts at the edge

Avoid using a small piece of turf right at the end of a row. This area is prone to damage, and a tiny bit of turf laid at the edge will be all the more susceptible. Instead, use a full-length piece of turf at the end, and fit the smaller piece further in along the row.

Make contact

Make sure that the roots of the grass are in firm contact with the moist soil beneath. Tread the surface of the lawn carefully once it is all laid. With small lawns, you may be able to use a flat-headed rake to tamp down the surface and so avoid walking on it.

Fill the cracks

Ideally, there will be no gaps between your pieces of turf. But if possible, having some finely crumbled or even sieved soil to sprinkle or sweep into the joint areas never hurts. It will fill any cracks, and the grass will soon spread into it.

Using a guide for a straight edge

For straight edges, use a gardening line – two pegs with string between them – held taut along the edge-to-be. Then stand on a plank, to minimize damage to the lawn, and make sure you are looking straight down at the string to cut an accurate line.

Shaping the edges

❀ It is always best to shape the turf to form the outline you want once the turf is in place, not before you lay it.

❀ You need to have a really sharp cutting tool, ideally a half-moon edger to make a firm, neat, vertical cut, or else the edge will look messy.

❀ If you do not have and cannot borrow a half-moon edger, then you can use a sharp spade, but the line will not be quite as smooth.

❀ When using a half-moon edger, position yourself so that you are standing immediately above the line you are cutting. This makes it easier to cut accurately, and also ensures that the cut you make along the edge is truly vertical.

For the neatest edges, try to use a half-moon edger.

If it does not rain, water the lawn well every two to three days, gradually tapering off over a month.

When to water

Never water a new turf lawn until you have finalized the edges; cutting wet turf is much harder and more inclined to make a messy edge. At the same time, standing on the adjacent turf increases the chances of you damaging it.

Keep watering

Keeping the newly laid lawn well watered is especially important while it is establishing itself and the roots are growing down into the garden soil. If they are allowed to dry out at all, the grass may never successfully root. If there's no rain, it's up to you.

A thorough soak

Once all the turf is in place and cut to shape, give the lawn a really thorough soaking. The water needs to penetrate right through the grass layer and the root layer, into the soil beneath. Although a new lawn won't appreciate waterlogging, it is better to overdo this first watering than risk the soil beneath not being adequately wetted.

Aftercare

❀ A new lawn created from turf should not be cut for at least two weeks after it is laid. Make the first cut higher – that is, longer – than normal.

❀ Keep off the lawn for at least two weeks and treat it gently for the first couple of months. After this, it should be well established and tougher.

Lawn pests and diseases

By keeping the lawn well maintained you can really reduce the amount of damage from pests and diseases, so make that your first task. If you do find you have a problem on your hands, deal with it promptly before it gets out of control.

Toadstools appear rapidly and need to be removed promptly.

Fungi on the march

If fungi appear on the lawn in a line, they are often growing from buried tree roots; the long-term solution is to remove the tree root.

Pick off fungi regularly

Fungi often spread effectively using spores produced from the lower surface of their caps. If you can, brush off toadstools growing in lawns as soon as they appear, and certainly before the caps open fully.

Fairy rings

Fairy rings are pretty much impossible to kill, but they do get wider every year. When the edges of the ring eventually reach adjacent borders or paths, the fungus usually dies out.

A charming name, but fairy rings can be a nightmare.

Practise good hygiene

If you do have fairy rings in your lawn, the spores can be spread on feet and on mowers, so make sure you mow the infected area of the lawn last, and clean the mower thoroughly afterwards.

Keep off the grass

If you can manage to avoid walking on the lawn when it is snow covered, frosted, or extremely wet, you will find that it remains more vigorous and is less prone to damage by fungal infections, such as snow mould.

Wildlife vandals

If you get problems with your lawn being ripped up or dug up by birds or small mammals, the chances are that they are looking for grubs, such as leatherjackets and chafer grubs. This tells you that you have a problem, and the only way you will stop them is by controlling the grubs. Biological nematode control drenches work well.

Mowing, watering, and feeding a lawn

Sowing grass seed and laying turf is only the beginning of the story. When the grass takes off, you then have to maintain it during the growing season – mowing, watering, edging and feeding as required.

It is obvious if you've left mowing too long.

Little and often

However boring you may find mowing a lawn, it really is a job you need to tackle fairly regularly when the grass is growing. If left too long, the lawn will look awful for a while when you do finally cut the grass, and it will take a long time to recover. Don't try to save time by cutting the lawn too short (also known as scalping it!), because this will put the grass under a lot of stress, making it more easily invaded by weeds.

Don't mow when wet

When the weather is very wet and the lawn is sodden there is an excellent excuse for not doing the mowing: you are likely to do more harm than good. The surface will become compacted, and drainage and aeration will be impeded.

Walking the plank

When edging the lawn use a straight-edged plank as a guide – lay the plank on the lawn with its long edge exactly where you want the lawn edge to be. Stand on the plank and cut directly along its edge. Trimmings from a repaired or edged lawn make a great addition to your compost heap, so don't waste them.

Don't cut too short during dry weather

If the weather is very dry, it pays to leave the blades on the mower slightly higher than normal. Keep mowing regularly, so that you only ever remove tiny, short clippings; these can safely be left to fall on the grass, where they will act like a miniature mulch and help to preserve moisture.

Finishing touches

If you want to make your lawn look really smart, neaten up the edges with a half-moon edger or, if they are still in shape but a bit overgrown, use edging shears.

Edging is a quick way to smarten up a lawn.

Watering

Lawns are more resilient than you might think. In most cases, even if they become brown and miserable-looking following a drought, they will re-green later in the year, especially if you ensure they get a bit of extra maintenance.

An evening drink

If you do feel the need to water your lawn, try to do this in the evening. As the day cools down, less water is lost to evaporation, and the grasses have a chance to take up the water more efficiently.

Lawns get the longest drink overnight, without evaporation caused by the sun.

Lawn stripes can be created with rotary and cylinder mowers, and can hide irregularities.

Keeping tabs on watering

If you are unsure about how much water a sprinkler is applying, once it is set up, leave a straight-sided jar or bowl on the grass within the range of the sprinkler. This will show you just how much water is being applied – it will be more than you think, so make sure you don't leave the sprinkler on for too long.

Feeding the lawn

Grass will survive perfectly well without being fed, but if you want a lawn that looks great and is better able to fight off problems such as weeds, moss, pests, and pathogens, you should feed with a specially formulated lawn fertilizer.

Feeding season by season

There are different formulations of lawn feed for the various times of year, so make sure that you use the appropriate one. For instance, if you applied a spring feed in the autumn you would be stimulating soft, lush grass growth at just the time of year when you need to be toughening up the grass in preparation for winter.

Some feeds come with devices to scatter them.

Using a dry fertilizer

When using a dry form of fertilizer, it is especially important to water it in well shortly after application. This minimizes the risk of scorching and increases the ability of the grass to make use of the feed. Avoid fertilizing a lawn suffering from drought stress; it is better to wait until it has recovered before applying the fertilizer.

Quantity control

Grass can be seriously damaged by excessive doses of fertilizer, so you must apply it at the correct rate. If you are using an applicator to spread granular feed, always make sure that it is correctly calibrated for the product that you are using.

Looking after your lawn

As your lawn matures, it may need special attention in places or you may want to make design changes. Whatever you do though, always remember that you can change your mind later down the line.

Reshaping an existing lawn

Mark out the edges of the shape you have in mind and stand back and look at it from all windows of the house, upstairs and downstairs, to make sure you have got the shape right… and don't start cutting until you are sure.

Make sure you are happy with the curve before you cut.

Cutting edge tools

A half-moon edger or a sharp border spade is the best tool to trim edges or cut a new shape. Try to keep the cut totally vertical and sharply defined.

Mix and match grass

In extreme cases of wear and tear, it may be necessary to re-turf parts of the lawn. Make sure that the new turf matches the type of the original lawn, and that you keep the patches extremely well watered and regularly tamped down until their roots have established.

Keep it simple

If changing your lawn's shape, think about why the old shape didn't work. Often, the problems are complex outlines or awkward corners that make mowing difficult.

Lawn repairs

Heavy foot traffic to get to frequently used parts of the garden, or the house itself, often mean far more wear and tear along those routes. Laying stepping stones in the lawn to allow direct access to these areas should keep the lawn in better condition, and means that you can even walk on it during wet, frosty, or snowy weather without feeling guilty.

Set slabs low enough to be mown over.

Sowing on the side

For extra-quick replacement seeding that is less reliant on the weather, chit or sprout the lawn seed first. Just mix the grass seed with some moist compost in a plastic bag and allow it to germinate before mixing with the soil on the bare area.

Seed fills gappy, sparse patches.

Overseed sparse grass

Areas that have become thin and sparse may respond well to overseeding. Just loosen the soil surface on the bare or sparse area, sprinkle on a matching grass seed, rake the soil over again, and water well. Overseed patches at the same time of year that you would sow a new lawn – but you can risk sowing much later into spring or even early summer if you can keep the new seed well watered.

Filling minor hollows

If minor hollows have developed, you may be able to even up the lawn surface by gradually filling the dents with a topsoil mixture in the autumn or spring.

Levelling hollows and bumps

Where hollows have developed in a lawn, cut an 'H' shape in the turf, centred over the hollow. Peel back the flaps of turf and add soil until the hollow is filled, before replacing the turf, tamping it down well, and watering thoroughly. If raised areas or humps have developed in the lawn, follow the same procedure in autumn or early spring. Remove excess soil from below the flaps of turf, then replace, tamp down, and water.

Use garden soil to fill in any hollows beneath the turf.

Reversing bad edges

Where lawn edges become worn or broken, cut out a square of turf including the damaged area. Lift it carefully, with the roots, and rotate it so that the damaged area now faces inwards and a new, perfect edge is on the outside. You can easily overseed the bare patch, and the cut edge will be much more resilient.

Patch and mend

If a your lawn gets damaged in a highly visible area, you can cut out the damaged patch and swap it with a matching piece of grass lifted from somewhere less obvious in the lawn. Tamp both pieces in well and water, then sow fresh seed on the damaged patch; it will recover quite quickly.

When to give up

If your lawn is persistently thin and miserable in shady, damp, or dry areas despite all your care, try planting groundcover instead.

Lawn problems

No matter how hard you try, it is nearly impossible to keep a beautiful, uniform lawn for long – weeds can't seem to resist marring the landscape and bad drainage may cause mossy patches. Learn how to stay in control with these helpful trouble-shooting tips.

Weeding

Deep-rooted perennial weeds can do a lot of damage to a lawn, not only spoiling its appearance, but competing with the turf grass for light, moisture, and nutrients. Even if you are not after a prefect sward of green, it is worth removing these weeds, especially those that are low-growing or rosette forming, such as dandelions, as they will not be affected by mowing.

Dandelions' foliage rosettes escape mower blades.

An invaluable weeding tool

An old, sturdy kitchen knife is a great tool for removing lawn weeds. Make sure you ease the knife right down around the roots, so that you can remove the whole root system, because some weeds are capable of regenerating a new plant from each chunk of root left in the soil.

A knife is useful for removing daisies.

For every weed, a killer

If you opt for the weedkiller approach, check the label of the product very carefully before you buy. There are numerous different weedkillers, available alone or in combination, and different products will not control precisely the same range of weeds. Make sure you know which weeds you have, and that the product will control all or most of them.

Cutting coarse grasses

❀ If coarse grass has developed in the lawn, it is especially difficult to control and weedkillers are obviously not an option. Instead, try fluffing it up before mowing; this ensures that more weed grass is cut by the blades and, if repeated each time you mow, it will have a seriously weakening effect and the problem will diminish.

❀ Use a sharp knife to slash closely spaced parallel lines across the patch of coarse grass. Repeat this every few weeks over the growing season and the problem will start to die out.

Weedkillers kill more than weeds

Every year a lot of damage is done to garden plants by careless weedkiller use, especially when weedkillers applied on windy, gusty, or very hot days drift onto neighbouring plants. Only spray during calm weather and read the instructions carefully.

A spring-tined rake is the perfect tool for scarifying.

Scarifying

❀ When you scarify the lawn, you are aiming to remove dead grass and other debris from the base of the lawn. The best tool for this is usually a spring-tined rake with long, flexible tines, but if you have a dauntingly large job to do, it may be worth hiring a mechanical scarifier.

❀ After you have scarified your lawn it invariably looks worse than it did before you started. Don't panic – this is how it should be, and the lawn will soon green up again, especially if it is kept well watered for the next few days.

❀ Provided the moss in your lawn has not been treated with a chemical moss killer, you can add it to your compost heap or use it as an attractive mulch for container plants.

Use lawn moss to create a mulch.

Improve aeration and drainage

❀ Fallen leaves from nearby trees can seriously damage a lawn, so it is important to rake them up regularly in the autumn. A spring-tined rake is the best type of rake for the job, but if the area is large you could use a leaf vacuum or blower.

Fallen leaves make a lawn prone to fungal diseases.

❀ If you really want to save time and effort, do two jobs in one. Provided you mow your lawn regularly, the mower will pick up and cut up fallen leaves that have not become firmly matted on the surface. This saves you having to rake up the leaves, and the ready-chopped leaves will rot down even more quickly in your compost bin because they have been chopped and are mixed with the moist, nitrogen-rich grass clippings.

❀ Poor drainage and aeration leads to poor grass growth and other problems. If time is short concentrate your efforts on the areas that have become most compacted, like areas near the barbecue and any children's play equipment.

❀ For the best longer term improvements in drainage, use a hollow-tine aerator. This removes plugs or cores of soil from the turf, and the holes created can then be filled with sand to create drainage channels. Otherwise, use a fork.

❀ If you have used a hollow-tine aerator, sweep up all the soil cores and add them to the compost heap.

Ease your fork back and forth to aerate.

Creating a meadow

A clipped and manicured patch of green is attractive and functional, but it can look a little formal and take hard work to maintain. If you want to go for the low-maintenance option that attracts local wildlife, create a wildflower meadow.

A haze of wild flowers in tall grass brings a natural tranquility to any garden.

The meadow effect

A wildflower meadow – or something to create that feel, however small – will help attract wildlife to your garden and provide a welcome relief, especially in a town garden.

Starting with plug plants

You can buy various formulations of wildflower lawn mixes, but the easiest way is to buy small plug plants. These tend to be far easier to establish and to keep than those raised within a developing lawn.

Natural methods

If you want to encourage natural wild flowers it is essential that you ignore all the usual instructions for lawn care, especially feeding. The grass needs to be treated more like natural turf and, if fed, it will simply swamp out wild flowers.

Keep choices local

When choosing flowers, consider the local environment and the soil type you have to offer. Annual poppies (*Papaver*), cornflowers (*Centaurea*) and field scabious like a well-drained, sunny spot; ragged robin (*Lychnis flos-cuculi*), and meadowsweet (*Filipendula ulmaria*) prefer damp sites.

Cornfield flowers suit drier sites.

Spring meadow colour

For spring colour and interest in a meadow-style planting, try growing wild daffodils (*Narcissus pseudonarcissus*) and species crocus such as *Crocus tommasinianus* and *C.vernus*.

Keeping a meadow looking good

Regularly remove pernicious weeds before they start to take over. Either cut them out carefully with a transplanting trowel or kitchen knife, or spot-treat with a weedkiller.

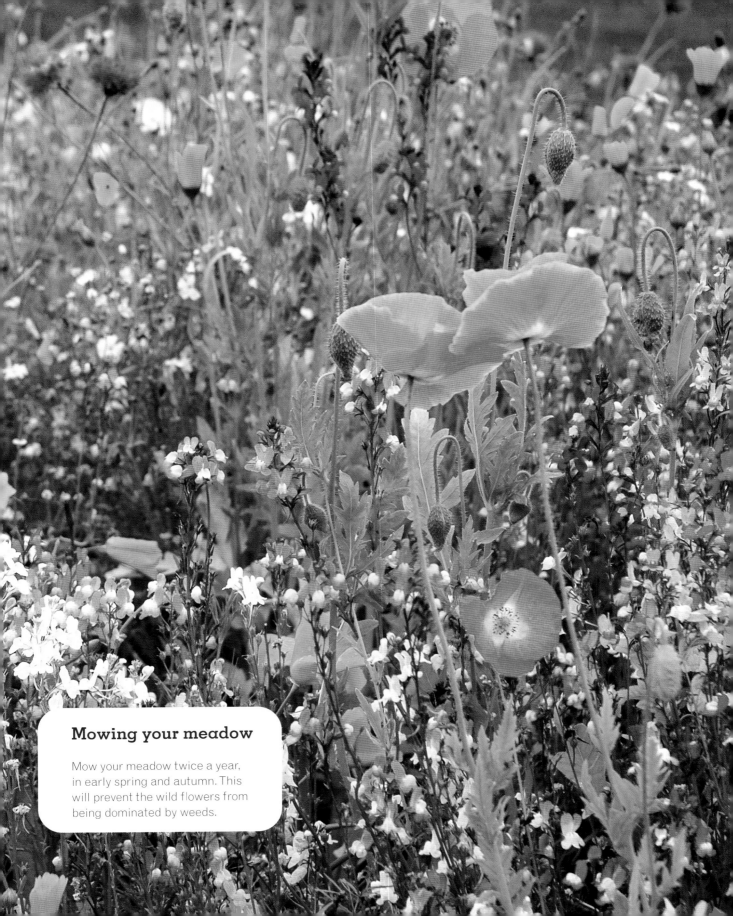

Mowing your meadow

Mow your meadow twice a year, in early spring and autumn. This will prevent the wild flowers from being dominated by weeds.

Naturalizing bulbs

You can make a lawn much more interesting by planting it with bulbs, which look great growing through grass. As you need to allow the bulb foliage to remain on the plants, plant the bulbs in an area that you are happy to leave the grass to grow long.

Do not plant bulbs under evergreen trees; they will not get enough light.

Where to position your bulbs

Before you go over the top, consider the site. Avoid areas where deteriorating foliage will be too unsightly or mowing around bulbs will be too fiddly. Remember that soil under a tree is likely to be dry, and in shade for much of the year.

Large or small?

Consider the site and the scale of the nearby plants when deciding what to plant. For a small-scale, delicate look, crocus, snowdrops (*Galanthus*), or miniature daffodils (*Narcissus*), such as 'Tête-à-tête' are ideal, while for a really bold planting on a larger scale, daffodils work well and are also very good value. If you hanker after a naturalistic meadow effect, snake's head fritillary (*Fritillaria meleagris*) is perfect.

Planning drifts

❀ Mow the lawn before you start to plant the bulbs. This makes it much easier to create the planting holes and to see what you are doing.

❀ Bulbs in grass look best if given the appearance of being a totally natural occurrence. Aim for random planting without even the slightest hint of regimentation.

❀ If you are planting more than one drift of bulbs of the same type for naturalizing, make sure that the drifts are not of exactly the same size and number of bulbs, and that each drift has a slightly different outline.

Stay on the level

Try to use either a single type of bulb, or at least varieties of a very similar or identical height, so you'll be able to enjoy them all. Avoid golden and yellow forms of crocus; these are always the first target for the birds, especially sparrows, who often shred them before they are even fully open.

Snowdrops multiply of their own accord.

Useful equipment

For planting larger bulbs in grass, you need either a very long transplanting trowel or a bulb planter. If you have more than a few to do, a long-handled planter, which you drive into the soil with your foot, saves a lot of strain on your back and knees – and a lot of time.

Scattering small bulbs

❀ Scatter bulbs and plant them where they fall, only moving any that fall far beyond the planned area or which are much too close to their neighbours.

Plant bulbs using the H-shape cut.

❀ Small bulbs, such as crocus, are time-consuming to plant in individual holes. Instead use a sharp spade or half-moon edger to cut an 'H' shape in the appropriate place. Peel back the two flaps of turf, gently fluff up the soil beneath, and scatter the bulbs. Plant in the usual way, and then replace the flaps of turf. Water well, so that the roots of the turf don't suffer too much and quickly re-establish.

Protect early leaves

As the bulbs start to grow in the spring, the first leaves are easily hidden by the grass, making them an easy target for passing feet, or even car tyres if they are next to your drive. A temporary fence of bamboo canes and twine helps to keep them from being damaged, and can be removed simply and quickly once the leaves are large enough to be impossible to miss.

Bed bulbs in firmly

When you are using a bulb planter or trowel, you are unlikely to be able to see the bottom of the hole clearly. Make sure that the bulb base (the root end) is pressed down fully so that it's in contact with soil at the bottom of the planting hole.

Use a bulb planter to remove a plug of soil that you put back on top of the bulb.

Divide to maintain flowering

Bulbs like daffodils (*Narcissus*) planted in fairly dense drifts soon need more space if they are to continue to flower well. Every five years or so, lift the bulbs (or at least half of them, randomly scattered through the planting) and re-plant in a new site – why not plant at the edge of the drift to make it bigger?

Feed and water

Bulbs in grass need extra watering, particularly near trees or during dry spells. Without moisture, they can't take up the nutrients they need to flower well the next year. They also need feeding; they are competing with each other and the grass. Apply foliar feed during the growing season while the leaves are green, or water in a granular fertilizer.

When to lift bulbs

Ideally, lifting bulbs for replanting should be done in the autumn, but at that time of year there will be no above-ground sign of where exactly each bulb is growing. Either mark the positions with sticks before the foliage dies down, or lift the bulbs "in the green", when they still have green leaves.

The kitchen garden

One of the most satisfying things you can do in your garden is to grow at least some of the food you eat. It is a fundamentally appealing activity, and there is no doubt that when you grow some of what you eat, it not only feels good, but tastes excellent too.

Whatever the size of your garden, try to find space for at least a few vegetables, herbs, or fruit. If you garden purely in containers then *see* pages 56–63 for some tips on growing a gorgeous selection of edibles in containers.

If you are worried that crops will be less appealing to look at than flowers and shrubs, then I say, think again. Many vegetables look stunning, whether they are grown amongst other vegetables or integrated into a flowerbed.

Growing your own crops
If you have never before entered into this exciting area of gardening, make this the year you start, because the rewards are huge. Once you've begun you'll find it truly addictive.

You can easily grow just about any of the non-exotic vegetables, and you'll be surprised at how straightforward it is to grow some of the more exotic ones. Make sure you start with the easier crops such as beans, tomatoes, and potatoes, plus perhaps a few fresh herbs. Once you've realized how easy these are, and gained some experience, you'll be even more likely to succeed with others. It is important to grow things that you really enjoy eating, and less rather than more of each crop, so you can avoid seasonal gluts.

This chapter shows you how to:
* Grow and look after herbs.
* Grow and maintain tree and soft fruits.
* Plan a vegetable garden.
* Grow vegetables from seed.
* Sow and grow under glass.
* Grow vegetables from sets, tubers, and young plants.
* Get the best from all your crops.

Making space for herbs

The easiest way to liven up an otherwise run-of-the-mill meal is to add some freshly picked herbs. Even a humble sandwich can be transformed into a truly delightful feast if you add some fresh, home-grown basil.

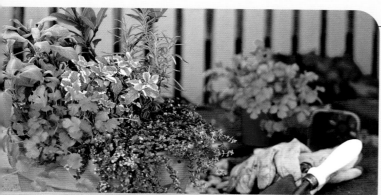

A mixed container of herbs near the kitchen door can be ideal, but remember to repot as the plants outgrow the space.

Basic soil requirements

Most herbs need very free-draining ground and will not last long if planted in a heavy, damp soil. If your soil doesn't fit their requirements, either grow the herbs in a container (*see* page 62) or a raised bed (*see* page 119), or make sure you dig in lots of grit, sand, and compost before planting, so that drainage is improved.

Not all herbs are hardy

Some herbs are not hardy and if planted out too early in the year, or left in too late in the year, they will die. Check the seed packet or plant label carefully.

Dressing the soil

Dressing the soil or compost surface with grit after planting slightly shallowly ensures a free-draining surface layer at the collar of the plants. This makes them much more likely to thrive, even when it's very wet. Always buy horticultural grit, and never use leftover builder's grit, shingle, or gravel because it can contain damaging materials.

Mint is invasive

The roots of mint are notorious for being aggressively invasive. Either grow mint in its own container above ground or plant it in a bed but keep it in its original container, plunged into the soil. When planted in a pot, the roots are much less likely to escape. The variegated mints are generally far less vigorous, and much less inclined to cause problems.

Different mints vary in flavour, so have a nibble to be sure the one you buy is to your taste.

Keep cats off your basil

Basil has an aroma that you either love or hate, and cats seem to love it. Perhaps because it is (to me at least) somewhat reminiscent of cat's urine, male cats in particular often spray or urinate on basil plants, so make sure that your basil is kept out of their way.

Statuesque and graceful, fennel is a herb that is worth growing in an ornamental bed or border.

Starve herbs for stronger flavour

Most herbs have a more intense flavour if they are not grown too "soft", so hold back on general or higher nitrogen feeds. Either don't feed at all, or use a high-potash fertilizer.

Herbs reach many heights

Make sure you check the ultimate or potential heights and spreads of the herbs you use – some, such as fennel, may look delicate in the garden centre, but check the label and you'll discover that it can grow to 1.8m (6ft).

Keep cutting herbs back

Even if you're not eating the herbs very quickly, it pays to cut them back regularly. This will keep the ones with woody stems compact with plenty of new growth, and prevent them from becoming leggy.

Sweet bay (*Laurus nobilis*) is a much more handsome plant if regularly harvested.

Ten great herbs to grow at home

1. Basil: mainstay of Italian cooking.
2. Bay: add to soups and stews.
3. Chives: garnish for salads.
4. Coriander: use in curries.
5. Mint: make into a sauce for lamb.
6. Parsley: garnish and fish sauces.
7. Rosemary: add sprigs to roast lamb.
8. Sage: use in savoury stuffings.
9. Tarragon: perks up egg dishes.
10. Thyme: delicious with fish.

Tree fruit

There is no flavour quite like fruit grown in your garden and eaten straight from the tree or bush. Almost no garden is too small: pick your crops carefully and consider growing in shapes other than the traditional tree, and you can grow fruit wherever there is sun.

White reflects light onto ripening fruit.

Best sites for tender fruits

Some of the more exotic fruits, such as nectarines, peaches, or vines, can be grown well out of doors, but for the heaviest crop a greenhouse or conservatory will help. A wall with all-day or afternoon sunshine is a good compromise because it acts as a heat store, accumulating warmth during the day and gradually releasing it when temperatures fall. A wall like this also provides some protection from the worst of the weather.

❀ Fruits invariably do better in a spot with plenty of sun; they won't crop that well if planted in a shady position.

❀ One of the more shade-tolerant fruits is the 'Morello' cherry. This does very well even on a north-facing wall.

❀ A moisture-retentive soil that isn't likely to get waterlogged is perfect for most fruit. In very dry weather it will often need watering, otherwise the crop will be smaller, and often a bit distorted or cracked.

Prune for productivity

Pruning fruit bushes and trees can make a phenomenal difference to the level of crop. Make sure you do your homework for the fruit you're growing, so that you know exactly how and when it should be pruned.

What to buy

When choosing fruit crops, consider whether they need a second plant as a pollinator. Some fruit is self-fertile, so only one tree is necessary for fruit set, but most need another pollinator. To be suitable, this must be in flower at the same time. Suppliers and nurseries should be able to tell you what they stock that would fit the bill.

Pruning the cherry family

Many fruit trees, particularly cherries, plums, peaches, nectarines, and almonds, are prone to silver leaf, a potentially fatal fungal infection. The spores gain access via open wounds. Infections are hugely reduced if trees are only pruned during the summer months, and if pruning cuts are kept as small as possible.

Using a wound paint may reduce the risk of silver leaf.

Hold the fruit and give the stalk a firm but gentle twist to test if it is ripe.

Spur and tip bearers

Most apples are "spur-bearers", producing crops on spurs along the shoot. Others are "tip-bearers", carrying much of their crop close to the shoot tip. Common tip-bearing apples include 'Discovery', 'Tydeman's Early Worcester', 'Worcester Pearmain', and 'Bramley's Seedling'. Avoid tip-bearers if you want to train your tree as an espalier, cordon or fan: they are much less easy to train into these shapes, and will have a lot of unproductive wood. A tip-bearer is better grown as a bush, half-standard, or standard.

Pollination improves productivity

Although so-called self-fertile trees can crop on their own, without you or an obliging neighbour having a suitable tree, I always find that they crop much more heavily when there is a pollinator close by. Make sure the extra pollinating tree is not removed if you can, otherwise you may find that your crops decrease.

Keep it in the family

If space is limited but you want several different varieties of apple, or to be sure that you have a suitable pollinator, then you could consider a "family tree" of different cultivars that have been grafted together to form one tree. Provided that they are all of a similar vigour, such as 'James Grieve', 'Sunset', and 'Egremont Russet', these can be fun. But if cultivars of different vigour have been used, pruning and fruiting can be a problem.

Training the branches of spur-bearing trees away from the vertical increases yields.

Fitting fruit in

❀ Fruit trees are not grown on their own roots, but are grafted onto a "rootstock" to limit their size. Broadly speaking, M26 means large apple trees, MM106 medium-sized, and M9 dwarf trees. With pears, Quince A and C are similar to an apple's M26 and M9, respectively.

❀ If space is limited, avoid apples described as biennial bearing: they often only bear a useful crop every other year. Ideally choose one that is described as "dual purpose": this means it can be used as a dessert apple or as a cooker.

❀ Fan-trained plums or cherries, and cordon or espalier apples or pears, can all be grown on a fence, trellis, or wires, and so take up very little room.

❀ Why not train a pair of cordon apples over a simple arch? If chosen well, they will pollinate each other, look great covered in blossom in spring, and fruit in summer, taking up little garden space.

Soft fruit

Soft fruit, such as strawberries, raspberries, and blueberries, add another dimension to your garden and certainly make a delicious addition to meal times. Most soft fruit is relatively compact, making it ideal for growing in the smaller garden.

Extending the strawberry crop

If you want to have lots of strawberries over a long period, choose the varieties carefully to include early, mid- and late-season types. Remember that the yield from a single plant on any one day is never going to be that great, so ideally you should grow several of each variety.

Raspberries need support

Raspberries are a crop I would recommend to anyone, but they do take up quite a bit of room. If you want to cut back on the preparation for growing these gorgeous berries, grow autumn-fruiting varieties; they do not need to have a support system like the summer-fruiters do.

Try tougher raspberries

If you garden on soil that is too alkaline and too heavy for raspberries, autumn-fruiting types may be the answer. For me, summer varieties never perform well after their first year, whereas autumn-fruiting ones seem much better able to cope in adverse conditions, and just keep on fruiting.

Soft fruit and birds

Raspberries, especially summer-fruiting types, are well loved by garden birds. I love feeding them, but there is a limit – I also love my raspberries. A fruit cage, netting, or bird scarers mean more of the crop goes to the humans.

A netting alternative

Standard fruit netting drives me mad, because it tangles and tears so easily; it is also easy for birds to become entangled in it. I prefer pond netting; it is less expensive, much easier to set up, doesn't tangle, and still has a small enough mesh to work brilliantly.

Pond netting is good for protecting fruit.

Build a fruit cage

To make a small cage, use Alkathene pipe, sturdy canes, and pond netting. Cut the pipe into lengths long enough to make a hoop over the plants, under which you can move to collect fruit. Push a cane in to each end, leaving about 20cm (8in) protruding. Drive one cane into the ground, bend the pipe into an arch, and drive the other cane into the ground. When all the hoops are up, attach the netting.

Make sure you leave a way into your cage.

Leave access for pollinators

Whatever method you are using to protect fruit, remember that to get a crop the flowers have to be pollinated, so don't put fine netting over the plants until most of the flowers have been pollinated.

Feed your fruit

With crops, you get out what you put in.

Most fruit produces a far lower or less appetizing crop if it is not well fed. Feeding needn't be complicated: give a general fertilizer in the early spring combined with a nutritious mulch, such as well-rotted manure or garden compost, and follow with sulphate of potash in early summer to encourage flowering and wood ripening.

Remember to water

In very dry years water will also be needed if you want a good crop that is relatively free from problems such as bitter pit (apples), or cracking (apples, pears, nectarines, plums, and cherries). Avoid frequent but light watering; a seriously thorough and deep watering at longer intervals is much more use.

Don't overfeed

Although feeding increases productivity, excessive feed, especially if it includes quite a bit of nitrogen, is likely to cause soft growth, easily damaged by pests, pathogens, and weather. It is generally better to err on the side of caution.

Blueberries like it boggy

A bush can yield 5kg (11lb) of blueberries.

Blueberries are popular for their lovely taste and texture and their brilliant anti-oxidant benefits. They perform well, but for the best crop, grow several plants and remember that these are lime-hating, boggy-ground dwellers. Unless you have or can create a suitable spot, they won't succeed. The best garden blueberries I have ever seen were in a compost bin full of acidic compost and soil. The compost volume was so great that it stayed moist.

Some fruit announces its ripeness through colour, smell, and softness.

When is it ripe?

With raspberries or strawberries, the change with fruit colour tells you when the crop is ripe; in gooseberries look for a slight yellowing and give the fruits a gentle squeeze – if it doesn't give, wait.

Planning a vegetable garden

Choosing a spot for growing vegetables is really important, but it's also vital that you then spend time preparing the soil… and last but certainly not least, planning what you want to grow. Get it right now to save problems later.

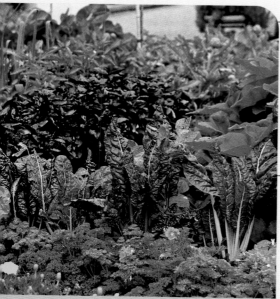

Textured leaves and dramatic colours make many vegetables attractive.

Get the site right

To grow vegetables easily and get a good crop, you really do need a sunny spot, and ideally a well-drained but fairly moisture-retentive soil. Everything will struggle if there is too much shade. But if the classic space for edibles, confined to the back of the garden, is not sunny enough, don't forget that crops can look great in amongst flowers and other ornamentals – or even in a prominent place of their own.

Adding lime

Most vegetables do best on a neutral to slightly alkaline soil, so adding lime may be necessary.

Watch out for wind

Windy spots are best avoided because they can cause a dramatic decrease in cropping. Even a slight to moderately windy spot may reduce yields by an average of 30 per cent.

Shield your crops

If there is no choice but to grow your vegetables somewhere rather windy, erect a wind-break fence or plant a shrubby wind-break before you start. Whatever you use, make sure it is at least partially permeable: a solid wall may cause problems as wind swirls over it. The effort really is worthwhile: every 1m (3ft) height of windbreak provides about 5m (16ft) of protection behind it.

A dense hedge slows the wind, reducing moisture loss from plants and raising air temperatures in the sheltered area.

Rotate your crops

However small your crop area, it is well worth using a rotation system. Ideally, move crops around three or four beds or areas in sequence, but always avoid growing the same or a closely related crop in the same ground two years running. This helps to reduce pathogen and pest problems and maintain fertility.

Crop rotation for weed control

Rotation can also help with weeding. If a plot is rather weedy, grow a crop of potatoes in it. These have a good weed-smothering effect, which saves you time, and also makes them a good crop to precede a difficult-to-weed crop, such as garlic.

Make a deep bed

You can create a "deep-bed" system, starting with very thorough soil improvement using a lot of organic matter. Avoid disturbing this soil over the coming years, only doing so when planting, and only add organic matter to the surface of the soil. This way you can save yourself a lot of work: firstly, there is a lot less digging and secondly, because the soil is not disturbed by digging, dormant weed seeds that are already in the soil do not germinate (as they do if the soil is dug over), so only weed seeds that are blown in need to be dealt with.

Companion planting confuses pests' sense of smell and their visual targeting of your crops.

Natural pest control

There are advantages to growing onions and carrots together – something a classic rotation system wouldn't allow. If you want to reduce the risk of carrots getting carrot fly and onions getting onion fly, grow these two crops on the same plot, perhaps even in alternating rows: the smell of the carrots masks the smell of the onions and *vice versa*, making both crops less likely to be tracked down by these pests.

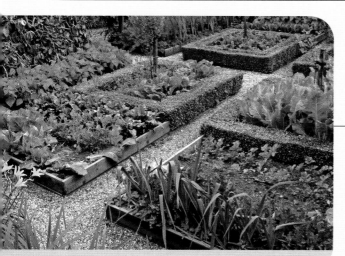

If you do not need to step into them, raised beds can be planted more densely than open ground.

Use raised beds

If the soil is very stony, very heavy, or very light and sandy, and you cannot improve it by the usual methods of digging in organic matter and/or grit, consider creating raised beds. Sink 15cm x 3cm (6in x 1in) boards about 5cm (2in) into the soil as edging, then fill with a more suitable soil.

Rotate crops for soil fertility

Rotation can help with soil fertility. Crops such as peas and beans (legumes) have the ability to "fix" nitrogen from the air into a form that is available to plants. This makes them a great crop to grow on a piece of soil which is then to be used for a nitrogen-hungry crop, such as cabbages, cauliflowers, Brussels sprouts or calabrese (the brassicas), or potatoes or spinach or chard. Because these crops use such a lot of nitrogen, it makes sense to grow a crop that does not need a lot of nitrogen, such as carrots or parsnips, on the same ground after them.

Keep a notebook

I'm not a great list-keeper or note-taker, but I would thoroughly recommend keeping a notebook if you grow vegetables. Recording the basics, such as varieties grown, sowing and planting dates, and perhaps even cropping dates and yields, makes decisions and planning easier the following year. It also ensures that you have a definitive record of the variety names, so you know what to choose (or perhaps what to avoid!) the following year.

Be adventurous

Try to be a bit adventurous if you're an experienced vegetable grower – by all means regularly grow those varieties that you know will do well and which have the flavour you love, but do try some of the new varieties too. Each year there is a whole host of new varieties put on the market, so don't miss out. F1 hybrid seed may seem expensive compared with standard seed but for uniformity and vigour, it may be money well spent.

Winter shopping

Raising your own vegetables from seed is very good value and immensely satisfying. Over the late autumn and early winter when things are generally a little quieter in the garden, take time to study seed catalogues and start to make lists of what you need.

As long as you group several plants in a clump, sweetcorn will crop well.

Grow beyond the vegetable plot

Some surprising vegetable crops can be used in ornamental areas of the garden. Sweetcorn, with its rustling leaves and feathery flowers, can make an architectural impact in a border.

Read catalogues carefully

To make life easier for yourself and to reduce the risk of pest and pathogen problems, take note of comments made in catalogues about each variety's resistance to common problems. Those sold as "suitable for beginners" or "for organic growers and gardeners" are generally a particularly good choice.

Space-saving plot design

If you are creating a vegetable plot from scratch, you'll want to maximize the amount you can cram into the space you have available — but don't forget to allow enough space on paths for a wheelbarrow to be pushed with ease and without damaging nearby crops. All areas of the beds should be easily accessible from the path: if they are too wide for this, lay a line of bricks or pieces of slab to create an access route for maintenance and harvesting.

Vegetables from seed

If you don't have a greenhouse, cold frame, or propagator, there are still plenty of vegetables you can grow by sowing the seed direct into the soil, or by investing in a few "ready-grown plants".

Get the soil ready

Make sure that the soil has been cleared of weeds, and if necessary incorporate some bulky organic matter. Digging in well-rotted manure or garden compost can make a huge difference to poor soil.

Don't work wet soil

Avoid working on soil that is very wet: it will be compacted very readily and this damages the soil's structure, increasing the chances of it becoming poorly aerated and waterlogged. In any case, many seeds will rot if the soil is too wet. It is better to wait for a week or so, even if this means sowing later than the suggested sowing times.

A plank will fit between rows of young plants.

Walking the plank

If the soil is nearly ready, but you still think it might get compacted if you stand on it, lay a plank or board down and stand on this. The plank spreads your weight over a much larger area and reduces the risk of compaction.

Attending to distances

However much of a hurry you are in, always take the time to check the suggested sowing depths and seed spacings. If buried too deeply or too shallowly, some seeds may germinate very poorly or even not at all. But don't get too worried about being very precise – a hairsbreadth here or there won't be significant.

How thin is thin?

Seed packets often suggest sowing "thinly" – a vague term, but one you should take note of; the thinner you sow the seed (within reason) the less thinning out you will have to do later. However, don't sow so thinly that there is a risk of the final spacing being too wide!

Sow three parsnip seeds together and thin to one.

Station-sowing

For some crops that are notoriously temperamental, such as parsnip, it is worth station-sowing. This is sowing about three seeds together, but with the suggested final spacing distance between each trio. It allows for one seed to fail, one to be a bit wimpy (and be removed) and the other to thrive, and avoids any more thinning!

Sow a marker crop

If you are sowing slow-germinating and somewhat erratic seeds, why not sow a fast-germinating crop, such as lettuce, along the row too? It'll be up and harvested before the slow crop needs all that space, and meanwhile it serves as a great marker, making it easier to see exactly where the crops are and where the emerging weeds are.

Some seeds don't like it hot

If the weather is very hot and drying when you sow the seed, prepare for heat-sensitive seeds, such as lettuce, to be slow and erratic in their germination. Ideally try to avoid these conditions because overall results tend to be very disappointing.

Coping with dry conditions

In very hot, drying conditions it can be difficult to keep the top layer of soil adequately moist. If it does not remain moist enough for long enough, the seeds may not germinate, or they may germinate but the germinated seeds or young seedlings may then die. There are several things you can do to avoid the problem.

❀ Make areas of newly sown seed and young seedlings high priority when it comes to watering.

❀ Make the drill into which you sow the seeds about 1cm (½in) deeper than normal, then put a layer of very wet soil in the bottom of the drill to a depth of about 1cm (½in) and sow the seed on this. Top the drill off with dry soil.

❀ After sowing, water well and then cover the soil surface with newspaper, a couple of layers of fleece, or similar material. This should help to reduce moisture loss from the surface. Make sure that you remove the covering before the seeds germinate, or they will perish.

Water will drain very rapidly through a layer of sand under your seeds.

Use sand when it's wet

If the soil is really too wet for seed sowing but you have no option but to go ahead, make the drill a tiny bit deeper than usual, and line it with horticultural sand before you sow the seed. This should prevent the seed from actually sitting in water and rotting off.

Cover rows with fleece

To get direct-sown seeds off to a somewhat speedier and more reliable start, cover the row with fleece held in place with metal pegs, or weighed down with large stones or bricks at the edges.

Thinning tips

❀ Seeds sown direct will need some thinning out unless you are unbelievably good at sowing thinly, and have been very lucky with your germination rates. But don't thin crops in very hot or very wet weather; either extreme is more likely to result in inadvertent damage to the seedlings you want to keep. Hot, dry weather is the most dangerous.

❀ When choosing what to thin, always take out the weakest-looking seedlings, or any showing signs of stunting, discolouration, or other problems.

❀ Using the thinnings: the thinnings of crops that transplant well (most things except the root crops) can always be used in other areas, if for some reason you suddenly find you need more of the crop or it has failed unexpectedly elsewhere.

❀ After thinning a row of seedlings, water the row straight away, even if the soil seems adequately moist. The water you apply now will help to re-settle the disturbed soil around the finer roots, so allowing the remaining seedlings to continue to grow away well.

❀ Always thin carrots in the evening, because however careful you are, you will bruise the foliage and this releases an aroma that attracts carrot fly, a serious pest of carrots. At night there are fewer flies around and less aroma is released into the cooler air.

A lolly stick, seed label, teaspoon handle, or even a pencil helps to ease out roots.

Handling small seeds

Sowing all but the largest seeds direct from your hand can be tricky if they stick to your hands because they are clammy or damp; when they do leave your hand, they will do so in clumps. Mixing the seed with plenty of dry horticultural sand will help. Alternatively, take a clean, dry piece of paper and fold a sharp crease down its centre. The seeds can be evenly distributed from this if you hold the paper in one hand and tap it sharply with the other as you move it along the row – although it takes a little practice.

Protecting seeds against birds

If wild birds have a habit of eating seeds before they germinate, temporarily cover the bed with fleece, newspaper, or net held taut between canes or pegs. The net must be kept taut to avoid birds getting tangled in it.

Protecting seeds against cats

Cats are not interested in your seeds, but they do find finely raked, crumbly soil irresistible, and see it as a huge litter tray! Lay lots of branching twigs over the newly sown ground to deter them from destroying your efforts.

Save your seed

If you have seed left over, it can often be saved easily and effectively from one year to the next, so don't waste it. Seed is most likely to remain in good condition if kept in cool, dry conditions, perhaps even in a sealed lunch box in the fridge. If you keep spare packets of opened seed, wherever you store it, make sure that it safe from rodents.

Save silica for seeds in storage

The packaging for electronic equipment, musical instruments, cameras, and other high-value items often contains small sachets of silica gel. Don't bin these: save them for use in the container in which you store your seeds because the gel helps to absorb moisture from the atmosphere around the seed packets and reduces the risk of dampness building up and damaging the seeds.

Extend your cropping season at both ends

❀ Successional sowing means sowing a relatively small proportion of the seed at, say, two-week intervals. It helps to reduce the extent of the seasonal gluts that are so common when you grow your own, and extends the period over which you can harvest each crop.

❀ Search the catalogues and take note of suggested harvest dates for any one crop: there are often distinct early, midseason or maincropping, and late-cropping varieties available. Choosing one from each category can hugely increase the harvest period.

❀ Covering the soil with plastic sheet or fleece before you sow allows it to warm up slightly, and may also keep off excessive rain. This allows earlier sowing and improves the chances of some crops, such as carrots and parsnips, which often fail due to damp, cold soil. Seeds germinate much better in the warmth.

❀ At the end of the season, cover developing crops with fleece or cloches to keep them viable and cropping for longer.

❀ Always start harvesting as soon as the vegetable is ready, or else the plant tends to slow down. With some crops, such as peas and beans or courgettes and marrows, this really makes a huge difference to the cropping season's length and the total yield.

Black plastic is best for warming soil. If you use a heavy-duty sheet, you can pack it away and use it again for years.

Using old seed

If you find a packet of seed that has been open for a while, or one that has past its suggested use-by date, there is no harm in sowing it anyway. Being opened or being old is likely to have reduced the percentage of viable seeds in the packet, so either sow more than you usually would, or be prepared to buy more if not enough germinate.

Sowing under glass

Some seeds need to be sown in a greenhouse or frame for a bit of extra heat; others that could be sown direct may give better results if protected from erratic temperatures or slugs and other pests. Whatever the reasons, try to supply suitable temperatures.

Using a heated propagator

❀ You get more reliable results for crops such as tomatoes, peppers, and aubergines if you can supply some bottom heat. Investing in a heated propagator may seem daunting, but it'll be less expensive than you might think and owning one opens up a whole new range of growing opportunities. If necessary, put it on your birthday or Christmas list!

Extra heat is invaluable for seeds of tender crops.

❀ If you have two or more types of vegetable seed that need slightly different temperatures to germinate, set the thermostat at the higher temperature or only very slightly lower, and stand the pots of those seeds requiring lower temperatures on inverted pots inside the propagator. Being raised off the capillary matting on the tray at the base means they are heated to a lesser degree.

❀ Seedlings soon suffer if kept in a heated propagator for too long. Once the majority of seedlings have appeared, gradually acclimatize them to a cooler life and then place them in a suitable position to grow on.

Small trays for small crops

If you only want small numbers of a crop, either use quarter size seed trays (harder to get hold of but well worth looking for) or sow in pots. Growing more than one type of seed in a single tray spells disaster.

Sow rows in guttering

Sow in lengths of plastic guttering; but be careful not to over-water. To plant out, squeeze the guttering to loosen the strip of compost and roots, and slide the row of young plants out into a channel dug in the soil. It saves time, and the plants suffer little if any check.

Use multi-cell seed trays

I'm a real fan of multi-cell or module trays for seed sowing. They allow you to sow just one or two seeds in each cell (rather like a mini pot), and this reduces the time spent pricking out, and also minimizes the disturbance to the seedling or small plant.

Module trays are ideal for tomato plants.

Potting on crowded seedlings

After years of carefully pricking out the grass-like seedlings of leeks into individual holes in new pots for growing on before planting out, one year I ran out of time and simply pulled the potful of tiny plants apart, replanting the whole lot in to a larger pot of fresh compost. Freed (to a degree), they grew away brilliantly, making plants just as good as those that had taken hours of work. This is only suitable for pretty chunky, tough seedlings like leeks.

Water before thinning

Make sure the compost in trays or pots is good and moist before you attempt to prick out seedlings. Dry compost means more root damage.

Sow thinly

If you sow seed in a tray, try to sow it thinly. This will dramatically reduce overcrowding and the time you later spend thinning out congested seedlings when you prick them out. It'll also mean an easier and less damaging move for the seedlings, and consequently better crops for you.

Sowing thickly may save space, but it will cost in time and yields.

Exposure to outdoor temperatures lets plants toughen up or "harden off" naturally.

Acclimatizing seedlings

❀ Move seedlings raised under protection outside during the day and back in at night for a week, to acclimatize before planting out.

❀ Use bell cloches or fleece draped over a frame as a temporary protection if you are worried, but don't leave them on for too long.

Planting out

❀ You can plant out most vegetables a bit deeper than you might expect: the extra depth gives them more support in the soil. Some, such as tomatoes, will form additional roots at the base of the stem.

❀ Avoid extreme conditions for planting out. Too much heat, cold, or wind, or a soil that is too wet or dry, will cause a check in growth that sets plants back. Wait a day or two until conditions improve.

❀ If the weather suddenly turns too hot, protect transplants with shade netting or even a sheet or two of newspaper for a few days. This gives their roots time to establish and they suffer less in the heat.

Vegetables from sets, tubers, and young plants

Some plants are generally grown using tubers (potatoes) or sets (garlic, onions, and shallots), while others are bought as young plants. This is a very easy way to raise an impressive crop, and the range of varieties available is huge, so take advantage of it.

Ridges give good drainage

If your soil is rather heavy and inclined to become very wet in winter, grow crops like garlic, which don't appreciate these conditions, on raised ridges for better drainage. I draw up a ridge of soil, about 15cm (6in) tall and 20–25cm (8–10in) wide at the base, and plant the individual cloves in the normal way, but into the top of the ridge. This works brilliantly – far better, I find, than the oft-quoted method of raising individual cloves in pots and then planting out once the soil conditions have improved.

A ridge of soil will be drier and warmer.

Choosing garlic

Garlic bought for cooking is best not used for planting. It might work brilliantly, but there is also a significant risk that it may be virus infected or that the variety itself is not actually a good performer in your climate. Buying special planting stock avoids both these problems.

For best crops use planting stock.

Use proper seed potatoes

It really isn't worth trying to economize and use potatoes that have started to sprout in your kitchen instead of buying certified disease-free tubers. Kitchen potatoes are much more likely to be virus infected, and also they are often covered with shoots that are much too long and break off when you try to plant them.

Protect sets with netting

When you plant onion or shallot sets, the necks of the bulbs will protrude slightly above the soil surface. This is a serious temptation to birds, which pull them out of the soil so they don't get a chance to root and you end up with gappy rows and fewer onions than you had hoped for. For the first four to six weeks after planting, keep the sets covered with netting – it'll keep the birds away and help your crop to get established.

Netting is the best way to keep birds off.

Planting leek seedlings

When you are raising leeks, wait until they are at least 20cm (8in) long before you plant them out in the open ground.

Allow for leek growth

After you have made a deep, narrow hole and placed a leek transplant into it, it is definitely best not to fill in the gap between the leek and the sides of the channel. Instead just wiggle it about a bit, to ensure that the roots are right at the base of the hole, and water it in well. This initial watering and any subsequent waterings will be enough to settle the soil around the root, while allowing maximum sideways expansion of the stem.

Buying young vegetable plants

Buying young vegetable plants is not a sin. If you've run out of time, missed sowing dates, or simply don't have the specialist equipment required for good germination, such as a heated propagator, or a frost-free or heated greenhouse, then they are a brilliant purchase. Don't be put off by people who say you should always do everything "properly" – short cuts can be equally successful.

Keeping tender veg warm

If you do buy in plants of tender vegetables, such as aubergines, peppers, or tomatoes, make sure you have somewhere suitable for them, with plenty of natural daylight and adequate warmth, until it is time for planting out. If you can't provide the accommodation they need, delay buying them.

Watering leeks and chives

Leeks and chives often succumb to devastating attacks of fungal rust. This is always worse when the foliage is damp, so always water these crops directly at the base.

Water leeks only at the base.

Toughen up plants to avoid rust

Fungal rust thrives on soft foliage, so avoid excessive feeds of nitrogen-rich fertilizers or manure. Instead apply sulphate of potash to the soil. Potash helps toughen up the growth and minimizes the risk of a fungus attack, without affecting the flavour in any way.

Raising plants in the house

If you are keeping plants on a house windowsill, they are at risk of becoming "drawn" or leggy because of the lack of natural light. Keep them as close as possible to the window and stand them on a sheet of aluminium foil (shiny side uppermost); this will help to reflect a lot more light back onto the plants.

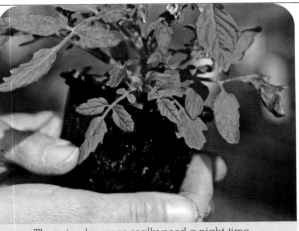

These tender crops really need a night-time minimum of 16°C (60°F) to thrive.

Top of the crops

Each and every crop you decide to grow will be worth the effort, but to get the best possible results – whether you're a first-time veg grower or a well-seasoned hand – give each what it needs.

Sweetcorn can be raised in pots; it prefers a warm start.

Grow sweetcorn in blocks

Whether you sow sweetcorn direct, or plant out the seedlings, always do so in blocks, not rows – this wind-pollinated crop gets much more thoroughly pollinated if grown in blocks, giving much higher yields.

Stick to one sweetcorn

Avoid growing more than one variety of sweetcorn, unless you have a very large garden, because cross-pollination between varieties often causes loss of quality. This is especially true if you are growing a "super-sweet" variety.

Avoiding tough tomatoes

You can reduce the likelihood of tough skins developing on tomatoes growing in your greenhouse by doing your best to avoid excessively high temperatures. Shading on the glazing both reduces the temperature and prevents too much direct sunlight from hitting the developing fruit.

Greenhouse soil care

If you grow tomatoes in the soil in a greenhouse border, you are likely to start to get problems after a few years, particularly with soil-borne infections. However much hard work it is, you will have to change the soil completely. Do this either as soon as problems start to occur, or, preferably, every three or four years, before crops start to fail.

Thinning tomato leaves

You can thin out the foliage on tomatoes, but don't go over the top. By all means remove some leaves if they are so numerous that they are shading the fruits heavily, but make sure there are still plenty left – they're needed to feed the plants.

Looking after cordon tomatoes

Cordon-type tomatoes, also called vine or indeterminate, such as 'Tigerella', 'Gardener's Delight', 'Mirabelle', and 'Shirley', need their sideshoots removed regularly so that the energy available can go to the developing fruit trusses. When the plants are as tall as you want them to be, usually towards the end of the summer, pinch out the top of the plant leaving a couple of leaves above the uppermost flower truss.

Limiting the size of a tomato plant means fewer trusses, but the fruit may be larger.

The bush-type tomato varieties are ideal for growing in containers.

Bush tomatoes

Bush-type or determinate tomatoes, such as 'Tumbler' and 'Totem', do not need pinching out and sideshooting – doing this would mean a lighter crop.

Pinching out shoots

Sideshoots are best removed when they are 3cm (1in) or shorter. Once they are any bigger than this, you can easily damage the plant when removing them. Never cut off sideshoots; instead hold the shoot between finger and thumb and quickly and firmly bend it down until it snaps off cleanly.

Snapping a sideshoot makes a clean break at a natural weak point that will heal quickly.

Supporting large tomatoes

Large-fruiting tomatoes, such as the beefsteak types, can produce very heavy fruit capable of breaking the stem to which they are attached. If you are worried that this might happen, place inverted flower pots beneath the lower trusses to support them, and either thin out upper trusses slightly or rig up a net to support them.

Use canes for support

When tying tomatoes to canes for support, always use a figure-of-eight system. Loop the string around the stem, then cross the two ends over, then pass them around the cane and tie them on the far side of it. The string must be loose around the stem to allow for plenty of room for expansion. Do not tie the knot next to the tomato: you are much less likely to injure the stem if you tie the knot against the cane.

Crossing the strings reduces the risk of the stem being chafed against the cane.

Avoid blossom end rot

Avoid the black, leathery sunken patches known as blossom end rot developing on the tomatoes by growing them in larger containers or ideally in the open ground. Erratic and inadequate watering causes this disorder so plants in containers are more susceptible, especially if the containers are relatively small. Keeping the soil constantly just moist is the key to avoiding the problem.

Avoid skin splitting

Erratic watering makes tomato skins split, so keep moisture levels even and never allow the soil or compost to get too dry before you apply the water. Consider a simple drip irrigation system if watering tomatoes in containers is difficult.

The right level of feed maximizes yields without losing flavour.

Feeding tomatoes

Regular applications of a liquid tomato fertilizer containing plenty of potash really help to maximize the crop. However, they often result in magnesium deficiency, showing on the leaves as yellowing or purple areas between the veins on the older or lower leaves. This rarely effects the cropping but, if it is severe, treat by watering the foliage with a solution of Epsom salts.

Magnesium deficiency is common later in the season.

Green tomatoes

If you have green tomatoes on the plant late in the season, when temperatures have dropped, you may be able to ripen them if you carefully lay the plant down on to a mat of dry straw and then cover with a cloche.

Everyone has encountered this end-of-season problem.

Blighted tomatoes

Outdoor tomatoes often succumb to the ravages of potato blight infection. If you want to avoid spraying against this infection, check catalogues regularly for varieties showing relatively high levels of resistance.

Dealing with blight

If blight does hit your tomatoes, promptly cut off the top growth and dig out the stem bases to reduce the risk of the spores getting into the soil. Bin or burn the infected material; do not compost it under any circumstances.

Ten great tomatoes

1. 'Gardener's Delight' (cherry, cordon)
2. 'Legend' (salad, bush)
3. 'Marmande' (beefsteak, cordon)
4. 'Oxheart' (beefsteak, cordon)
5. 'Piccolo' (cherry, cordon)
6. 'Sweet Million' (cherry, cordon)
7. 'Tigerella' (striped salad, cordon)
8. 'Tornado' F1 (salad, bush)
9. 'Totem' F1 (salad, bush)
10. 'Tumbler' (cherry, bush)

Ripening the plant

You can ripen healthy green tomatoes once picked – just put a few in a dry paper bag containing a slightly over-ripe banana. The ethylene gas produced by the banana is a natural ripening agent.

Watch the temperature

Erratic temperatures can cause distorted fruit, so try to ensure even, warm temperatures all summer.

Feed your pepper plants

Make sure that peppers are fed regularly with a liquid feed containing plenty of potash to keep them flowering and fruiting.

Try aubergines

Don't be deterred from growing aubergines – they're as easy to grow as indoor tomatoes. They need greenhouse protection, and perform best with plenty of natural light. If you have the luxury of space, they are ideally grown in a separate greenhouse from tomatoes, which develop tough skins in too much light.

Courgettes, marrows, squash, and pumpkins

All these crops need plenty of moisture if they are to produce a really heavy crop, so make sure they are planted in moisture-retentive soil and that the surface is kept mulched.

Pick crops when young and shiny; older ones turn bitter.

Don't over-water

Aubergines are much easier to over-water than tomatoes or even peppers. Make sure the compost is just dry to about 5cm (2in) depth before you water.

Harvesting aubergines

Always keep a pair of secateurs or a sharp knife to hand when it's time to harvest aubergines. They are extremely spiny around the calyx or stalk end, and the stems are very tough.

Courgette flowers

❀ If conditions are too dry, plants form more male flowers. This means fewer fruit, but it does make good eating picked fresh and fried in batter; leave some to fertilize female flowers.

❀ Male flowers are easily identified by their slim, straight-sided stem; there is a slight swelling just below the base of female flowers.

❀ One of the most common causes of damage to fruit is rot from a wet flower spreading into the developing fruit. You cannot stop rain, but only water at the base of the plant. When flowers start to deteriorate, quickly pinch them off.

Only a few males are needed for fruit.

Remove leaves dusty with mildew, but don't worry about these silver marks.

Don't panic over leaf markings

Many courgette and marrow varieties form distinct silver markings on their leaves. This is perfectly natural and nothing to worry about, but is often mistakenly thought to indicate mildew or, worse still, virus infections.

Dealing with blighted potatoes

If potato blight strikes, immediately cut back all the haulms (top growth) of infected or suspect plants and bin or burn them; never compost diseased material. If this is done rapidly and if conditions are relatively dry, you can prevent the tubers becoming infected. Lift the crop as soon as possible, and make sure it is thoroughly dry before storing.

Brown patches spreading on leaves are the depressing symptom of blight.

Potatoes and lime

Avoid growing potatoes on ground that has just been limed (perhaps for a crop of brassicas) for a year or two. Limey soil is more likely to produce potato tubers infected with scab – not a major problem, but best avoided!

Resistant varieties

There are a few varieties of potato now available that do show good resistance to potato blight, such as 'Sarpo Mira' and 'Sarpo Axona'. They are well worth tracking down if your potato crops are always badly damaged by blight.

Avoid wireworm tunnels

Soil that has only been cultivated for a year or two is very likely to have a high population of wireworms. These small, ginger-coloured pests tunnel into the tubers and can wreck the crop. Try to avoid growing potatoes until the third or fourth year: if you just cannot bear to wait, concentrate on early potatoes, which can often be lifted before the wireworms have had time to do much damage.

Mildly blighted potatoes may look sound but will soon deteriorate.

Early potatoes make efficient use of space.

Choose early potatoes

If you are short of space but still want to grow potatoes, then early varieties are best. They take up less room, and because they are in the ground for a short time, the site can be used for another crop once they are lifted.

Earth-up potatoes

Potato blight fungus is the most serious problem affecting potatoes, and earthing-up well will help to reduce the likelihood of it infecting the tubers when the spores are washed down through the soil.

Plenty of earth above developing tubers helps stop them turning green and possibly toxic.

Slug control

Large, deep tunnels in potatoes are caused by keeled slugs, probably the second most serious potato problem. Try using a biological control nematode, growing the varieties described as relatively slug-resistant, or growing mostly early varieties that can be lifted before the worst of the slug damage can occur.

Check stored potatoes

Checking stored potatoes regularly is always a good idea: infections often spread rapidly with so many tubers in close proximity. It is essential to check very regularly if your crop had blight because this infection makes the tubers very prone to secondary bacterial rotting.

Try sweet potatoes

❀ If you want to branch out a bit, try growing some sweet potatoes. You raise these from "slips" (rather like cuttings), but they do need warmer conditions than standard potatoes.

❀ To increase the chances of a heavy crop, move the slips to individual pots before planting out in very early summer.

❀ Planting through thick, black plastic (I use cut-open compost bags, laid black side up) and covering with horticultural fleece really helps to increase soil and air temperature, and makes for a better crop.

Sort your potatoes

When sorting potatoes for storage, it pays to have at least three grades – seemingly perfect, minor damage (such as surface slug or wireworm attack), and eat now (more seriously damaged). Provided the tubers are perfectly dry when stored, I have kept slightly damaged tubers for months with no problem.

Lift potatoes on a dry day and dry them off before storing in breathable sacks or boxes.

Choosing lettuce

If your lettuce crops are often ravaged by slugs and snails, try to choose at least some varieties that have red or purple leaves. I find that they are rarely as badly damaged by these pests as the green varieties.

Sow cool

Lettuce seed is unusually sensitive to heat, and does not perform well if the conditions are very hot, so plan your sowings accordingly.

Ten great lettuces

1. 'Bijou' (red loose-leaf)
2. 'Chartwell' (romaine)
3. 'Corsair' (cos)
4. 'Freckles' (red-freckled romaine)
5. 'Little Gem' (mini-cos)
6. 'Lollo Rossa' (red loose-leaf)
7. 'Mascara' (red oak-leaf)
8. 'Revolution' (red loose-leaf)
9. 'Salad Bowl' (oak-leaf)
10. 'Sioux' (iceberg)

Grow a range of lettuces for colourful salads.

Protecting oriental vegetables

Flea beetle – a tiny pest responsible for causing numerous equally tiny holes in the foliage – is a serious problem on many of the leafy oriental vegetables. Before it gets a chance to attack, cover the crop with fleece. This serves a dual purpose, because many oriental vegetables enjoy the somewhat more protected and slightly more humid conditions beneath the covering. If you can, cover the row straight after sowing.

Horticultural fleece or mesh are perfect alternatives to pesticides.

Cut and come again

Many leafy vegetables can be cropped more than once. Loose-leaf lettuces, which don't develop a tight, dense heart, are ideal, as are chard, spinach, and even kale. Three to six weeks after sowing, when the young plants have reached about 10–15cm (4–6in) in height, simply cut them off 3cm (1in) above ground level with a sharp knife. The stump will regrow, giving enough for a second crop of baby leaves within another few weeks, and a third after that.

Avoid bolting

Lettuces will bolt, rocketing up into tall plants and turning bitter, if they become too hot or dry. Keep moisture levels constant, and be prepared to harvest before bolting strikes in a hot spell.

Avoiding pea moth

Pea moth, which leaves tiny maggots to develop within the pods, can be avoided by growing the crop beneath a layer of fleece or very fine mesh. Making sowings early and late in the day also helps avoid the problem.

Mulch peas and beans

Mulching beans will make a huge difference to the crop, especially during dry weather. Always mulch when the soil is really moist.

Pick peas

It is essential to keep on picking peas and sugarsnaps as fast as the pods develop. If the seeds within are left on the plants to ripen, the flowering will diminish and the yield will suffer accordingly.

Frequent picking means tender peas and high yields.

Prepare a bean trench

Beans are a very thirsty crop, so do all you can to prepare the soil well before sowing or planting, incorporating plenty of bulky organic matter. It is often said that you must prepare the bean trench the autumn or winter before, but I regularly do it minutes before planting and find it works just as well.

Climbing French beans have greater yields than dwarf types.

Try French beans

If runner beans regularly disappoint because the young beans abort, this is almost always due to dryness in the soil. If lots of organic matter and mulching don't do the trick, grow some climbing French beans; these are far more tolerant of slight dryness.

Ten great beans and peas

1. 'Aquadulce Claudia' (broad)
2. 'Blue Lake' (climbing French)
3. 'Borlotti' (climbing French)
4. 'Cobra' (climbing French)
5. 'Kelvedon Wonder' (pea)
6. 'Meteor' (pea)
7. 'Oregon Sugar Pod' (mangetout)
8. 'Pickwick' (dwarf runner)
9. 'Purple Teepee' (dwarf French)
10. 'Red Rum' (runner)

Fleece tunnels are quick to put up, and provide warmth as well.

Avoiding carrot fly

Carrot fly is a serious pest. The maggot-like young pests tunnel into the root, making it more prone to rotting and a lot less appealing to eat. Avoid by covering the crop with fleece or very fine mesh as soon as the seed is sown, or as the seedlings start to emerge. To make weeding and harvesting easier, put an open-topped barrier of fleece or fine mesh around the row. If this is at least 45cm (18in) tall, the low-flying carrot fly will not be able to fly over it to lay her eggs.

Sowing times for carrot

If the soil is too wet and/or cold, carrot seed readily rots off. Ignore the directions on the packet; make a decision about sowing times on the basis of the soil conditions.

Grow shorter carrots

Try the stump-rooted carrot varieties if your soil is shallow, rather stony, or in any other way not great for growing carrots. They naturally produce shorter, stubbier roots which may not look as elegant, but they taste just as good and will perform better in less than perfect soils.

Stump-rooted carrots are best in stony soils and even containers.

Try a range of carrots

❀ It is worth trying carrot varieties, such as 'Flyaway', 'Sytan', or 'Resistafly', sold as showing a degree of resistance to attack.

❀ Round-rooted varieties of carrot include 'Parmex' and 'Paris Market'. These work relatively well in stony soil.

❀ Different carrots suit early and late crops. Try 'Amsterdam Forcing' or 'Nantes' types for summer salads, 'Autumn King' or 'Chantenay' for later in the season.

❀ For different colours, try 'Purple Haze', 'Purple Dragon', or 'Yellowstone'.

Water features & ponds

Being able to have a pond or water feature in your garden adds a certain touch of magic. There is nothing quite like the sound of gently moving water to add to the feeling of tranquility that being in a garden brings.

Bringing water into your garden need not be hugely time-consuming or expensive. You can scale up (or down) what you create to fit in with the size of your garden and your budget.

If your garden is on a slope, you will have to take this into account in the design you choose.

If you just want a single pool or pond, make sure you are prepared to create an adequately sized level area first, and to make a pond with pools leading to or from it look relatively natural, think carefully about where you position each part.

Planning each element

If you want moving water, you will need to have a power source close by. If you are just starting to plan a new garden, take this into account, perhaps trying to keep your water

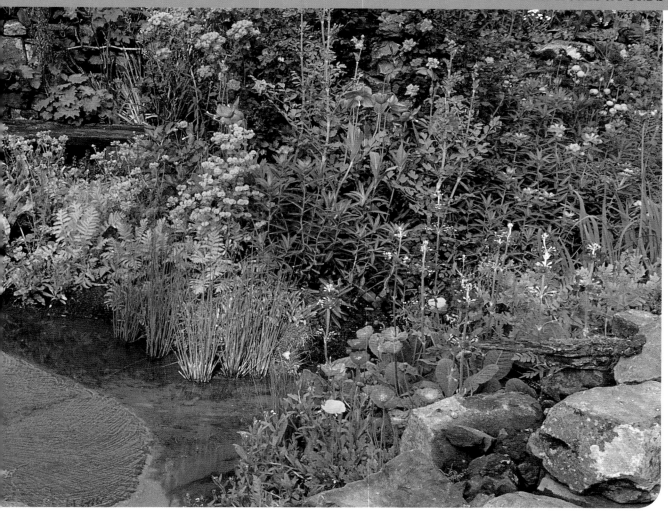

feature close to any other part of the garden that will need an exterior power source so this may influence where you make your water feature.

Water, particularly in the form of ponds, can pose a serious and potentially life-threatening risk to children. If you do introduce water to a garden that young children use or might visit, bear this in mind and perhaps choose a self-contained feature that has no significantly deep water.

This chapter shows you how to:

❀ Choose a water feature.

❀ Plan a pond.

❀ Choose a liner for your new pond.

❀ Edge a pond with plants and boulders.

❀ Plant up your new pond, and the best plants to use.

❀ Look after your water feature.

❀ Care for your pond, all year round.

Choosing a water feature

There is such a huge choice of ready-constructed and kit-form water features available these days, you will have no difficulty finding something to suit your garden. Look through catalogues, and then visit a specialist supplier for advice.

The importance of proportion

Powered water features, such as fountains, can only spray or move water to a maximum height or spread. Always check what it is, whether this force is appropriate to your pool or pond, and that the feature is in proportion to the pool and the rest of the garden.

Safe features

If you have small children or are likely to have any visiting your garden, then always consider the safety aspect. You may dream of a large pond, but perhaps this could replace a safer short-term feature in a few years, when the children are older?

Pebble fountains are safe and simple.

Self-contained features

For small gardens or for use within a small area of a garden, look for the many self-contained water features available. These will allow you to have moving water despite these limitations.

Go with the flow

If, like me, you garden on a steep slope, a pond can be an extremely difficult feature to create. Better to make use of the natural slope and instead make a stream or even a waterfall that can come down the slope, end up in a small pool and then be pumped back up to the top again.

Types of pump

There are two main types of pump you may come across in a garden centre. A submersible pump is installed so that it works from under the water, while surface pumps need to be sited out of the water and so need to have some sort of housing created for them. Surface pumps generally create a noticeable noise.

Submersible pumps are simple to install.

Water can be directed down a slope through a natural-looking stream or more formal rills.

You can fit a surprising amount into a simple, small pool of still water.

Make a mini-pond in a container

❀ If you don't have enough space for a pond, you can make a mini-pond in a large ceramic container. It should be at least 45cm (18in) deep; any shallower, and the water will get too warm and may turn green.

❀ A half barrel makes a good miniature pond, but make sure that it is totally water tight – ideally line it with butyl. Fold down the liner at the top edge, so that it does not quite reach the rim, and then use short, galvanized tacks to hold it in place.

❀ Choose a container that is frost-proof, but if you get extremely cold weather be prepared to insulate the sides of the container too.

❀ A pot or container with drainage holes in it will be more difficult to use, but you can often achieve a water-tight effect if you plug the holes with corks from bottles of wine.

❀ Ceramic containers that are not glazed on their inner surface will need to be made waterproof by treating the un-glazed surface with neoprene paint.

❀ In a small container pool there will be no space for planting shelves, but you can create these by submerging bricks.

❀ Make sure you choose suitably sized plants for a very small water feature. Check the ultimate heights and, even more importantly, the spreads of the plants carefully before buying.

Adjustable pumps

If you are buying a pump to power a cascading pots-of-water feature, spouting gargoyle, or miniature fountain, make sure that you check the pump's flow rate and that it can be adjusted if necessary, allowing you to create just the right look.

Pump power

To check if the pump you have in mind will be powerful enough, work out the volume of your pond: this is its depth x length x width. For a pump to work well, its flow rate per hour must be greater than the total volume of the pond.

Plan your electrics

Powered water features and fountains will need to be connected to an electricity supply. Consider the distance from the mains and the time, trouble, and expense needed to extend the existing supply. Installation of proper armoured cables is a specialist business, and cables need to be labelled and buried at the correct depth by a qualified electrician.

Always use clean, mortar-free bricks.

Planning a pond

A pond is a long-term addition to any garden, so make sure you spend plenty of time working out what will work best, look most appealing, and be of maximum benefit and least risk to your garden.

A good site means less maintenance.

Where to site your pond

❀ Avoid a position beneath or even very close to deciduous trees: this will obviously increase the problem of leaves falling into the pond when the autumn arrives.

❀ Too much sunlight will increase the rate at which algae build up. A partially shaded spot is ideal: it should have enough sunshine for healthy plant growth without encouraging algal growth.

How to keep shapes smooth

If you are aiming for anything other than a straight-edged pool, make sure that the shape is flowing and smooth. The easiest way to achieve this is to make the edges relatively simple and to use a flexible garden hose to mark out where the outline should be. This will allow curves and smooth lines without sharp angles.

Simple shapes, like a circular pool, create the greatest impact.

Design intricacy increases costs

Flexible liners can be used to make an elaborately shaped pond but a simple design will use up considerably less butyl and underlay. This allows you to save money or have a bigger pond for the same outlay.

Shelf planting

Make sure that you create or install your pond so that most of the shelf-planting will be at the back, making it easier to enjoy the water and shallower planting in the foreground.

Put the widest part of the shelf at the back of the pond.

Hidden depths

Design your pond with water of varying depths. This allows you to use a wider range of plants and attract more varied wildlife (*see* pages 150–51). Remember that the shallower water will heat up more rapidly in the summer, and so be more likely to become breeding grounds for algae.

Shaping your steps or shelves

Steps or shelves at the sides of large ponds are invaluable for plants that require shallower depths of water. Make sure that the horizontal surface of each planting shelf is wide enough to hold a planting basket and that it is either totally level or sloped very slightly, with the lip edge very slightly higher; this makes it even less likely that the pond basket will fall off.

Plants like this gracefully nodding *Dierama* love the moist conditions of a bog garden.

Plan your shelves

Before creating planting shelves, try to decide roughly which plants you intend to use and make sure you create enough shelves at suitable depths to have what you want. It is much easier to get it right at this stage than to alter shelf heights later on.

Create a boggy area

❀ A pond looks more natural with a bog garden beside or around it. This gives perfect conditions for plants from hostas up to a giant gunnera.

❀ If you are creating boggy areas at the edges of, or adjacent to, your pond, these will need some sort of liner, perhaps off-cuts of the main piece of butyl (*see* page 146).

❀ To keep the area within boggy but not too wet, use a garden fork to puncture the liner. With no holes, the water and soil would soon become unsuitable for plants, and be likely to get rather smelly as oxygen levels drop.

❀ Keep these mini-drainage holes open and avoid them becoming blocked with silty soil by placing a 5–10cm (2–4in) layer of stones in the base of the area that you have punctured.

Level off

It is essential that you create a pond on a totally horizontal site: whatever you do, the water will always find the level, and a lopsided pond looks awful. Make things easier for yourself and choose a relatively level spot.

Check the levels

At regular intervals as you dig out the pond, check that the top is level. If you are installing a rigid pre-formed liner, it is vital that it too is on the level. An ordinary spirit level will do: lay a plank across the pond and place the level on it.

Never rely on judging the horizontal by eye.

Filling your pond

Ideally ponds should be filled with rain water but it may be difficult to get hold of adequate quantities. If you resort to tap water, allow it to stand for at least a week before you start to plant it up. This will allow at least some of the additives to disperse.

Choosing a liner for a pond

Many garden centres supply some pond equipment, but if you want the best selection of liners of any type, and often at the most reasonable prices, it is generally best to go to specialist suppliers, many of which offer a mail-order scheme.

Rigid liners

Rigid, pre-formed liners provide the easiest way to create a pond and generally come complete with shelves to allow for planting at varying depths. Their main disadvantage is that there is a limited range of shapes.

Draining rigid liners

Some pre-formed liners have a drainage hole built in to them to allow you to empty and clean the pond relatively easily. For this to work, it is essential to make a small soakaway beneath the plug hole when you install the pond – a rubble filled pit is perfect.

Protect the liner from stones

Remember that for flexible liners, such as PVC, butyl, or plastic, you will need to put down some sort of underlay. Otherwise there is a great risk of the liner being punctured by underlying stones, tree roots, or other sharp objects. You can buy special underlay, or use old carpet underlay; for smaller areas, a thick layer of straw will work well.

A layer of sand and underlay are vital.

Butyl liner

Using butyl allows for the greatest flexibility, literally giving you the freedom to create as many different depths and outline variations as you wish. Although butyl liners are the most expensive option, their life expectancy is about 30 years, so they are good value.

The water's weight will pull the liner in gradually.

Plastic or butyl?

Plastic flexible liners are readily available and considerably less expensive than butyl, but they are more prone to degrading in sunlight and rarely last more than five years.

Measuring up for a liner

Butyl is expensive so it is important to order the right quantity; the only way to do this is to do your sums! Measure the greatest length (L) and greatest width (W). Then measure the deepest point and double it (call this 2D). You'll also need an extra 45cm (18in) on all sides for the overhang at the edge. Now grab a calculator. You'll need a sheet of butyl L + 2D + 90cm long, and 2D + W + 90cm wide.

Edging a pond

It is important to consider what you want the edge of your pond to look like, especially if you are installing a formal pool. Wildlife ponds are generally well-planted so the appearance of the edge matters less.

Make sure of a perfect fit

Before laying your edging material, you will probably have to adjust the levels around the pond edges, especially if you are using a rigid pre-formed liner. These must fit snugly in to the hole – gaps increase the likelihood of damage because the weight of the water exerts considerable pressure. Dry sand or dry garden soil works well, and the drier it is the easier it is to pack it tightly down the sides and beneath the outer lip of the liner.

Place stones at the edges

❀ Large, rounded stones at the edges of a pond are not only useful for small animals (see page 150), they are also a great way to hide the uppermost and outermost edges of the pond liner and will help to avoid soil from adjacent areas falling into the water.

❀ For a natural effect, use large stones on the outermost edge, gradually moving to smaller stones at the water's edge and into the water. Plenty of marginal plants will complete the look and be useful to wildlife.

A "beach" at the edge is better for wildlife.

Decks and jetties

Timber decking can be used up to the edge of a pond and even extend out over it, creating the illusion of a much larger pond under the deck. Supporting a wooden structure on piers over water is not simple, however, and you may want to get professional help.

Edging bricks

If using an edging of bricks for a formal pond, choose engineering bricks. These are very frost-resistant, and so less likely to disintegrate after a hard winter. Make sure that you avoid letting any cement fall into the water – if it does, fish it out or it can alter the water's pH and may poison wildlife.

Overhanging bricks or slabs are neat and formal.

Keeping stones in place

Make sure that an edging of stones can remain in place and look good by creating a depression for them around the edges of the pond. A slight flat shelf at the water line that's partly submerged, on which the smaller stones can lie, completes the effect.

Pond plants and planting

If you are after a very formal pool or pond design, plants may not feature too highly on your list of priorities, but if chosen carefully they can certainly add a touch of drama and interest.

Hardy plants

Always check whether pond and marginal plants are hardy before you buy – there is no need to rely totally on hardy plants, but if any are in the slightest bit tender you will have to either provide winter protection for them, bring them in to a frost-free temporary home each winter, or regard them as annuals and be prepared to replace them if they are damaged by adverse weather.

Buy healthy plants

Only buy plants that appear perfectly healthy and free from pest infestations. Once they are planted in the pond, problems are even harder to deal with than when things go wrong with plants in flower borders.

Invasive plants
(to be avoided)

Azolla caroliniana

Canadian pondweed
(*Elodea canadensis*)

Flag iris (*Iris pseudacorus*)

Floating pennywort
(*Hydrocotyle
ranunculoides*)

Juncus effusus

Myriophyllum aquaticum

*Myriophyllum
proserpinacoides*

New Zealand pygmy weed
(*Crassula helmsii*)

Check plant sizes carefully

Check each plant's ultimate height and spread, but if you are unsure after reading the comments on the label or in the garden centre or nursery, check in a book. Some water plants might be invasive or prove too vigorous for any but the largest pond – don't risk introducing something that could end up swamping out all your other plants.

Flag iris is attractive, but it is suitable only for large areas of water.

Mesh baskets may be rigid or more flexible and bag-like.

Essential mesh

Pond baskets are a must – the mesh sides allow plenty of through-flow of water while keeping the compost and the plant in position. They are readily available from outlets selling pond and marginal plants.

Avoid hessian

If you cannot get hold of pond baskets with fine mesh, keep trying. If you still cannot succeed, line a large-meshed basket with plastic mesh. It is best to avoid hessian.

Seal plants with gravel

Once the baskets are planted up, cover the surface of the soil in each with a layer of good-sized pebbles or gravel; this will help to keep the soil in place, reduce the risk of it falling into the water and, if you intend to have fish in the pond, it will also help to prevent them stirring up the soil.

Still water

Waterlilies require still water, so will not be happy in moving water. Plant them a still pond, pool, or rill, but avoid any with fountains or other pumped or circulated water, unless it is big enough for the plants to be sited well away from the movement.

Smaller, less vigorous waterlilies can be grown in a mini-pond.

Waterlilies need the right depth and several hours of full sun daily to flower well.

Plant at the correct depth

❀ Provided you put water plants into the pool at their correct final depth there is no need to panic if the leaves are submerged when you first lower their planting basket into position. They will soon re-orientate themselves and grow so that they are at the surface.

❀ Waterlilies in particular often have very specific requirements when it comes to depth of water. They will either not thrive or simply fail to flower if planted at the incorrect depth. Check that those you like the look of will actually perform well in the pond you have – there is almost always an alternative waterlily if they won't.

Focus on wildlife

Wildlife really benefits if you install a pool, pond, or indeed most sorts of water feature. The water provides a place to drink and bathe if it is easily accessible and created in a wildlife-friendly design. It can also be a suitable place to breed and live.

A beach area makes a pond safer and more accessible for wildlife in search of a drink.

Beach attraction for wildlife

Straight-sided ponds are potentially lethal for wildlife such as hedgehogs which may tumble in and not be able to climb out. Make sure that your pond has at least one "beach" of progressively shallower water ending up on a pebble-covered area, perfect for less able swimmers.

Life on the edge

Plenty of marginal planting makes a pond appealing and ensures safe places for wildlife to hide from predators.

When a pond turns bright green...

❀ Algae are the most common reason for this. If your new pond is green, don't be tempted to empty it and start again: be patient. The settling-in period invariably includes a few weeks of green water. This starts to clear as the pond gains its natural balance.

❀ Reducing the amount of light that hits the water's surface will generally help to decrease problems with algae – using more surface-floating plants, including water lilies and oxygenators, will help.

❀ Oxygenating plants include *Ceratophyllum demersum*, *Callitriche*, *Myriophyllum verticilliatum*, and *Ranunculus aquatilis*.

Fish are for fish ponds

If you want to encourage wildlife to your pond and to make it a safe place for it to stay, do not introduce carp or other fish because they prey upon wildlife species, their young and their eggs.

Goldfish will eat tadpoles, newt eggs, and dragonfly larvae.

❀ Fish and their faecal matter raise nitrogen levels in the water, in turn increasing algae.

❀ Use barley straw (*see* opposite).

This problem is worse on ponds in sunny places.

Introduce pond snails

A good population of pond snails helps to keep algal levels down because they eat algae. Make sure you get either the ramshorn snail or the small round pond snail and that you avoid the giant pond snail – this one may also start to munch your pond plants!

Clear dead foliage regularly throughout autumn to limit sludge build-up.

Barley straw "soaks up" excess nitrogen in the water, starving algae.

Autumn slowdown

You will need to do some maintenance throughout the year (*see* pages 154–55), but do any major work in early autumn when it will have least impact on any wildlife in your pond. Make sure any creatures in the removed debris have a chance to get back into the pond.

Use barley straw to control algae

Barley straw really helps to control algae. Buy a pre-formed "pad" or simply put straw into a fine mesh bag kept submerged by the weight of a brick. Use about 50g (2oz) of barley straw for every 1sq m (11sq ft) of the pond's surface. Put it in early spring, and replace it every six months or so.

Trapping giant pond snails

If you find you have the wrong sort of snail in your pond (the giant pond snail) then set a trap for them. Float good-sized lettuce leaves on the pond's surface: the snails will be attracted onto the lettuce, and then you can scoop up the snail-infested lettuce with a pond net at regular intervals.

Giant pond snails find lettuce irresistible; use it as a lure to trap these pests.

General maintenance

Like any other part of your garden, ponds and water features benefit from some timely maintenance. Even wildlife ponds and wildflower meadows will work better if not left totally to their own devices.

Check carefully for duckweed

Numerous, tiny, green, floating leaves are duckweed (*Lemna*), which seems to appear from nowhere. Always check new plants for duckweed before planting them; a single leaf-like plant multiplies rapidly.

Duckweed soon builds up, and can spoil the appearance and functioning of a pond or water feature.

All about blanket weed

❀ Blanket weed is made up of filamentous algae, and is a serious and common problem, often clogging ponds. It will be encouraged by the same factors that encourage the pea-soup effect algae: sunlight, high nutrient levels, and low oxygen levels. It can be discouraged in the same ways, including the use of barley straw (*see* pages 150–51).

❀ The easiest way to remove blanket weed is with a sturdy bamboo cane. Insert it into a mass of weed, twizzle it around a few times, and you'll soon scoop up a lot of weed.

❀ Blanket weed can be composted in your compost bin or heap, but before you take it too far from the pond, give wildlife that may have been caught up when you removed it a chance to escape. Lay the weed on the ground in clumps, with a small amount trailing into the water, for a couple of days before composting it.

Ponds need to be promptly cleared of blanket and duckweed.

Feeding pond plants

Some pond plants may eventually need feeding, but as there is a serious risk of fertilizer contaminating the water, you should only do this when really necessary. Feed very carefully, applying a small amount of slow-release fertilizer directly into the pond basket. Don't attempt to feed surface-floating plants.

Don't feed an algae problem

Make sure that no fertilizers (including manure and artificial feeds) are applied in large quantities to flower beds or lawns that are close to a pond. Run-off can cause additional nutrients to flow into the water and so increase problems with algae.

Year-round pond care

Spring is a good time to remove, re-plant or divide and then re-plant pond and marginal plants. To keep the pond at its best, make sure you only introduce healthy, clean stock and discard unhealthy looking divisions.

Feed fish after winter

If you have fish in your pond, take care when you start giving the fish food again in spring after a winter-break from feeding. Start with small quantities and then only apply every three days or so – excess, uneaten food messes up the water.

Trim deteriorating foliage

Throughout the summer even healthy pond plants will have the odd damaged or dead bit of growth. It is essential to cut this off and compost it before it gets a chance to rot in the water. Decaying foliage will raise nutrient levels and so increase algae.

Regular top-ups

Water levels are likely to drop in hot summer weather, so top them up occasionally. Doing this using a hose spray sprinkled onto the water's surface will also help to raise oxygen levels, which are inclined to fall during spells of hot weather.

Keep an eye out for dying leaves and snip them off quickly.

Both fountains and top-ups applied from above the water surface keep a pool aerated.

Clear away the debris

Regular removal of larger quantities of faded pond and marginal plants is essential during autumn, when die-back is greater and more widespread. If you end up also thinning out a plant that has been growing a bit too rapidly, great, but make sure that any pond wildlife clinging to it is given the chance to escape back into the water before you compost it!

Catch the falling leaves

Net the surface of the pond to prevent leaves from nearby trees and shrubs falling into it. Make sure the net is in place by early autumn, so you catch the maximum possible amount. Remove the net at regular intervals, before it becomes too laden down with leaves, and empty them into a leaf mould or compost heap.

The more vegetation falls into your pond, the more often you will have to clean it out.

Reduce fish food in autumn

In autumn fish are starting to slow down considerably, so if there are any in your pond, reduce the frequency and quantity of food.

Double netting

It can be difficult getting a net properly positioned over a large pond, and removing it regularly becomes a horrendous chore. The best solution is to get a relatively sturdy, easy-to-handle net in place and anchor it over the pond's surface for the whole of the autumn into early winter. You can then lay a relatively lightweight net over the top. The latter can easily be removed and replaced because the lower one helps to support it.

Melt ice gently: never smash it or pour boiling water onto it because you could shock or kill fish.

Winter maintenance

In winter the only bit of real pond maintenance is attempting to keep the surface free from ice in at least one place. A total covering of ice prevents potentially toxic gases, such as methane, from escaping, and this can kill fish or small pond wildlife, such as newts. The age-old trick of floating a football on the water's surface helps to slow the rate at which it freezes.

Creature comforts

If the pond freezes over in winter, the best way to create a hole without endangering creatures below is to hold a saucepan full of hot water on the ice until a circle melts beneath it – just don't let go of the handle!

Structures & surfaces

Pretty well every garden has a boundary, and to some extent every garden needs one so that it's clear to everyone precisely where your garden ends and theirs begins. This provides you with another planting surface that you may not necessarily think of using, and countless creative opportunities. A fence or wall, or even well-installed trellis, can look great when decorated with a well-chosen planting scheme.

Although maximum boundary heights often exist, you need not have a full-sized boundary,

and in some situations quite a low-level fence, hurdle, or wall fits the bill. You could fill out adjacent beds with attractive plantings to cover the wall, or use containers.

As an added bonus, any vertical structure instantly provides support for some gorgeous plants, bringing height and variety to your planting schemes. With a bit of thought, even the most uninspiring of boundaries can be adequately disguised and concealed beneath a mass of foliage and flowers.

Creative design possibilities

With patios and decks there is a huge range of styles and types to choose from, and like your garden boundary, these too can really bring your own hallmark to a garden, whatever its size and style. Both boundaries and patios and decked areas play an important role in a garden, and at the same time may also affect the microclimate and the extent to which the garden can be used as an "outside room" or area for entertaining.

This chapter shows you how to:

❀ Choose a boundary style – walls, fences, or trellis?

❀ Plan and build walls.

❀ Install paved, gravel, or decked areas.

❀ Look after your patio or deck.

❀ Install and maintain arches and pergolas.

❀ Buy and care for garden furniture.

Setting boundaries

Before you decide on a new garden boundary, take a look at what your neighbours have used, to assess its style and how it has fared in the local conditions. The strength and direction of prevailing winds may mean that flimsy options are best avoided.

Walls or fences?

Don't forget that although the cost of building a wall is much greater than the cost of a fence, even a brilliantly made and beautifully erected fence will need more care and more regular replacement than a wall.

Trellis shapes and styles

Take a while to find out what is available before you take the plunge. Rounded trellis sections designed to be fitted on top of a fence come in convex or concave styles, which not only add extra planting space and a little more privacy, but can look attractive in their own right before covered.

Curved trellis tops give a softer look.

Shop for quality

Fence panels can be a relatively low-cost and quick way to erect a fence, but it is worth buying from a reputable supplier and paying more for high quality, well-constructed panels. Don't buy any with loose parts: securing them is a fiddly and splinter-ridden task, best avoided.

Sturdy panels are a good investment.

Using trellis

Large, full-length panels of trellis can be used to create either a garden boundary or divisions within your garden. You will need to like your neighbours or indulge in some very extensive planting if you use them for boundaries, but within the garden they can provide a great support for lightweight climbers, partitioning off an area while still allowing you to see some of what lies on the other side.

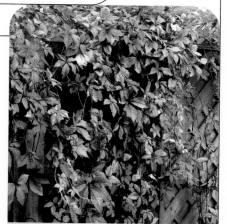

Latticed panels imitate trellis and bear more weight.

Make sure posts are rot-proofed

Fence posts should always be tanalized or pressure treated with preservative. If you need to cut fence posts to size, you may be exposing untreated areas of wood. If so, stand the cut post in a bucket of wood treatment for a day or two before erecting it. This will allow it to absorb some of the preservative before you use it.

Brass fittings

Always use galvanized (zinc-coated) or brass fixtures and fittings when erecting a fence or trellis because these will be much slower to rust and may not rust at all. The initial cost is a small price to pay for not having to re-do the job in a few years time when ordinary fixtures and fittings will have rusted.

Matt, grey, galvanized nails resist corrosion.

Keep off the soil

The lower edge of a fence is most prone to rotting because it will regularly be damp. Fix a timber or concrete board along the lower edge of the fence so that this, not the panel, is in contact with soil and plants. It's easier and cheaper to replace the board, and if you use concrete it may last longer than the fence!

Fine-tuning the fit

❀ Standard-sized fence panes are quick to install, but if a panel is too short for the space, insert a strip of wood between the post and the panel and nail it in place.

❀ If the fence panel is just too wide to fit snugly in the space, use a plane to carefully remove a small amount of wood, but check the fit frequently so you don't remove too much.

Keep it safe

If a fence post shows signs of decay, do not attempt to repair it; it will not be strong enough for the job. Grasp the nettle and replace the entire post, but before you do, check other posts too. It is likely that if one has started to go, others may need attention.

Blending in

If you replace a fence panel, there will be noticeable differences in colour between old and new. Unless your planting is extremely dense and evergreen, this will show. Take the plunge and treat the whole fence, old and new, so that it all matches.

Preparation saves a lot of time later on.

Treating surfaces

❀ Avoid applying a wood treatment in very hot weather; sometimes it dries too fast. A warm or overcast day is best.

❀ Don't take short cuts with dirty or algae- and moss-covered wood. If a paint or stain doesn't stick well, it will quickly need re-applying. A stiff wire brush removes grime and roughens the surface, making applications adhere better.

❀ Re-paint plant-clad fences in late autumn when the leaves have fallen.

159

All about walls

There is something seriously permanent about a garden wall. Even one that has just been erected looks imposing and creates an air of stability – however flamboyant the adjacent planting.

Know your limits

Unless you are experienced at building walls, this is a job you should leave to the professionals. A poorly built wall looks awful and may be unsafe.

Save time and your back

If you are building a large wall and need a lot of concrete for the foundations, it really is worth hiring or borrowing a concrete mixer – the amount of time and energy it will save you makes it a worthwhile expense. Ready-mixed mortar is a good buy unless you have a lot of mortar-making experience.

Mixing mortar

To minimize wastage, as well as unpleasant and potentially harmful dust clouds when mixing mortar, dampen the surface of the mixing board slightly before slowly adding the mortar powder. Use the trowel to firm the powder gently and flatten the surface, then make a dip in the centre. You can then slowly pour the water into this and draw the powder in.

Mixing mortar takes a bit of practice.

Brisk, dry, brushing is the only way to remove efflorescence.

Special treatments

If a wall is in a particularly damp area it may be worth using a special treatment paint that minimizes the penetration of water. This reduces the formation of deposits and perhaps even extends the life of the wall.

Dealing with blooming walls

New bricks often produce a white, crystalline deposit called efflorescence. This looks bad, but it's only deposits of salts coming out of the brickwork. Don't wash it off because that will make the problem recur with a vengeance; instead use a stiff wire brush to gently scrape off the efflorescence.

Feature walls

In a large garden, a freestanding wall incorporating an archway – separate from the boundary – makes a beautiful support for classic planting and will perfectly frame a view.

Is ivy destructive?

Self-clinging climbers, such as ivies (*Hedera*) and Virginia creeper (*Parthenocissus quinquefolia*), can damage a wall, but only if it is already not in the best condition. Flaking bricks or loose mortar may be made worse by a vigorous self-clinging climber, but neither is likely to be initiated by the climber.

Roots and pads on climbing stems are used to "stick" the climber to a support. They will not penetrate a solid surface.

Check for cracks

Walls need relatively little maintenance, but it is still worth checking them over from time to time. Any repairs are generally easier, quicker, and cheaper to make if carried out promptly.

Clean with care

If you use a pressure washer to clean off deposits of algae, mosses, and lichens from a wall, take care not to use it on too aggressive a setting. The protective surface layer of the bricks can be loosened and damaged, especially on older walls.

Test settings on a hidden area of wall before letting loose.

Removing old mortar

❀ If the mortar or pointing is starting to fall from between the bricks of your wall, use a chisel or screwdriver to remove chunks that are loose and then remove any sandy mix that lurks behind, using a soft brush.

❀ To do the job of re-pointing properly, you will need to remove the old mortar to about 3cm (1in) into the joint. This will ensure a longer lasting repair.

Prepare properly for repointing

If the bricks are left covered with dusty and sandy deposits after you have removed the loose mortar, the new mortar will not adhere properly so make sure you clean these deposits off thoroughly before re-pointing. A damp sponge or sturdy rag should do the job.

Colour-match mortar

Do take the time to match the colour of the mortar for the areas you are re-pointing. This may seem like an arduous process, but a wall with assorted colours of pointing looks awful. You will end up spending a fortune on climbers as you try to cover the mess, and it's still likely to show despite your efforts.

Let it dry

Once dry, mortar changes colour quite noticeably. When you are trying to colour-match, mix up tiny amounts of each mortar you make, allow them to dry and then compare each of them with the existing mortar in the wall.

Ironed joints

If the mortar joints have this slightly concave profile, mimic it using a short length of garden hose pressed evenly but firmly along the length of the moist mortar.

Your joints may look terrible at first, but persevere – they will get better!

A special trowel can be bought for this, but is only worth it for large areas of pointing.

Weatherstruck joints

It is worth taking some time to match the profile of the mortar between each brick with that on the existing brickwork. A slanting, weatherstruck joint is best achieved using a bricklayer's trowel. The mortar is angled so that the upper end is slightly recessed into the space beneath the course of bricks above, and the base of the mortar is very slightly protruding or level with the top of the bricks below.

Re-colouring bricks

If some of the bricks have become discoloured and are spoiling the look of the wall, take a spare brick of matching colour, wet it thoroughly and then rub it really firmly over the discoloured or stained bricks, wetting the spare brick regularly as you go. Some colour from the surface of the wetted brick should rub off and help to mask any staining on the wall.

Paving, gravel, and decking areas

If you want to be able to enjoy your garden as an "outside room", a level place for a few chairs or seats and a table is essential. Make your choice of surface with care as it will have a big impact.

Where would you like to sit?

There are a number of factors to consider when deciding where best to construct a patio or terrace.

❀ A sheltered and preferably sunny spot is generally going to get the most use, particularly early and late in the year when a more exposed site is likely to be too cool.

❀ Although a nearby tree may appeal because it will create some shade during hotter, sunnier weather, consider how much shade it will cast and at what time of day. Even if you want to create a shaded patio so that you can escape the sun, at least part of the area needs to be beyond the reach of the tree's branches because long after it has stopped raining, there will still be water dripping from the tree's canopy.

❀ If the site you have to use is rather exposed, or if it is overlooked by neighbours or passers-by, incorporate enough space to plant a windbreak, erect trellis, or use plants to create a little more privacy.

❀ A patio, especially one on which you are intending to enjoy food and drink, will benefit from being relatively close to the house. At the same time, consider the view that you will get when sitting out and eating, drinking, or simply relaxing.

A secluded seat is always enticing.

What surface?

The surface you go for is up to you, but factors such as the initial cost of material and installation (either your time or a landscaper's bill), and the amount of maintenance, will all need to be considered.

A raised deck lets you enjoy greater views of the garden.

Matching the surroundings

If you have a wall or other hard surface nearby, make sure you consider this and its colour and texture before deciding what materials to use. It is often best to restrict materials to a maximum of two types in any one area, for example stone and brick or stone and gravel, rather than all three together.

Two materials are company, three would be a crowd.

Think long-term

Check that paving or slabs are all fully frost-proof, and if possible that there is an acceptable degree of colour fastness over time – or at least that you like the colour to which the slabs fade. You should also consider where natural stone and slate materials have come from, and whether you are happy with this.

Get a firm footing

A properly levelled and firmed or compacted base layer is essential beneath surfaces of gravel or paving. If necessary, consider hiring a machine to do the hard work of compacting the ground for you.

Never lay surfaces without a spirit level.

Planting holes

Think about the next step in the creation of your new patio or terrace, and when you make your paved, shingled, or decked area ensure that you create a few planting opportunities too. Plants generally prefer growing in open ground to growing in a container, and climbers in particular rarely thrive if kept in containers permanently.

Plants instantly soften a new deck or patio.

Make space for plants

If you are going to create planting holes or use planters, do take care with the location. In particular, consider whether a plant grown there will become a trip hazard or be in the way of garden furniture. Any new planting opportunity should be in a good, out-of-the-way place. You should also make sure that you include areas of open ground for planting adjacent to any walls or fences that abut the surface you are creating.

Clear the ground

Weed seeds or the roots of pernicious weeds beneath surfaces can cause constant problems that get worse with time. Always try to clear the area of weeds completely before starting to level or compact the surface ready for a new area of hardstanding.

Weeds are particularly problematic under gravel.

The worst weeds

Weed-prevention fabrics can be a real help beneath gravel or shingle surfaces or under decks, preventing all but the most aggressive weeds making an appearance. If you have problems with weeds such as brambles, horsetail, Japanese knotweed or other notorious thugs, you should try to eliminate these as best you can before you lay the fabric.

Cut at the edges

Slabs may need to be cut to fit in. Try to make sure that cut slabs are in out-of-the-way places, hopefully to be concealed by plants later on, and not in a position where they will be subjected to a lot of wear and tear.

Paving on a dry base

With paving slabs laid onto a bed of aggregate or rubble, there is often some initial movement for a few days after the slabs have been laid. Allow the newly laid paving to settle for a few days, then re-check the levels and adjust as necessary. Only add mortar between the slabs once you are certain everything has settled properly.

Substantial slabs can be laid on a dry bed of hardcore.

Cutting slabs

To cut a slab to fit a gap, you need to score both sides of the slab with a chisel, making sure each scored line is exactly lined up with the other. Each groove needs to be cut to a depth of about 3mm (⅛in). If in doubt always cut the slab slightly too small, ideally about 5mm (¼in) all around. This will allow the slab section to fit into the gap despite any uneven edges. Once the grooves are complete, place a length of smooth, flat wood beneath the groove on the lower surface and then tap the upper surface of the slab with the handle of the hammer just to one side of the groove you have made. The slab should then break neatly along the scored line.

Use a broad bolster and a heavy hammer to cut.

The weakened line will break under pressure.

Be prepared to top up

With areas of shingle, pebble, or gravel, keep a note of the code number and name of the material you have used, plus the contact details for the supplier. I really do not know where it goes, but after a few years I always find that levels of these materials need topping up. It is also worth keeping a small, new sample of the material in a jar in the shed because if you cannot get hold of exactly the same material when the time comes, then at least you know what the original looked like when new, so you should be able to do some accurate matching.

Safety first

When cutting a slab to create a new area or fit accurately into a gap, make sure that you wear goggles and tough gloves. The cut slab edges and fragments can be extremely sharp.

Keep work areas clear

Always place a slab on a firm, flat and level surface before attempting to cut it. Any unevenness beneath means wobbly cuts.

Get even

If at the end you find you have the odd uneven slab, it is essential that you sort these out, or they are likely to cause people to trip and fall. You may need to remove hardcore or add to it, and then replace the slab.

Incorporate a slope

Where possible, introduce a slight slope or camber on the surface, especially those that will be impenetrable to rain (or virtually so). This camber should allow rain to be shed more easily and so prevent problems of standing water after heavy rain, and later growth of algae. You need a fall of about 3cm (1in) for every 2m (6½ft) of patio or deck.

Spread the impact

To level up slabs that are slightly uneven, get a block of wood or section of a plank, place it on the edge that is too high and then gently but firmly tap it with a club hammer until you achieve the desired level. The wood will dramatically reduce the possibility of your damaging the slab.

A rubber mallet can be used gently all over a slab to bed it down once level.

Abandon broken slabs

Instead of replacing broken, badly discoloured, or missing slabs, why not remove them completely. Then replace the hardcore beneath with good soil mixed with compost, and make it into a low-level planter. If it is in the middle of the space, remove a slab from elsewhere to make a planting hole and replace the broken one.

Don't skimp with mortar

Thin, light slabs should be laid on a mortar base. Lay a solid base, not "dabs"; if some mortar dabs settle differently, the slab will rock. Spaces under the slab also make it more likely to break under pressure, let water accumulate and wash out soil, and make a lovely home for ants.

Mortar edges

Even if laying slabs on a dry bed, it is worth mortaring at least under the last half slab along any "free" edge leading onto a lawn or gravel: this stops the slabs slipping, and is simpler than installing a retaining kerb.

Looking after your patio or deck

Maintaining patios and decking helps to keep them looking good and also reduces the risk of excessive build-up of algae and mosses. It might be a time-consuming job, but it rarely needs attention more than once a year.

Clear fallen leaves regularly in autumn.

Keep it clean

Any soil, compost or even organic debris, such as fallen leaves and flowers, will create a potential seedbed for weeds if allowed to accumulate on a pebble or gravel surface, so always do your best to keep these surfaces free from materials like this.

Outdoor vacuuming

A good quality leaf-blower or garden vacuum can be a real help in trying to keep pebble or gravel surfaces clear of leaves and faded flowers. The materials you collect up can always be added to the compost heap.

Easing in new slabs

If you have to replace broken slabs within an area of paving, it is often difficult to get them into place without damaging or scuffing the adjacent slabs. Lay a broom handle or spare piece of copper water pipe across the space that you need to fill. You can then place one end of the new slab into the space and the support will allow you to ease the slab down into position.

Check your deck

Decking may need regular treatment with a wood preservative, but the frequency and the best material to use will depend on exactly what the deck was made from and where it is, so check before you treat.

Clear treatments provide the least UV protection.

Solving slippery decks

❀ Deck paint has gritty material in it, and should be slip-free in any weather.

❀ Galvanized chicken wire fixed over the wood with galvanized staples isn't pretty, but it is effective.

Clean and treat

Before treating timber decking, use a stiff wire brush to remove surface deposits of algae and moss, and repair or replace any seriously damaged or deteriorating timber.

Arches and pergolas

There is something really appealing about an arch or arbour, helping to give the feel of an established relaxed garden and also to add charm and often a touch of romance, too.

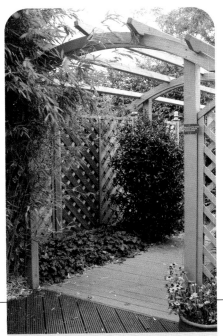

Keep pergolas wide: narrow spaces tend to feel mean.

Using arches, arbours, and pergolas

❀ The style of any garden feature like this needs to fit in with your existing house and garden, or at least with the garden you are planning to create. A very modern-looking metal arch will look rather out of place in a cottage-style garden, and similarly an elaborate or rustic-style construction will not be best suited to a geometric, formal, or modern garden.

❀ If you want to keep maintenance to a minimum, consider coated metal structures. For me they do not have the initial appeal of a wooden structure, but if you plan your planting carefully, pretty soon you will be able to see very little of the underlying structure, and it will require minimal maintenance.

Sizing arches and pergolas

❀ There is nothing worse than an arch or pergola that is not tall enough. When deciding on the dimensions of an arch consider the tallest person likely to walk through it, add on about 30cm (12in) for plant growth to hang down, ideally making it a total of 2.5m (8ft) or more, and don't forget that the supporting posts or uprights will need to be buried in the ground.

❀ The width of an arch or pergola that spans a path needs some thought too, and again plant growth on the uprights needs to be considered or else you will end up with more of a tunnel than a pergola.

If buying a kit, you may need additional support for climbers.

Buying and caring for garden furniture

Good quality, very comfortable garden furniture makes your garden all the more appealing, even to the non-gardening residents. So do your research, and take time and care to choose well.

Even if your table is on the lawn in summer, move it onto a deck or paving when damper weather sets in.

Keep off the grass

Wooden garden furniture will last a lot longer if you make sure that over the winter months it is kept on a surface where rain water does not accumulate. Avoid standing it on grass – it is likely to sink into the turf during wet weather and the legs are then more likely to rot.

Undercover

Furniture of all types lasts longer if taken into a shed or other protected place over winter or, failing this, covered up. If, like me, you like to sit out in your garden on the odd wintry day, then just make sure you are vigilant about regular applications of wood treatments.

Leg treatment

Stand each leg of wooden garden furniture in its own pot of wood treatment for several hours to ensure that adequate amounts are absorbed to keep this high-risk area really well protected. Re-treat at the recommended intervals.

Use the best material you can get for this job.

Caring for joints

Joints on wooden furniture are likely to hold moisture more than other areas, so check them more regularly and use a medium-firm paintbrush to really press the wood treatment into those awkward corners.

Oil your teak

Teak oil makes a great annual treatment for hardwood furniture. Although hardwoods are much less inclined to rot than softwoods, teak oil will help to keep the wood in better condition for even longer and preserves the original colour.

Plastic renewal

If your plastic or resin garden furniture is faded and grotty-looking but still perfectly sound, don't discard it, paint it. With a suitable proprietary paint, designed specifically for plastic, it can have a new lease of life.

Keep the shine

Plastic garden furniture benefits from a regular washing with water – not only to keep it clean, but also because any grit or grime that accumulates on it could cause scratching of the surface.

Hinges and pivots on folding chairs need regular attention.

Oil for protection

Metal furniture that is kept in the garden throughout the year will stay in better condition for longer if it is dried off thoroughly and then given an annual application of oil. If you do this right at the end of the main season you can then leave the oil in place, only wiping off excess just before you need it again in the spring.

Lubricate moving parts

An aerosol of oil or water-displacing lubricant with a thin extension tube is perfect for hard-to-reach places on your furniture, and for lubricating hinges and springs. It is so much easier than trying to reach these areas with an oily rag or a brush.

Dry before repairs

❀ If wooden furniture needs repairing, with the odd rotted bit being removed and filled, bring it under cover for a couple of weeks first. The wood must be completely dry before you tackle the job; fillers will not work on moist wood.

❀ Small areas of wood can be dried a little more speedily if you can get the furniture close to the house – a hairdryer works wonders.

Removing the rot

If you need to cut out rotted wood, make sure you cut out adjacent discoloured or suspect areas too, because these are likely to be in the early stages of decay. It is better to cut a bit more than you need to, rather than not removing enough – filler will soon fall out if more wood starts to rot around it.

Sustainable wood

When buying wooden furniture, look for the logo of a certification scheme that ensures it comes from sustainable sources, such as the Forestry Stewardship Council (FSC).

Caring for plants

No matter how much time and money you spend choosing and planting new plants for your garden, this can all be lost in a matter of days if you do not give the plants the TLC they deserve. As soon as they are home and in your care, there are things they will need, and without this initial aftercare, their chances of surviving, let alone thriving, are very poor. Basic needs such as adequate water, and later on some extra food, are essential to the plants, especially in that initial establishment period.

Even when the plants are established, most will not perform as they could unless you look after them. Most aftercare need not take more than a few minutes, but it can make all the difference between a miserable, poorly performing plant and one that is living up to and above any expectations you had of it.

Maintaining your plants
Taking time to care for your plants can be incredibly satisfying, and means you can

really observe what's going on and how things are progressing – and perhaps even catch and deal with an early infestation of a pest or pathogen attacking your plants.

The amount of time and effort you need to allow depends on your garden's size and style; formal gardens generally require much higher maintenance than more naturalistic ones. Just remember that plants and garden features need some input, but every second you spend will be well worth it.

This chapter shows you how to:

❀ Care for your plants in the first few weeks after planting.

❀ Water your plants efficiently and economically.

❀ Feed and mulch your plants – plus organic and chemical fertilizer options.

❀ Weed your plants, and techniques for effective weeding.

Initial aftercare

The first few weeks or months after planting are generally the most critical. Once out of its pot, a new plant needs to get its roots into place quickly and get itself established, so if your time per plant is limited, make this initial aftercare period your top priority.

Beware of shocking your plants

If the conditions in the garden differ noticeably from the conditions in the nursery, garden centre, or shop where the plants were before, make sure you give them the chance to acclimatize and try to avoid too dramatic a change.

Overnight protection can ease a plant into its new conditions, but remove it in the morning.

This mesh may not look like much, but it slows the wind enough to make a real difference.

Put up a windbreak

A temporary windbreak is a good idea: you can use fleece, or for a larger planting get special windbreak fabric. Whatever you use, the important thing is to get it in position as soon as (or preferably before) you plant.

Gently does it

Covering a new plant with fleece or even old net curtains for a few nights after planting should help it to acclimatize to a less protected, cooler environment. This will also help to prevent wind damage, but it is important that you gradually allow the plant to get used to the harsher conditions – don't cosset it too much or too long.

Hardy plants aren't always totally hardy

Even a plant which is described as hardy may often prove to be slightly tender in its first winter, especially if you buy it relatively late in the year and it has been in the protected environment of a polytunnel or a warm site. If there are any signs of fairly soft growth, or you are even the slightest bit doubtful, it is worth taking precautions because the plant may not have had sufficient chance for its growth to harden before the onset of winter in your garden.

Keep well watered

To encourage the roots to grow out into the soil, and so allow the plant to become established, the soil needs to be kept really moist. If there is plenty of rain that is penetrating deeply enough into the soil, that will do, but if in any doubt, grab the watering can.

Unless there is a spell of wet weather, water to ensure the ground stays moist.

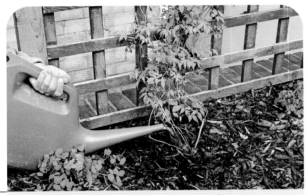

Water a wide area around a new plant to encourage the roots to grow outwards.

Drought tolerance takes time

Don't forget that even drought-tolerant plants, which should need little extra watering once established, will need watering if the soil is very dry in the first few weeks (for annuals) or months (for perennials and woody plants) after planting.

Sacrifice the first flowers

You may think it sounds crazy but, to get the best long-term performance from a new plant, it often helps to cut off all or at least some of the flowers when you plant it, or any that appear shortly afterwards. These flowers may look appealing, but they will have a draining effect on the plant, drawing resources away from where the plant needs it most, in its roots and general structure.

For best results, deadhead for the duration of the plant's flowering period.

Deadhead for good health

As soon as a new plant is in the ground – or earlier if you have a moment – grab scissors or secateurs and do a thorough deadheading. This ensures that no resources are used on the formation of seeds and associated structures instead of on the vital early stages of establishment.

Watering your plants

When it comes to watering, it is essential that you know the moisture requirements of your plants. Just as many plants may be killed by over-watering and excessive kindness as die through neglect and under-watering.

Watering when dry

Water is lost from the plant in especially large quantities during hot, dry weather, but windy weather often has an extremely dehydrating effect too. Always check soil and compost moisture levels after windy periods, even if the weather has appeared quite cool and overcast.

Probe the soil to test how deeply water has penetrated.

Too little, too shallow

It is essential that any watering you do has a useful effect, and does not just moisten the soil on the surface or immediately below it. If only this area of the soil is moist, the plant's roots will tend to move towards this area, sometimes even growing in an upwards direction. Once in the upper regions of the soil, they will be more prone to the effects of drought and heat than if they were in their usual place, lower down in the soil.

Winter drought

Unlike most deciduous trees, shrubs, and climbers, conifers and other evergreens are especially prone to drought during dry periods in the winter, late autumn, and very early spring because their foliage is still in place. During dry weather make sure that they are watered adequately.

Wait and see

It can be very difficult to know just how far down into the soil the water you have applied has penetrated. On first inspection, if you dig into the soil, the water may not have gone very deep at all, but if you wait an hour or so before checking, you will tend to form a much more accurate picture of the moisture levels.

It is important to water conifers because they are always in leaf.

When to water

In the heat of the day the soil surface temperature can become very high. This means that watering done then is more likely to allow a lot of moisture to be lost by evaporation, so whenever possible water in the evening or very early in the morning.

Keep the pegs long or the hose may slip over.

Avoiding hose damage

If you use a hosepipe to water your garden, it is all too easy to drag the hose over or against precious garden plants as you move the hose from one area to another, causing a lot of damage. To avoid this, drive sturdy wooden pegs into the soil on the bed edges and at intervals along the edges of very large beds. As you drag the hose it should always hit a peg rather than the plants in the border.

Soft and low

❁ Avoid strong jets of water. Plant top growth is easily damaged, and if you direct the jet at the ground, you are likely to displace the soil from around the roots.

❁ Many plant pathogens, such as powdery mildews and rusts, thrive when the foliage is wet, so always try to avoid wetting the foliage when you water.

Reaching inaccessible parts

If there are areas in a bed, or perhaps within rows of vegetables, that become inaccessible later in the season, they can be difficult to water. When planting, lay a piece of guttering with holes drilled at frequent intervals along its length, in the inaccessible place. Provided the guttering is kept level, you can simply pour water in at the accessible end of the pipe and the water should move along the guttering to reach the soil beneath it.

When jets can help

It helps to use jets of water when you have an infestation of red spider mites on the foliage of your plants. This pest really detests getting wet feet, so it pays to wet the foliage whenever you can, provided it is not during very bright sunlight.

Keep the water in

To encourage water to stay in the most useful place, create a slight ridge of soil in a circle around the base of the plant, large enough to encompass the feeding roots of the plant. You can then direct water into this "bowl" and it should all penetrate within the circle.

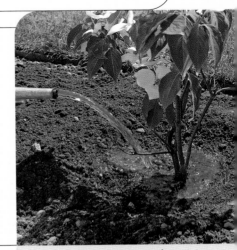

If all the water stays where it is needed, you can use less.

Once you have checked the flow is what you want, cover the hose.

Reducing watering loss

❀ A porous hose allows very gentle and slow seepage of water into the soil. Perfect for watering newly installed plants, and less wasteful because the water does not run off.

❀ If you are using a porous hose pipe, make sure you cover the hose with mulch. This not only hides the hose from view, but ensures that even less water is lost through evaporation.

Don't wet the petals

The petals of flowers are generally far more easily damaged than the leaves, so take extra care not to wet these when you are watering. This is especially important in sunny weather: the combination of water and hot, bright sunlight causes scorching of the petals or soft foliage.

Welcome rainwater

❀ Make sure you recycle water whenever possible. It makes such a lot of sense environmentally, and natural rainwater is generally the plants' first choice as well. (*see* pages 228–29)

❀ If you have hard water in your area it will not be ideal for lime-hating or ericaceous plants so, wherever possible, water these plants with rain water.

❀ Lime-hating or ericaceous plants may definitely do better when fed rainwater, but if there is no rainfall and your water butts are empty it is still essential to water these plants if their soil or compost becomes too dry, especially if they are growing in the confines of a pot. Hard water is definitely better than no water.

❀ Small quantities of hard water can be made suitable for these plants by boiling it and allowing it to cool. Adding a few old tea bags or tea leaves to the water will help to acidify it slightly.

Watering in the shadows

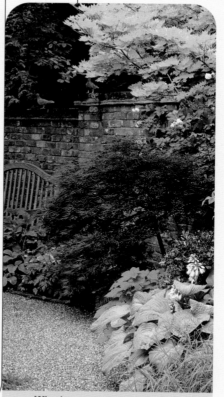

Whether sunny or shady, a bed by a wall is often dry.

Plants growing close to a wall, especially a house wall, are especially prone to dry soil conditions because the base and the foundations of the wall act rather like a sponge and absorb water from the soil. Plants on a house wall have the added problem of the roof overhang which creates a very effective "rain shadow". Make plants in these areas a watering priority, and avoid planting very drought-intolerant plants in this sort of position.

To sprinkle or not to sprinkle?

It is tempting to use a sprinkler system to water the plants over the summer as it can be left to its own devices. Sprinklers also make light work of watering lawns and areas of dense planting. However, if they are left in one place for too long, they can be wasteful, and can end up giving the leaves of the plants a light sprinkling, as opposed to delivering the water to where it is needed – at the roots. As hosepipe bans are frequently enforced over the summer months, another watering method, such as a spray-gun hose, may be a more environmentally sound option.

Feeding and mulching

There is no need to apply excessive quantities of fertilizer to your plants – indeed it may damage them – but the truth is: gardening creates some unnatural situations, and with plants packed in or cropping heavily, they do benefit from feeding.

A balanced diet

Plants require nutrients as well as water and the energy they can create using sunlight. If you want your plants to perform to perfection, some supplementary feeding is generally a good idea, but don't forget that you can over-feed or feed incorrectly. Doing this is just as likely to result in problems as if you under-feed, so take care not to over-do it.

Keep on composting

Keep your soil in good health by regularly incorporating garden compost and well-rotted manure. This helps to ensure that soil micro-organisms are plentiful, as well as topping up many nutrient levels. It is cheap (or even free) and means you are less likely to need artificial fertilizers.

Organic matter is beneficial to the soil.

The power of potash

Sulphate of potash is used to promote flowering, ripening of stems, and toughening up of foliage. Potash is leached out of the soil readily, so this can be applied earlier in the year or later in the year, as well as during the classic feeding times. Because it does not promote soft growth, it is also perfectly safe to apply it during "off-season" times.

Sprinkle potash around the base of the plant; it will wash down to the roots.

Feeding – the basic rules

❀ Reduce the risk of soft growth being produced too late in the year by feeding only until midsummer. Applying feeds that stimulate growth in autumn would make the plant very vulnerable to frost.

❀ Feeding excessively, or too late in the season, may cause flowering shrubs or trees to bloom less well than they should because buds are more likely to fail or to drop.

❀ Never feed plants that are seriously stressed, especially if they are suffering from the effects of drought. They are unlikely to be able to make use of the fertilizer, and may even be damaged by it.

Don't starve seedlings

If seedlings or small plants waiting to be pricked out or potted on cannot be given the treatment they need immediately, apply a foliar feed to their leaves. This gives them a boost and at least partially makes up for the low nutrient levels in the compost. To avoid the risk of scorching, dilute the liquid so that it is half its normal strength.

Growth cycle

Plants generally grow more during the spring and summer, start to slow down in autumn and pretty much come to a standstill during winter. This is in part a natural protection mechanism: any soft, new growth produced would be damaged by winter frosts. As a result, the best time to feed most garden plants with general or complete fertilizers is midspring to midsummer.

Fertilizer rules

Never use a fertilizer except in the way described by the manufacturers. A standard fertilizer, even if in liquid form, should not be used as a foliar feed. It has not been formulated for this, and so doing could mean that the plant does not benefit, or worse still may actually be damaged.

Always mix feeds as directed: a little bit more "for good measure" can be harmful.

Foliar feeds are the ultimate fast food for plants, giving an almost instant boost.

Quick feed

❀ If you are looking for a quick-fix feed with relatively fast results, choose a liquid feed. These are taken up and used very rapidly.

❀ Using a foliar feed – that is, one that is applied directly to the foliage – is generally regarded as being the quickest way to get nutrients into a plant. Make sure you apply this type of fertilizer on a dull day because using it during hot, bright sunlight may cause scorching on the leaves.

❀ Since foliar feeding seems to stimulate root growth, it is an excellent way to encourage either initial plant establishment, or re-establishment after transplanting, or replacement root growth after the roots have been injured.

❀ Because foliar feeds take effect relatively quickly, you can safely apply these to plants a little later in the season than when you are using root-applied feeds.

When to avoid lime

Avoid using lime if you have recently dug manure into your soil, have used it as a mulch, or are intending to do so soon. Lime will react with the nitrogen in the manure and release ammonia, which may damage the plants.

Feed and forget

Controlled-release fertilizer granules are useful in situations where you need to be sure that the plant will get food even if you forget to feed it. They have a resin coating that is permeable and allows more nutrients to be released when the soil or compost is moist and damp, less when it is very dry or cold. The result of this is that the plants get more food when they need it most, and less when they don't need it so much.

Granules may be loose or in "plugs" to push into pots.

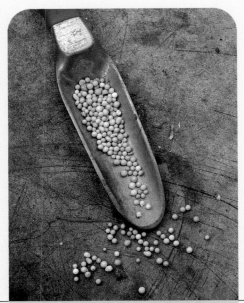

Fertilizers come in many shapes and forms, so check labels carefully.

Granular fertilizers

Granular fertilizers need to be dissolved into their liquid form if they are to be of use to the plant and not scorch it, so make sure that you feed plants either when the soil is already very moist or just before a heavy fall of rain. If in doubt, or if neither of these options is possible, water the plant and the fertilized area thoroughly straight after application.

Avoid touching the leaves

Always try to keep fertilizers (except foliar feeds) off the plant's foliage. They may cause scorching, especially if the plant is stressed or the weather is particularly hot and sunny. If the fertilizer has contaminated the foliage, try to brush it off straight away; ideally you do not want to wet it. If this is not possible, then you could thoroughly drench all the affected plants with large quantities of water in an attempt to wash it off.

Concentrated fertilizer will scorch leaves: wash it off and down to the roots.

Avoid contact with roots

If you are incorporating a fertilizer into the soil before planting, make sure that it is mixed in thoroughly with the soil and that the roots of the plant will not come in direct contact with the concentrated fertilizer. If they do, root damage may occur.

Lack of balance

Sometimes the presence of large quantities of one nutrient may cause others to become less readily available to plants. For instance, if a lot of potash is used, perhaps to encourage fruiting of tomatoes or flowering of roses, then it is likely that the plant will start to show symptoms of magnesium deficiency.

Magnesium deficiency

❀ Magnesium deficiency affects the older, larger leaves first, showing as yellowing between the veins on the affected leaves. It may also show as browning or purple discolouration between the veins.

❀ Epsom salts is the most widely used treatment for magnesium deficiency. This can be watered into the soil or applied directly to the leaves for a much more rapid effect. Any solution that runs off is not wasted because it will also be taken up by the plant's roots.

Hose-end feeders can be adjusted to give a solution of the correct strength, saving time.

Quick feeding with a hose

Save time by using a hose-end fixture to get feed onto the plants. These are suitable for either a liquid feed or a granular or powdered one that has to be diluted with water before applying,

Magnesium deficiency can look alarming but is easily treated.

Phosphate for roots

Since phosphate helps to encourage root growth, it is particularly useful for new plants. Bonemeal is often used, but it can sometimes attract wildlife, such as foxes, that then excavate in the area looking for what appears to be a source of food.

Using ash safely

Wood ash contains useful amounts of potassium, but make sure that no unsuitable materials, such as firelighters, plastics, or painted or treated wood, have been burned on the fire. Only use the ash on the garden if it originates purely from plant materials. Ash from a garden bonfire will have lower levels of potassium if most of the wood burned was old and woody, and more if the materials included fresher, younger plant growth.

If you burn plant material that cannot be composted, it can still be useful.

Nitrogen-fixing plants

There are a number of plants, in particular the legumes – including beans, peas, lupins, and sweet peas (*Lathyrus*) – which have root nodules containing nitrogen-fixing bacteria in them. These are able to convert unavailable soil nitrogen into a form that is available to plants. Make sure you always include some peas and beans in a vegetable plot rotation system (*see* page 119). If possible, leave the roots of all these plants to die off and break down in the soil once their cropping or flowering period is over; this will allow them to continue to be useful for even longer.

Gloves for safety

It is always advisable to wear gloves when handling fertilizers. If you are using a dust formulation, wear a dust mask as well.

Always be careful when handling concentrated substances.

Make your own liquid feed

Make a very useful and totally free liquid feed for your plants by rotting down the top-growth of nettles and/comfrey plants. You need about 1kg (2½ lb) of nettles for every 10l (2¼ gallons) of water. Just mix the nettles with the water and ensure that they are completely covered with water. Keep the container tightly covered and stir regularly and then, when the leaves have rotted down in a few weeks time, you can strain off the liquid. Dilute the concentrated fertilizer with about one part fertilizer to 10 parts water.

Replenish mulches

Top up all organic mulches regularly, because the material will gradually become incorporated into the soil. Make sure that the mulch is not actually in contact with the stems or trunk of the plants; this can cause the stem to start to deteriorate.

Top up the mulch, then pull it back from around the stems.

Mulching for weeds

Mulching helps to smother small weeds or to create a barrier that prevents weed seeds from germinating. Keeping mulch levels topped up helps to reduce problems with weeds.

Small weeds will die under a light-excluding mulch.

Mulches for moisture

Help moist soil to stay moist by applying a bulky organic mulch to the soil surface in spring. This prevents the surface from getting too hot and reduces moisture loss by evaporation.

Heavy-duty woven landscape fabric stops all but the toughest.

A barrier to weeds

It may not suit all areas of the garden, but if you use a covering of gravel or even large pebbles on the soil surface this woven plastic sheet will allow water to reach the roots while providing a serious barrier to weeds trying to come up from the soil, and to weed seed germination.

Depth of mulch

To be most effective an organic mulch layer needs to be 5–8cm (2–3½in) deep, but if you run short, just put on what you can and then add to it as soon as you can. Some mulch is definitely better than no mulch.

Weeding

Weeds compete for those basic needs of your garden plants – water, light, and nutrients. Everything from the smallest bedding plant to a young tree with the potential to be a giant one day can suffer, so don't underestimate weeds, either annual or perennial.

Make weeding a priority

Most weeds are extremely rapid growers that flower and set seed far more quickly than garden plants. Weeding needs to be a high-priority job because it is essential to remove weeds before they get a chance to set seed and multiply.

Which weeds make compost

❀ Weeds make an excellent addition to your compost heap – but avoid using any that have been treated with a weedkiller, are just about to set seed or have set seed. You should also leave out the roots of any that have pernicious root systems.

❀ Weeds with seeds and roots can form new weed plants in the compost heap. They are best left to rot in a large tub or barrel of water. Within a few weeks they will rot down, producing liquid feed. The liquid tends to be rather smelly, so keep the barrel in an out-of-the-way place!

❀ Perennial weeds often have seriously pernicious roots that are extremely difficult to remove in their entirety. Deal with them slowly, and try to ensure that you do get all of the root out – in many cases, each section of root left behind will have the potential to form a new plant.

A sharp hoe uproots weed top growth.

How to hoe

❀ A sharp hoe is a really good way to deal with annual weeds. Invest in a tiny hoe, usually sold as an onion hoe, which has the head only a few centimetres wide. This is perfect for weeding around small or closely packed plants with accuracy.

❀ Try to hoe weeds on a hot, sunny day, when they can be left on the soil surface and will dry to a crisp.

Digging out deep weeds

An old but sturdy table knife is a great tool for digging out longer-rooted perennial weeds, such as dandelions, because it can be inserted right down into the soil adjacent to the root.

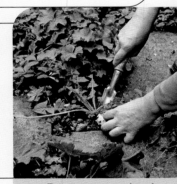

Removing every bit of a tap root is tricky work.

Handle with care

Chemical weedkillers can be used but remember that they are, basically, plant-killers; they have to be used with extreme care and precisely according to the manufacturer's instructions.

Avoid drifting weedkiller

Weedkiller drift is a serious risk, especially if you are using a sprayer, because tiny droplets are easily wafted around on air currents and thermals. Wherever possible use a watering can to apply weedkiller.

A dribble bar is ideal for targeting weeds fairly accurately and efficiently.

Bruise the leaves

Some weeds are tough to control because they have a tough outer surface. To increase uptake of the weedkiller, gently crush the foliage before applying.

Leave it late

Some weeds, such as nettles, benefit from a late-season spray, applied just before the foliage starts to die back – it seems that the weedkiller is carried down into the base of the plant as the plant re-absorbs nutrients from its foliage.

Plants pull everything into their roots just before winter.

Applying with care

❀ If you are applying weedkillers using a sprayer, plant mister, or watering can make sure that it is really clearly and indelibly labelled and is only ever used for applying weedkillers. Even extremely tiny traces of weedkiller can cause a lot of damage.

❀ Always check that the product you have in mind is suitable for the job, and that it can be used on the type of weeds you are trying to control.

❀ A watering can fitted with a dribble bar allows direct application of weedkiller and little if any drift. If you are applying a weedkiller in a bed that has other plants in it, make sure you protect these first, otherwise they may be damaged or even killed.

❀ Only apply weedkillers during suitable weather conditions. The day must be calm, with no signs of excessive heat, wind, or rain.

❀ Cover or shield nearby plants with plastic bags, cardboard boxes, or sheets, or even disposable plastic dust sheets for larger plants. Remove these only when the weedkiller has dried on the weed foliage.

❀ If you feel tempted not to bother with these precautions, just think how long it would take and how much it would cost to replace any plants killed by the weedkiller!

Simple propagation

Propagating your own plants need not be either complicated or expensive. There are several ways you can build up your plant numbers with little effort, no well-honed skills, and sometimes no outlay.

You may be trying your hand at seed sowing, taking cuttings, or layering for the first time, or perhaps you have tried these techniques before. In either case, there are sure to be a few ways to make plant propagation easier and more successful.

The beauty of propagation

One of the great things about propagating your own plants is that you can raise exactly what you want. When you grow your own plants from seed, you can search the catalogues until you find what you want, or even collect and save the seed from the plant you've fallen in love with.

For woody climbers, shrubs, and trees, if you can take cuttings or do simple layering using that perfect plant as your propagation material, then you're guaranteed extra numbers.

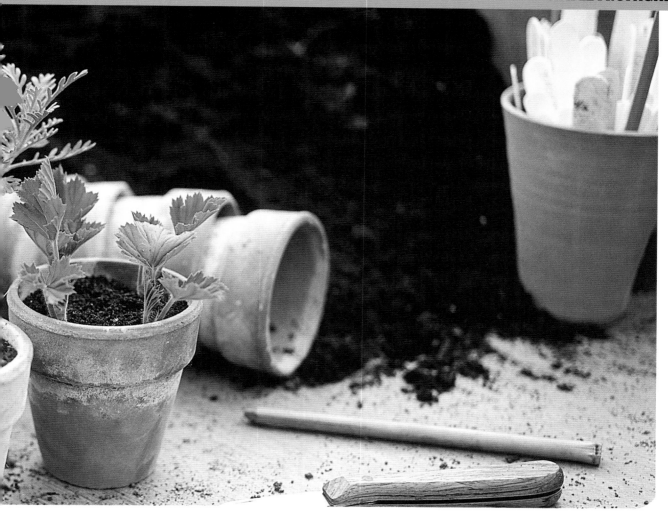

Some plants are easier to propagate at home than others, and there is no doubt that in many cases a little bit of specialist equipment – perhaps just a heated propagator – will make it easier to successfully propagate a wide range of plants. This said, the outlay will not be huge and is nothing compared to the money you can save when you propagate your own plants, and the satisfaction and pride you will feel when you see your little "fledglings" growing in the garden!

This chapter shows you how to:

❀ Prepare and sow in trays and pots.

❀ Sow in a heated propagator.

❀ Manage without a greenhouse.

❀ Prick out and plant out seedlings.

❀ Sow direct and collect seed.

❀ Take cuttings from a variety of plants.

❀ Divide plants and propagate by layering.

Starting with seed

Most of the plants that you might want in your flowerbeds or vegetable plot can be raised from seed, including some trees and shrubs. It is worth gathering a selection of seed catalogues, and buying or making some simple equipment to get started.

Choose easy seed

If you are new to seed sowing, it is worth starting with seeds that are relatively easy, or at least avoiding those that are described as needing "some experience". There is plenty of time for those later – first prove to yourself that you can do the basics.

Read the instructions

Seed packets will always tell you which months are suitable for sowing the seed. It's worth noting these because the weather conditions that follow will determine whether or not the plants you produce will do what they need to, and each plant has different needs.

Badges of merit

Some seed packets bear logos that show they have been assessed in trials and found to be plants of particular worth in the garden. The Fleuroselect Gold Medal or Quality Mark and the Royal Horticultural Society's Award of Garden Merit (AGM) all indicate good buys.

You can start with just a few seed trays for most seeds. More equipment allows you to grow a wider range of plants.

Seasonal adjustments

There is margin for common sense when it comes to sowing dates. If you are living in a particularly cold or especially mild part of the country, or have reason to believe that this will be a year with an Indian summer, adjust sowing dates by a week or two, so the plants are ready when the weather is right.

Tools of the trade

What you can sow depends on the equipment you have (some seed needs a heat source, such as a heated propagator, to germinate), and also on the time of year. The right equipment lets you cheat a little on sowing dates, letting you sow seeds indoors (and with heat) either to make an early start or to catch up if you've left things a bit late.

Wait and sow

For seed that is to be sown direct in the garden (*see* pages 202–3), let your common sense prevail. If the ground is very wet and cold, don't sow, even if the seed packet says it is the right time. Wait until it gets a bit drier or milder.

Recycling at home

Using old food containers as seed trays is sensible, because these are generally made from the sort of plastics that are not widely accepted for recycling.

Don't drown your seeds

There are all sorts of seed trays available, but make sure yours is equipped with drainage holes. I have seen a surprising number of seed sowing pots and trays provided in kits that are hole-free and will cause the seeds to rot off or the seedlings to fail in days.

Drainage holes should be plentiful and not too small.

Don't skimp on drainage holes – it is hard to make too many. One every 3cm (1in) should be enough.

Make your own

If you want to do your bit to recycle, create your own seed-sowing containers from thoroughly cleaned margarine tubs, ready-made salad pots or fresh fruit containers and punnets. Use a sharp knife or a heated skewer to make plenty of drainage holes.

Save trays with lids

Some containers with potential for a second life as a seed tray are especially useful because they come complete with a clear plastic lid. This makes them perfect miniature propagators.

A lid keeps in heat and moisture, but take it off before the seedlings brush against it.

Preparing trays and pots

Getting pots and seed trays ready for sowing is rather like making up the spare bed for a very special guest – you need to get the conditions just right for them to do well and enjoy their stay. But, like guests, they will need moving on before too long!

Don't mix seeds

Full-sized seed trays are great if you have a lot of one type of seed to sow, but you will usually want to sow less than this. It is possible to sow more than one type of seed in a single tray, but it is harder for you and for the emerging seedlings, which are likely to germinate at different rates or even require different conditions for optimum germination. Smaller half- or quarter- trays are generally much better for smaller quantities.

The beauty of seed cells

I often use sowing cells – numerous tiny pots or cells together in one tray shape. The advantage is that you can dramatically reduce the amount of thinning out and transplanting you need to do, and the seedlings will get much less root disturbance when they are finally transplanted, because each has its own mini-pot for its own root system. The disadvantage is that the smaller individual volumes of compost are more inclined to dry out rapidly, so you will need to keep a closer eye on watering.

Sow seed in modules if it hates disruption.

Seed sowing composts

For all but the most fiddly seeds, you can get perfectly good results using a good quality multi-purpose compost. For the more difficult customers, choose a special compost sold specifically as seed-sowing compost, or sometimes as seed and cuttings compost.

A compost sieve is handy for seed trays, and also for smaller potted plants that won't like lumpy compost.

Fine tuning the compost

If your compost is lumpy, the best solution is to invest in a compost sieve of medium mesh size. Failing that, you can use an old kitchen colander or rigid vegetable steamer to sieve your compost ready for seed sowing. Avoid using a kitchen sieve: the mesh size is so small that virtually nothing comes through.

Avoid older compost

If you find some oldish compost in an open bag lurking around in the greenhouse, shed or garden, use it as a mulch for the garden, or perhaps mix it in with fresh compost for a large plant. Use only fresh compost for sowing because older compost may harbour pathogens.

Using garden soil

You can sometimes successfully sow and germinate seed in garden soil but the risks are high. Sowing in open ground is one thing, but in the confines of a pot or tray problems such as damping off are more common, especially if extra warmth is provided.

Shake out lumpy compost

❀ If you are desperate to sow some seeds but have no sieve, you can remove the largest lumps from compost fairly effectively if you put a quantity of it in a large pot or bowl and repeatedly shake it quite firmly and tap the base of the bowl on the work surface. The lumps should come to the surface in much the same way as the lumps of butter come to the surface when you are making pastry or a crumble topping.

❀ Don't waste the larger lumps and twiggy bits left after sieving the compost. They can either be used in the very base of the seed tray or as part of the potting mix for larger plants.

Removing lumps by hand is not ideal, but most seeds clearly benefit.

Stand the compost in a sunny place or, ideally, a greenhouse.

Warm up cold compost

If you are buying compost in cold weather it too will be cold, so if time permits put the compost somewhere relatively warm for a day or two before you sow the seed. Warming the compost will help to get things off to a quicker start, and if you are using a heated propagator it will take little electricity to bring the compost up to the right temperature.

193

Sowing in trays and pots

Once the compost is in the trays or pots, the seed can go in and the process of growing your own plants from seed really begins. For the best results, take time over this seemingly simple process, and it'll pay dividends.

Filling the tray

Seeds do need a decent depth of compost to develop their roots, but don't fill the tray to the brim. Doing this uses more compost than you need and can make the compost difficult to water later on. It is best to fill the tray to within about 0.5–1cm (¼–½in) of the rim.

A flat tamper will level compost better than your hands can.

Firming the compost

Compost needs firming, but not compacting, and the surface needs to be levelled. If you do a lot of seed sowing or intend to do so, then it is worth making your own compost tamper. Use a piece of wooden board the same dimensions as the surface of the tray minus a few millimetres all round, with a block of wood attached centrally. You can then use the block as a handle to gently but firmly tamp the compost.

Tamp with a tray

As an alternative to a compost tamper, use the bottom of another seed tray the same size as the one full of compost. Hold the empty tray level on the compost surface, then press it down. The surface will be levelled, and in many cases it will also have some slight furrows in it (from the drainage grooves on the tray's base), and these can be used as guides for sowing in straight lines.

Sowing at the correct depth

The depth that seed should be sown should be stated clearly on the seed packet. Although seeds have an amazing determination to succeed in germinating, if you bury them far too deeply they need to use up a lot of energy to produce all that extra growth just to get to the surface.

Estimating depth

For seed saved from the garden or given by a friend, you may have to guess the correct depth. The general rule is that the smaller the seed, the smaller its reserves, and the closer to the light it should be. Scatter dust-like seed on the surface, and bury larger seeds to about their own depth.

Make sure you know what's what!

❀ Always label your seed trays as you sow them. It is easy to assume that you'll remember what you sowed and when, but this is not always the case, and seedlings often bear little resemblance to the mature plant, especially when very small.

❀ If there are children in the house, I recommend also writing labels on the pots and trays themselves, just in case small hands decide to collect up the labels for you. I've had this happen to me too!

Labels written with non-water-soluble pen or pencil are essential.

Sowing thinly means finding more space for seed trays, but yields much better results.

Don't crowd seeds

Always sow seeds thinly in pots and trays. Sowing too thickly produces seedlings that are more likely to become etiolated or "leggy", and be more prone to damping off diseases. They will also be that will be much trickier to prick out when the time comes.

Mix fine seed with sand

Very fine seed from plants such as lobelias is difficult to sow thinly. One way to make it easier is to mix the seed with several times its own volume of dry silver sand before sowing. Scattering this larger quantity of sand over compost is much easier.

A pinch of dust-like seed is easier to sow if mixed into a teaspoon or two of sand.

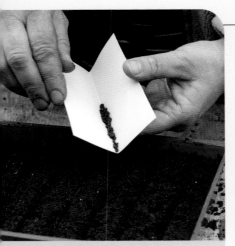

With a little practice, you can sow very evenly from paper.

Small, fiddly seeds

If you find small seeds sticking to your hands, take a piece of stiff paper or card and fold it so that it has a crisp crease along the centre, and tip some of the seed from the packet into it. You can then hold the paper in one hand and tap it sharply with the other hand to release a controlled stream of seeds onto the compost.

Covering seeds

If you sow in furrows at the correct sowing depth, you can simply flick the compost from the sides back over the seeds. For seeds that are randomly scattered or very small, it is easiest to use finely sieved compost, applied directly from the sieve and shaken over them.

How to sow seeds

Sowing seeds in straight lines rather than randomly scattering them makes it easier to prick the seedlings out later on. Large seeds can go into individual holes created with a dibber or pencil; for smaller ones, make a furrow of the appropriate depth using a plant label drawn over the compost surface.

A little time spent making furrows saves a lot of fiddling and frustration later.

A light covering

Some seeds need light to germinate, but would not survive if left on the open compost surface. You can cover them with a thin layer of a material such as vermiculite, which will hold them in place, prevent them becoming dehydrated too easily, and yet allow some light through. Alternatively, cover the tray with cling film, a sealed clear plastic bag, or a sheet of glass.

Sowing deep-rooting seeds

It is best to use deeper containers for sowing some larger seeds, such as sweet peas (*Lathyrus*), that need to develop a good, sizeable root system before planting out. If you want to engage in a bit of recycling, roll newspaper into cylinders about 4–5cm (1½–2in) across to make individual pots. When the seedlings are ready to go into the garden you can even plant them without removing the pots; the roots will grow through the newspaper as it disintegrates in the moist soil.

Grouped in a tray, paper pots keep their shape.

Use warm water

Use tepid or warm water for watering seed trays. Cold water will chill the seed and lower the temperature of the compost, and you will have to raise it again for germination to be successful.

When to water

I prefer to sow seeds into dry compost, rather than watering it first because I find the compost easier to work with, but if you do this you will need to water the compost thoroughly after sowing. If you water from above, the water hitting the compost surface will wash seeds, especially small seeds, around and into clumps. This will happen no matter how careful you are. Instead, I put the trays of sown seed into a container or sink with just a little tap water in it – not enough for the tray to float. After about ten minutes (the time depends on the type and quantity of compost in the tray) the compost will be thoroughly moistened, and the seeds will still be where you positioned them.

Let the compost pull up water gradually from below to avoid disturbing seed.

Dreaded damping off

The most common reason for seedlings dying is an infection known as damping off. It is caused by one or more microscopic fungi that kill off the plant roots or stem bases, making the seedlings flop and die. There are several ways you can easily reduce the risk of this.

❀ Only use mains water on seedlings: water from a butt is more likely to contain fungal spores.

❀ Use only fresh, proprietary compost for seed sowing.

❀ Avoid over-watering seeds and seedlings; they should be just moist.

❀ Sow seed thinly and make sure that you keep it at the temperature required. Temperatures that are significantly too high or low can cause problems.

❀ Consider watering the compost at the suggested intervals with a copper-based fungicide recommended for this purpose.

❀ Make sure the seedlings have plenty of natural light and don't leave them in the propagator for too long, putting on lush, soft growth.

Top-dressing seed trays

If trays or pots are going to be standing outside, a layer of grit can protect the seeds from pests and colonization by weed seeds. Indoors, a layer of vermiculite is ideal for covering small seeds, retaining moisture, and ensuring a well-drained surface around young seedling stems, but it is far from essential for most.

Sowing with heat

The range of plants that you can raise from seed is greatly increased if you have access to a heated propagator. These are really useful and simple to use, and worth the investment – even a small, inexpensive propagator will increase your options.

Plan your seeding

If you want to germinate several different types of seed at the same time, you may be faced with a problem: some seeds require lower temperatures than others to achieve a good germination rate. Try to sow your seeds in batches, grouping the seeds so that those requiring similar temperatures are sown together; there is room for a degree of compromise. You can also place pots of seeds requiring slightly lower temperatures on the base of upturned pots or trays within the propagator: introducing a little space between the compost and the heat source in the base of the propagator results in slightly lower temperatures.

Uneven heating

Quite often the heating element in a propagator seems to supply heat unevenly. Take advantage of this by noting which areas are the warmest and which are the coolest, and you can position trays and pots of different seeds accordingly.

Capillary matting

Most propagators come with a piece of capillary matting that fits snugly onto the base. This allows the water you put in the base of the propagator tray to be drawn up to the seeds, but without the risk of them becoming waterlogged. For this effective watering system to work, you need to keep the matting just moist at all times. Wash it really well before each use, just in case it is harbouring any fungal pathogens.

Ordinary detergent and hot water are great for cleaning.

Clean every time

After each use, thoroughly clean the tray and lid of the propagator. This will help to reduce the potential for disease problems, and cuts down on the build-up of algae on the lid, which would otherwise reduce the amount of light reaching the seedlings. Make sure you do not wet the electrical apparatus when you clean it out.

Don't bake seedlings

Most propagators have vents in their lids, allowing some air circulation. It is essential to keep these open on hot, sunny days: even in a thermostatically controlled propagator, temperatures can build up to potentially fatal levels, and seeds or seedlings will literally bake to death. It is best to keep seeds and seedlings out of direct, very hot sunlight, even with the vents open.

Managing without a greenhouse

If you don't have a greenhouse and need to raise seeds in a warm environment, you can generally get reasonable results on a sunny windowsill during the summer months. If the windowsill faces south or west, you may even need some shading on hotter days.

A cut down, foil-lined box maximizes light.

Limited light

Plants on windowsills generally only get sunlight from one direction, and they have a tendency to become etiolated (leggy, pale and rather weak) and to grow towards that light source and so become lopsided. You can take steps to avoid this.

❀ Stand your pots or seed trays on a sheet of aluminium cooking foil, or even better, stand a foil-covered card on the room side of the sill. The foil reflects the daylight back onto the plants.

❀ Rotate your pots and trays at least once a day, preferably more frequently, so that the effect of one-sided light is reduced.

Stroke your seedlings

Research shows that seedlings develop sturdier stems and are less inclined to become lanky if they are stroked regularly! Gently brush over the tops of the seedlings with a piece of paper or card, back and forth, several times a day. It may sound funny but it works, and the more you do it the better the results. This technique also works really well for seedlings in greenhouses, probably mimicking the effects of a gentle breeze.

Cheap insulation

Covering pots of seedlings with a clean, clear plastic bag or a miniature plastic cloche allows them to receive maximum light while dramatically reducing problems associated with fluctuating temperatures or the compost drying out. Do make sure you don't let them get too hot.

Into the frame

If you need a place to grow on seedlings after they have left the confines of a seed tray or propagator, a cold frame should work well. It must be well insulated, and adjustable enough to keep temperatures at a suitable level.

Homemade propagator

Make your own miniature unheated propagator to fit over a single flower pot: cut the base off a clear plastic lemonade or water bottle, and use the upper half to pop over the pot like a cloche. You can even remove or replace the lid to regulate the temperature.

Less stylish than Victorian glass cloches, but just as effective.

Pricking out and planting out

When you need to move small seedlings on to a larger home – known as pricking out – or plant them in the garden, make sure they are well watered before you move them. Dry growing medium clinging tightly to fine roots is likely to cause them to get torn.

Before pricking out

Prepare the new pots before you start to prick out seedlings. That way you can pop the delicate roots straight into the compost and reduce the risk of them drying out or becoming damaged.

Watering

Watering seedlings straight after they are transplanted is worthwhile, even if the compost was already quite moist. The extra water helps to settle the compost around the plants' roots, and also ensures that they establish in the new position quite quickly.

Water from below

If water pours onto the compost surface too rapidly, it may dislodge the compost from around the base of the seedling. If in doubt, stand the pots of newly transplanted seedlings in a tray of water until the surface of the compost starts to glisten, indicating it has taken up plenty of water.

A brief soaking ensures good contact between roots and soil.

Hardening off

Even hardy plants need hardening off before they can safely be planted outside. This just means toughening the plants up gradually before permanently moving them from a windowsill, propagator, greenhouse, or frame. Nights are often much cooler than days, so for the first few days bring plants in at night.

Prime time for damping off

If you are dealing with seedlings that are particularly prone to damping off, try using a copper fungicide for the first watering after pricking out.

Handle with care

Holding a seedling by the stem is potentially lethal for it. Only pick up or manoeuvre seedlings by the "seed leaves", which are much tougher.

Making a frame

If you have a lot of seedlings and small plants to deal with, it may be worth constructing an inexpensive cold frame. It can be as simple as bricks or breeze blocks topped with an old window frame or several layers of fleece.

Sowing direct

Many seeds can be sown straight into the soil without the need for any compost, trays, or special equipment. Some, such as poppies (*Papaver*) and candytuft (*Iberis*), invariably perform significantly better if sown direct.

Remove stones

Before you sow, make sure the soil surface is pretty well levelled. Raking over will bring some larger stones to the surface: remove these because each blocks an area of soil surface, preventing you from sowing there.

Which seeds?

Not all flower or vegetable seeds can be sown direct, so always check the seed packet. For flower seeds, look for the words "hardy annual" (often abbreviated to HA on the packets), and on vegetables, look for a mention of "sowing direct".

Concentrated fertilizers may harm seedlings, but a little manure is ideal.

Sowing early

❀ If you want to make an early sowing, soil conditions may be a bit too cold. Covering the soil with a sheet of black plastic sheet for a week before you intend to sow will help to increase the soil's temperature and may also shelter it from excess rain. Make sure the sheet is well anchored with large stones or bricks.

❀ You can use black bin liners but these can be quite thin. Compost bags are generally made from much thicker plastic – just cut the bag open to create a flat sheet, then anchor it to the soil with the printed side down and the black uppermost.

A black sheet will warm the soil and dry out a wet surface.

Prime conditions

For best results make sure that the spot you have in mind is sunny and adequately fertile. Digging in some well-rotted manure or garden compost before you sow will help to improve texture as well as fertility. At the same time, it also improves the soil's ability to retain moisture, so it really is worth the effort.

Judging the conditions

Sowing times are important, but always take local conditions into account. If the soil is wet and cold, many seeds are likely to rot off before they get a chance to germinate, so it is worth waiting.

201

Top hardy annuals for sowing direct

Bright eschscholtzia are easy sown direct.

Nigella has masses of jewel-like flowers.

Agrostemma
Calendula officinalis
Centaurea cyanus
Clarkia elegans
Eschscholtzia californica
Gypsophila elegans
Iberis
Limnanthes douglasii
Linanthus androsaceus
Linaria
Linum grandiflorum
Malcolmia maritima
Nemophila menziesii
Nigella damascena
Papaver rhoeas
Papaver somniferum
Phacelia campanularia
Scabiosa atropurpurea

Aim for a natural look

Mark out different areas with horticultural sand. This soon disappears, but shows where to sow each type of seed. Avoid using builder's sand; it may contain contaminants. The sand sold as "play sand" is perfectly good, and if you have children and a sandpit they won't miss a little.

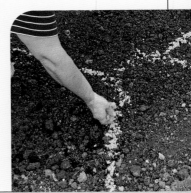

Areas with irregular outlines look more natural.

Protecting the seeds

If cats or seed-hungry birds visit your garden, it may be worth putting up a temporary scaring device on the seedbed or using randomly spaced canes and taut strings to keep them off. If you use strings it is absolutely essential that they are kept taut, because loose strings may entangle birds.

Check the heights

When you are planning your annual summer flower display, consider not only flower colour but also the plant's expected height. It is easy to be misled by the pretty picture on the seed packet, and you need to make sure none of the flowers tower over their neighbours.

Gauzy, tall plants can come to the front, but generally taller plants are best kept to the back of a bed.

Sow annuals in rows

It may be tempting to simply scatter the seed within each sowing area, but if you sow annual flowers in rows it is much easier for you to tell which are seedlings and which are "weedlings" when the growth appears. Once the plants have started to put on growth, the fact that they started off in straight lines will be completely masked, so you won't end up with regimented rows.

Sow thinly

I like to sow hardy annual seeds thinly, ideally aiming for a distance of only about one-third of the suggested final spacing distance between each seed. This allows for a bit of wastage through failure or pest attack, and dramatically reduces the amount of thinning out you have to do later on.

Labelling rows

Once you have covered the seed over with soil to the suggested depth, make sure you label each area clearly. This means you know what you are expecting, and can spot complete failure before it is too late to re-sow. I find that pens sold as laundry markers or good quality permanent marker pens are generally better for writing on plant labels than those sold in garden centres.

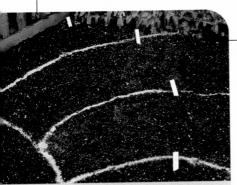

You can forget what you have sown surprisingly quickly.

Make your furrows

A piece of bamboo cane or a sturdy stick from the garden makes a perfect tool to draw across the soil surface to create the furrows into which you can sow the seeds.

Shallow furrows are all you need.

Weeding out

❀ However well you prepare the ground, some weeds will always appear. Most weeds germinate and grow more rapidly than garden flowers, so hand weed carefully and regularly.

❀ A small-headed onion hoe can be used with care on weeds that appear between the rows.

❀ After removing weeds, always water the area thoroughly, even if the soil is moist. This will help to re-settle the disturbed soil.

Use thinnings

You can re-use thinned seedlings or plants in other areas of the garden. To minimize root damage, water the soil before thinning. Thin in the evening or early morning, when the temperature is relatively low, and pop the thinned seedlings into a plastic bag to reduce moisture loss before replanting them straight away.

Don't thin all at once

Thin over a period of time: if you thin plants out to the suggested final distance the first time you thin, some disaster in the form of a pest or a pathogen may leave you with a rather sparse display.

Water thoroughly

Always water the area thoroughly after thinning so that the soil settles back closely around the roots of the remaining plants. You need to do this even if the soil appears quite moist.

Collecting seeds

One way to make plant propagation even more economical is to collect your own seed. You can build up large numbers of your favourite plants, and you already know that they will thrive in the conditions you have to offer.

Most poppies will self-seed with abandon.

Self-seeding plants

Take advantage of natural self-seeders. When you remove faded hardy annual seedheads, give them a few sharp shakes over the areas where you would like some plants next year.

Natural fall-out

Many plants shed seed which then germinates and thrives, so take advantage of self-sown seedlings of plants such as hellebores, aquilegias, forget-me-nots (*Myosotis*), and hollyhocks (*Alcea*). They often do very well in the spot they have "chosen", but may need transplanting to fit in with your plans or prevent paths being blocked or other plants over-shadowed.

Collecting and saving seeds

Although saving seeds produced by plants growing in your garden may seem like a great idea, remember that many will not come "true". That is to say, the seedlings may look good, but will not necessarily be the same as the plants from which you collected them.

Self-sown plants have done half the job for you, so keep an eye out for them.

Picky seeds

Some seeds have quite specific requirements for germination – periods of cold and warmth, the heat of fire, even chemicals in smoke. With the trickiest, bought seed is more reliable – but you might be lucky with your own.

F1 seeds

Of all the plants in the garden, those sold as F1 hybrids are least likely to come true. These are vigorous hybrids of two distinct parents. Their offspring may be worthwhile, but can be quite different from the parent plants.

Bide your time

If you have your eye on seed from a plant in your garden, avoid the temptation to collect seedheads or seeds before they are ripe. Generally there is little if any more development once the seeds are removed from the plant, and they will remain immature and non-viable if removed too early.

Collect on a dry day

Always try to collect seed on a dry day and when the plants themselves are not rain-soaked or damp from dew. The drier the seed is when gathered, the more likely it is to store successfully.

Most seeds can be rubbed from seedheads with your fingers.

Clean seeds for storage

If you save your own seed, clean it up by removing attached bits of seedhead, which may harbour moisture and possibly even pests or pathogens. Label it and store in a cool, dry place until it can be sown.

Seed catcher

A paper bag attached loosely around the nearly ripe seedhead will catch seeds as they ripen. This prevents them being shed and falling to the ground and, provided the bag is paper, they should be fine in there for a day or two. Plastic bags would cause condensation to build up, and the seeds would be more likely to be damaged.

Keeping dry

A small amount of silica gel helps to keep the air inside a container adequately dry. I re-use the little sachets that sometimes come with electrical equipment.

Berry seeds

To remove seed from berries, squash the berries gently by hand and remove the flesh as thoroughly as you can. Then place all that remains in a bowl of warm water, and rub gently and wash until the flesh floats off.

Chemicals in the flesh of fruits can prevent germination.

Don't be greedy

Plants generally succeed better when sown with care than when self-seeding: you won't need masses of seed.

205

Simple softwood cuttings

Most softwood cuttings need to be taken in the spring. At this stage the new shoot growth is still very flexible or soft, and will be in a perfect state to root quickly, often in the simplest of set-ups.

Morning cuttings

The best time to collect material for softwood cuttings is early in the morning, when the stems have not yet lost any moisture in the heat of the day. If weather conditions have been dry, it also helps if you can water the plants the night before.

Cutting practice

❀ Use really sharp secateurs to minimize damage to the material and the plant.

❀ Take a few clean, clear plastic bags with you. Put each type of cutting in a separate bag immediately: this will really help to prevent the cuttings from flopping.

Taking cuttings does not harm the plant.

Short-term storage

Ideally you should get on and root the cuttings immediately after taking them. If for some reason there is an unavoidable delay, fold the top of the bag of cuttings over and put the bag in the vegetable compartment of your refrigerator.

Cuttings will keep for a few hours in a fridge.

Healthy sideshoots

Always choose the best looking, healthiest sideshoots for softwood cuttings. Avoid any that are damaged or looking miserable, and try to avoid any sideshoots that are bearing flowers or buds.

Pinch out the buds

If all the sideshoots are bearing small buds, then you will have to use some of them. Carefully pinch out each bud, taking it right back to the point where it joins the stem.

Pinching out buds avoids energy being wasted on the flowers.

Leaf nodes contain plant hormones that help rooting.

Rooting preparation

Before rooting, trim each cutting so that it is 7–12cm (2½–5in) long and remove the lowermost leaves to leave a bare stem. Then use a very sharp knife to make a straight cut just below a leaf node – this is the junction on the stem where the leaves were attached.

Rooting in compost

Softwood cuttings can be rooted in well-drained cuttings compost. Rooting in compost means that it is particularly easy to pot them on once rooted. If you use this method, it is worth dipping the ends of each cutting in hormone rooting powder to assist rooting.

Rooting in water or gel

Softwood cuttings can be rooted in a jar of tap water or in a proprietary rooting gel. If you are using water, make sure the jar is really clean and support the cuttings so that their leaves do not flop into the water. Fixing a piece of chicken wire or some aluminium foil over the top of the jar creates a good support system, but if using foil, you will need to make holes in it with a pencil before inserting the cuttings.

Supported by foil, the cutting hangs with its end in the water.

You can watch the roots form and then pot up.

Protection for cuttings

Enclose each jar or pot of rooting cuttings with a clean, clear plastic bag, fixed around the rim so that it is not in direct contact with any part of the cuttings. This will help to prevent them losing too much moisture from their leaves, and protect them from extremes of temperature.

Top plants for softwood cuttings

Abelia	*Erica*
Abutilon	*Forsythia*
Caryopteris	*Fuchsia*
Ceanothus	*Hydrangea*
Ceratostigma	*Kolkwitzia*
Cotoneaster	*Lavatera*
Cytisus	*Perovskia*
Enkianthus	*Philadelphus*

Fuchsias are perhaps the easiest plants from cuttings.

Semi-ripe and hardwood cuttings

Semi-ripe cuttings are cut just below a node, and ideally have a soft or flexible tip and a slightly hardened or woody base, known as a heel. Hardwood cuttings are taken from fully ripened, woody stems. Both are taken from the current season's growth.

Heeled cuttings

Rooting can be stimulated by paring away a sliver of bark about 3cm (1in) long on one side of the base of a semi-ripe cutting. Then trim off any sideshoots, the lowermost leaves, and the soft tip.

This heeled cutting is a good starting point.

Top plants for semi-ripe cuttings

Aucuba*	Garrya*
Azara*	Ilex
Berberis*	Lavandula
Buxus	Mahonia
Callistemon*	Olearia
Camellia	Photinia*
Carpenteria*	Pieris*
Ceanothus*	Pyracantha
Choisya	Rhododendron*
Cotoneaster*	Skimmia*
Daphne	Viburnum
Deutzia	Weigela
Elaeagnus*	*Needs to be taken
Escallonia*	with a heel.

Penstemons are easy to propagate this way.

Trim large leaves

Cuttings taken from shrubs with large leaves can fail because they lose too much moisture. Cut across each leaf, half-way down with sharp scissors before rooting the cuttings.

Crowd control

Semi-ripe cuttings should root well in good quality cuttings compost. You can put several in one pot, but the foliage from one must not touch that of its neighbour because this may encourage fungal problems.

Rooting powder

Dipping the base of the cutting into hormone rooting powder will help stimulate root growth. Excessive hormones can damage the cutting's base, so make sure that not too much powder adheres to the cutting by tapping it sharply before inserting it into the rooting compost.

Scrape the surface to promote rooting.

Use fresh hormone rooting powder.

When to take different cuttings

❀ Choosing the right moment for the best semi-ripe cuttings can be difficult. If you can, take a few every two weeks or so: that way at least some of them are bound to hit the perfect date for best rooting.

❀ Hardwood cuttings are generally taken in late autumn or early to midwinter. They are simple, but take the longest of all cuttings to produce roots.

Cut at the very base of this year's growth.

Hardwood cuttings

Hardwood cuttings are best cut 25–38cm (10–15in) long from the area where this year's growth meets last year's, on stems about as thick as a pencil. Most hardwood cuttings can be rooted either in pots kept in a cold-frame or simply in a trench in open ground. Once watered in, cuttings can be placed in a propagator for faster results, or if you do not have one, a clear plastic bag, making sure that the bag does not touch any foliage left on the cuttings.

Preparing a trench

If you decide to root hardwood cuttings in a trench, prepare this before you take the cuttings. Weed the ground, then dig out a trench about 15cm (6in) deep. Just before you are ready to use it, add a layer of coarse horticultural sand about 5cm (2in) deep in the base. This will ensure adequate drainage during wetter weather.

Into the trench

Use sharp secateurs to remove the very tip of the cutting, taking it back to just above a bud or a pair of buds. Insert the cuttings into the trench so that each one is about 12–15cm (5–6in) deep into the soil, and has 15–30cm (6–12in) of stem protruding.

These cuttings can be set quite close.

Planting out

Hardwood cuttings rooted in pots in a cold frame have usually formed sufficient roots by the spring to allow them to be planted out. Cuttings rooted in open ground are generally a little slower to root, so transplant these to their permanent homes the following autumn.

Top plants for hardwood cuttings

Buddleja

Cornus alba

Forsythia

Ligustrum ovalifolium

Philadelphus

Ribes

Rosa

Rubus

Salix

Sambucus

Spiraea

Symphoricarpos

Tamarix

Weigela

Easy divisions and layers

Many herbaceous plants benefit from being divided. After a few years the older, central part of a clump becomes less vigorous. Lift the plant, remove decrepit parts, and replant smaller, vigorous sections. Layering is good for shrubs that are tricky to grow from cuttings.

Spring divisions

If you garden on heavy clay soil, divide perennials in the early spring. At this time they are less likely to suffer the serious setback that winter wet could cause.

Dividing perennials

Generally speaking, herbaceous perennials are best divided in either autumn or spring. If the plant gets too dry or flops in the heat when lifted, the new divisions are less likely to thrive. Divide plants only when they are not suffering from drought stress, and ideally do it in the cooler early evening. They can then have the evening and night to recover before facing the tougher daytime conditions.

Dividing with forks

The age-old idea of using two forks, inserted back-to-back into the clump to be divided, really does work. Make sure you drive each fork in firmly and to an equal extent before you start to ease them apart, dividing the plant into clumps. There is no need to use full-sized forks on a tiny but well-established clump that needs dividing – use a pair of hand forks instead.

Sturdy forks divide the toughest clumps.

Top plants for propagating by division

Achillea	Lychnis	Rudbeckia
Anemone	Nepeta	Sedum
Aster	Paeonia	Solidago
Astilbe	Polemonium	Thalictrum
Bergenia	Pulmonaria	Veronica
Campanula		
Coreopsis		
Crambe		
Doronicum		
Epilobium		
Geranium		
Heuchera		
Hosta		
Liatris		

Check plant roots carefully for weeds.

Check the roots

If there is a problem with pernicious weeds, such as couch grass, nettles, oxalis, or docks, in your garden or the garden from which the division came, check the root system over carefully. Remove even the tiniest bits of weed root.

Anemone hupehensis and similar autumn-flowering types divide well.

Pin down runners

On plants that naturally produce runners, you can pin a runner down with a U-shaped piece of galvanized wire. Once the runner has rooted, simply sever it from the parent plant.

Encouraging roots

❀ Strip leaves from the section you peg down, except at the shoot tip.

❀ Wound the lower surface of the stem at the point where you want the roots to form, about 25–30cm (10–12in) from the shoot tip.

❀ Dust the cut with hormone rooting powder to stimulate more root growth.

Cut shallowly to leave a tongue.

Layering is natural

A number of shrubs naturally propagate themselves by simple layering: you may find well-rooted branches around existing shrubs. They can be severed from the parent, and grown on to form a better root system, then planted.

Peg the stem down and then cover it with more soil. You may want to label the spot.

Pegging the layer

Use galvanized, sturdy wire to form a U-shape with which you can peg the stem into the prepared soil. If you have wounded the stem, and this area is kept open and in contact with the soil, rooting will be further encouraged.

Encourage low growth

Encourage vigorously growing shoots low down on the shrub because these root best. About one year before you want to try layering, prune stems low on the plant so that plenty of new, vigorous shoots are produced. These can then be used for layering.

Shrubs for easy layering

Aucuba

Carpenteria

Chaenomeles

Corylopsis

Erica

Fothergilla

Gaultheria

Laurus

Magnolia

Rhododendron

Skimmia

Syringa

Layering is by far the easiest way to propagate lilac (*Syringa*).

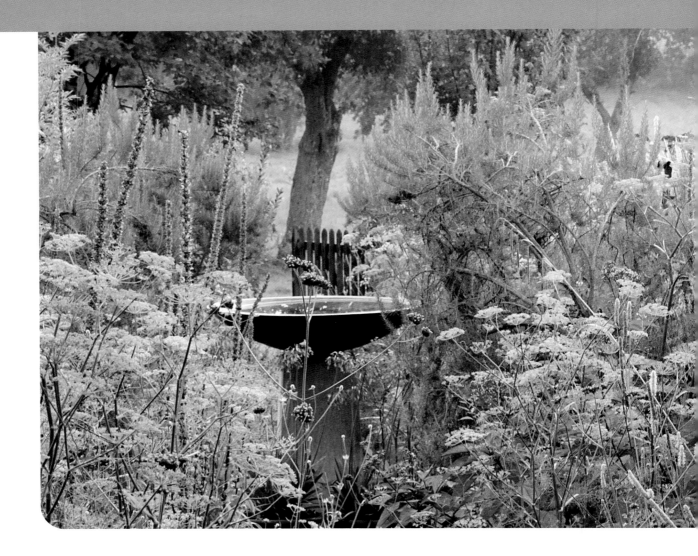

Friends & foes

Every garden is teeming with creatures, from the large to the microscopic. Some of these are pests that can spoil your plants, while others should be encouraged. Many are neither friend nor foe, simply an integral part of your garden.

It is essential to get to know which to make welcome and which to reject – and this isn't always straightforward. All too often, people assume that because they don't recognize an insect on their plant, it is the one responsible for the holes on nearby leaves.

Not all pests are equally easy to track down or spot in the garden. Identifying which pests are significant and which can be left to their own devices is key to successful gardening, especially if you want to avoid using pesticides.

Combating the pests
Pests can be a problem for any gardener, whatever their level of experience or size of plot. There are all sorts of ways that you can try to tackle pest infestations when they do get a grip,

but the idea of getting something else to control them for you may tempt you more. Your garden is full of potential allies, creatures that won't attack your plants but will prey upon or parasitize pests. It makes sense to identify the creatures in your natural pest-control team, and learn how to encourage them to breed and live in your plot. If your gardening is restricted to a tiny yard, or even a window box, there are still some creatures waiting to help you perfect low-maintenance, chemical-free pest control.

This chapter shows you how to:

❀ Provide for natural allies – which creatures to encourage and how.

❀ Garden for natural allies – entice the natural pest-control team onto your plot.

❀ Identify common pests and diseases.

❀ Deal with slugs, snails, and vine weevils – three pests that will challenge your green convictions.

Providing for natural allies

Most birds are welcome in a garden, and in my view we should encourage them all –
even finches that nip off fruit tree buds, and pigeons that shred brassicas, although you
may want to protect your plants! Don't forget to provide for your smaller allies too.

Invitation to dine

Hanging up bird feeders encourages birds to regard your garden as part
of their potential territory. Not only will you enjoy seeing them on the
feeders, but when pests are about in your garden, the birds will help you
to keep those under control.

Buy a protected feeder if you
have squirrels in your garden.

Fresh water helps to keep
thirsty birds off summer fruit.

Bath time

A supply of easily accessible
clean water provides a welcome
spot for birds to drink and bathe.
Make sure it is in a position
where they need not be at risk
from the neighbourhood cats.

Bed and breakfast

Use roosting pouches and
encourage thick, dense
hedge growth so that birds
can have a relatively safe,
warm spot to roost at night.

Pecking order

Suspending a peanut feeder
on a tree branch is a sure
way to bring in small and
very useful garden birds. I've
often seen tits form what
amounts to a queue on a
branch, and those that are
waiting for their turn on the
nut dispenser invariably peck
away at cracks and crevices
on the tree bark and stems,
removing aphids, insect eggs,
and caterpillars.

A range of birds, including
many finches, eat rose hips.

Fruitful harvest

Grow plenty of seed- and berry-
bearing plants, like viburnum
and amelanchier, that can supply
a natural food source for birds.

Nesting instinct

Put up some nesting boxes to encourage birds to take up residence and breed in your garden. Make sure you choose those that have been properly designed and constructed so that the birds will be safe in them: look out for logos of national bird protection organizations. Remember to site boxes in a sheltered place out of direct sunlight, so they aren't too cold or too hot.

Stripes are stars

Bees in all shapes and sizes are an integral part of a garden, and many are brilliant pollinators too, helping ensure that your vegetable and fruit crops are prolific. Similarly striped hoverflies are also great pollinators and one of the best aphid predators; they can look like wasps, but with a thicker waist, so don't swat them.

Flowers in your garden are pollinated by a huge range of insects, from large bees to tiny flies.

Indiscriminate pesticides kill the creatures you enjoy seeing, as well as the pests.

Don't harm visitors

Avoiding using any pesticides will go a long way towards encouraging good populations of all sorts of insects, including butterflies, moths, and bees, as well as potential predators and parasites of pests.

Home comforts

There is now a wide range of "hotels" and "feeding stations" that you can site in your garden. These will instantly provide hideouts for birds, butterflies, bees, and other creatures that are great to have in the garden.

A string of birch bark makes an attractive insect habitat.

Natural enemies

I love cats, but it has to be said that they are generally considered to be one of the worst enemies of garden birds.

Gardening for natural allies

There are lots of pretty plants that both look good and bring in those beneficial insects. On the whole the simple, non-double flowers are the most insect friendly, so make sure that you include some. Small changes in your gardening habits make a big difference.

Fancy hybrids offer less

Make sure that you grow plenty of "natural" flowers, and not just wall-to-wall hybrids. Many of these are sterile, so do not produce pollen or nectar to feed insects.

Recycle plant stems

Some of the chunkier herbaceous plants, such as hollyhocks (*Alcea*), have hollow stems. Come the winter, the dead stems provide a perfect overwintering site for ladybirds and lacewings. If the foliage is diseased, at least save a few stems, having first cleared them of the old, dead leaves.

Leave stems in place or use them as part of a "hotel".

Flat flowerheads offer more

A plant that produces a sizeable flowerhead composed of lots of tiny flowers is often a particularly good and safe nectar source. Some of the tinier beneficial insects are likely to drown as they attempt to feed in very large flowers. Nectar in very deep flowers may also be inaccessible, especially to some parasitic wasps and predatory insects that have particularly short mouthparts. So grow some plants such as fennel, dill, or elder (*Sambucus*).

Sedums are superb nectar plants.

Time of their lives

Many potential garden allies, such as lacewings and hoverflies, have more than one distinct life stage, and it is only the larval stage that preys upon pests. Of course, you need adults to get larvae, so it is important to treat all life stages with respect. Make sure you know how to identify the adults, larvae, and (if possible), the eggs of any potentially beneficial insects.

Adults have their own needs

Do all you can to encourage the adults of hoverflies and lacewings to visit and breed in your garden so that they can then produce pest-eating larvae. The adults feed on protein- and sugar-rich pollen and nectar. By growing suitable flowers, ideally the non-double, open-centred kind, with easily accessible nectar, you should increase the appeal of your flowerbeds.

Delay the tidy up until spring

Even if your beds and borders need a tidy up after summer, try to avoid being too hasty. By leaving some areas of the garden unkempt over the autumn and winter, you will be providing hiding places and safer, warmer overwintering sites for some of the beneficial creatures you need to encourage. Try to leave most of the tidy-up until spring.

Top flowers for attracting beneficial insects

✽ *Phacelia* This hardy annual with bluish, scented flowers is perfect for direct sowing.

✽ **Coriander** An annual herb producing masses of tiny white flowers, that is perfect for direct sowing.

✽ **Fennel** The flowerheads of both the green and bronze forms of this hardy perennial are great for beneficial insects.

✽ **Poached egg plant** The yellow-and-white flowered *Limnanthes douglasii* is a hardy annual loved by hoverflies.

✽ **Californian poppy** Thriving in sunny, well-drained, sites, pretty *Eschscholtzia* with yellow, orange, or cream flowers can be direct sown.

✽ **Goldenrod** A really tough herbaceous perennial, *Solidago* can be direct sown and has showy, golden flowers.

✽ **Candytuft** With readily available pollen and nectar, perfect for beneficial insects, *Iberis* is of the easiest hardy annuals.

✽ **Pot marigolds** Gorgeous, bright gold *Calendula officinalis* can be direct sown and keeps on flowering until hit by frosts.

Useful allies in pest control

✽ **Ladybirds** are very attractive, and both the soft-bodied larvae and the adults consume huge numbers of aphids.

✽ **Lacewing** young or larvae are brilliant predators, eating mainly aphids, but also other pests such as thrips and the eggs of moths.

Lacewings are easy to recognize.

✽ **Hoverflies** have soft-bodied, yellow-grey larvae that are great aphid eaters, a single one eating up to 50 in a day, nearing 1,000 in its lifetime.

✽ **Ground beetles** are often seen scuttling off at speed when you move pots, low-growing plants, or loose slabs. They are mostly black and often shiny, and are excellent predators of many pests including slugs, vine weevils, and some insect eggs.

✽ **Some solitary wasps** feed their larvae on aphids, weevils, and other insects.

✽ **Fast-moving centipedes** eat a lot of soil-dwelling creatures and their eggs.

✽ **Anthocorids or flower bugs** feed on aphids, mites, thrips, and a range of small insects with their sharp mouths.

Leaf litter and logs protect centipedes.

✽ **Devil's coach horse** beetles are predators of soil pests including slugs, cutworms, and leatherjackets.

Common pests and diseases

It would take far too much time to get the know all the potential pests and pathogens of every plant that you might possibly want to grow, but there are some that just seem to crop up everywhere, so get to know them first.

Keeping perspective

Before you sink into misery because there is a sizeable range of pests and problems in your garden, remember that there are also plenty of plants in your garden that are healthy and performing just fine.

Check it out

It is worth taking the time to have a quick check over plants on a regular basis. This should mean you will be able to spot problems before they get out of hand, and in turn this should mean that you are much more likely to succeed in controlling them quickly and efficiently.

Timing counts

Just how much an infestation of pests or an outbreak of a pathogen really matters depends on many things, including the plants that are under attack and the time of year. With some problems, such as an attack of rust or powdery mildew on a shrub, do not worry too much if the problem arises towards the end of the summer or into early autumn on a deciduous plant. Whatever the effect, the foliage would soon be about to deteriorate anyway.

Getting into the habit of regular health checks also lets you appreciate your plants close up.

Autumn clean-up

A very thorough clean-up of infected material after the leaves have fallen, possibly combined with some pruning to remove stem infections, may often be sufficient to achieve a perfectly good clean-up after a problem.

Select chemicals carefully

If you do decide to use a chemical spray against a pest or pathogen, make sure that you choose something which mentions that particular problem on the label. An unsuitable chemical will have little if any useful effect, wasting time, energy, and money, and in the process you may endanger other organisms that are susceptible to the chemical.

Understanding aphid pests

Commonly known as greenfly and blackfly, aphids in reality come in numerous shades of green, brown, grey, yellow, pink, and black. They damage the plants on which they feed, and they may also transmit viral infections that do more serious damage. Aphids often cause leaf curling and yellowing, and their sugary excreta is called honeydew. When splattered on plants or other surfaces, honeydew may attract harmless but unsightly grey-black sooty mould fungi.

Aphids love luscious, sappy growth, so are very fond of well-fed garden plants.

Dealing with aphids

There are several useful and naturally occurring predators and parasites of aphids. They include hoverfly, ladybird, and lacewing larvae, parasitic wasps, a predatory midge larva, and several bird species. There are also several proprietary sprays available that should control aphids. Some of these are systemic in action, moving through the plant, so could be useful for infestations that are difficult to reach.

Ladybirds eat aphids at any life stage.

Finding ants' nests

Ants can be a real nuisance, especially in a hot, dry summer, and their ant hills and the soil loosening activities can do some indirect damage to garden plants. If you find ants but not where they are living, the best thing to do is to put down something with serious ant-appeal, like a dollop of jam, and trace the line of ants back to the source – that way you will quickly find the location of the nest.

Ants will find a sweet bait like this and carry it off surprisingly quickly.

Treating ants

Proprietary ant killers or boiling hot water are the most widely used methods of controlling ants, but you are most likely to have success if you first disturb their nests using a garden fork.

Hungry caterpillars

Caterpillar pests are common. For crops, it is best to try to prevent the adult butterfly or moth from getting access to the plants in the first place – fleece or very fine netting should do the trick. If you pick caterpillars off an infested plant, remember that they make a welcome snack for garden birds on the bird table.

You don't need to wash the mites off, just wet the plants.

Red spider mite

Red spider mite thrive in hot, dry conditions, so anything you can do to raise humidity in a greenhouse will help to decrease their numbers. Regular misting with plain water works a treat because these mites hate wet feet! A very thorough tidy-up and scrub down of all the interior glass and staging at the end of the season will help to reduce numbers considerably the following year.

Hungry for red spider mite

There is a useful predatory mite that will eat red spider mite, their young and their eggs. Called *Phytoseiulus persimilis*, it works well, but is best used in protected environments, such as greenhouses and conservatories.

Bio-controls can be ordered for delivery at the ideal time.

Greener sprays

There is no resistance to sprays based on fatty acids, plant oils, or starches. These smother insects rather than poison them, and are generally considered greener than toxins.

Sprays for mites

There are several proprietary mite sprays available if you choose to use the chemical route, but some glasshouse red spider mite are showing resistance to many of them, so you may have to try several.

Preventing mildew

Damp foliage or humid air both encourage powdery mildew growth, so try to improve air circulation around your plants and avoid wetting the foliage if at all possible.

Dairy solution

Proprietary fungicides for use against powdery mildews work well, but if you prefer to go for a greener option, many gardeners report finding that a 10 per cent solution of milk in water is an effective treatment.

Making mildew worse

There is a definite correlation between dry soil conditions and the extent and severity of powdery mildews. If the soil is dry, mildews are generally much more of a problem, so keep the soil moist and well mulched (*see* page 185).

Larger fungi

If you see larger fungi, such as toadstools or bracket fungi, appearing on or around a large tree in your garden, it is essential you find out exactly what the fungus is. Some are of no consequence, but others can indicate that the tree is potentially dangerous. Always get the precise identity checked out and take prompt action if necessary. Removing a fungal growth from a tree does not remove the problem – it may help to limit spore production, but the damage is likely to continue within the tree.

Even in a moist soil some plants, such as *Aster novi-belgii*, are prone to mildew.

Powdery mildews

Fungal powdery mildews are very common and show as powdery white fungal growth. This is generally most extensive on the upper surfaces of leaves, but can appear on the lower leaf surfaces, stems, and even petals and prickles.

Gather rust-spotted leaves and bin or burn them, rather than composting.

Rust spots

Fungal rusts are almost always much more problematic during damp years or if conditions on the foliage are wet. Rust fungi need a film of moisture (albeit minute) on the leaf surface if they are to spread and infect. Try to avoid wetting the foliage unnecessarily, and improve air circulation.

Resisting rust

Using a dressing of sulphate of potash, and also avoiding excessive use of high-nitrogen feeds, will help to increase a plant's resistance to rust by keeping the leaf growth just that little bit tougher.

Leaf spots

Most fungal leaf spots, with the notable exception of blackspot of roses, are generally fairly weak pathogens and only likely to cause significant damage on a plant that is already in trouble. Improving growing conditions and cultivation techniques should reduce the risk of pathogens causing a problem.

Fungal leaf spots are usually dark, often greyish, and may bear minute, fungal-fruiting bodies.

Slugs, snails, and vine weevils

In any gardening pest survey, these "big three" always rank highly due to the frequency with which they terrorize our gardens. They are loathed by gardeners. So, what can you do?

Larger black slugs feed mainly on decaying organic matter.

Does size matter?

Most of the damage done to garden plants is from the smaller slugs, especially the greyish-black keeled slugs, and from the pinky-grey field slugs. The larger slugs generally feed primarily on dead or decaying organic matter.

No place to hide

Keeled slugs spend most of their time below ground, venturing above ground to feed but returning again quite promptly. Using a soil-applied and soil-acting treatment, such as the nematode bio-control for slugs, therefore makes a lot of sense.

Barrier methods

Barriers work quite well against slugs and snails, but nearby plant material must not form a bridge over them. They also need to be put right up against the plant stem, otherwise slugs may come up from below within the confines of a barrier even if they cannot get over it.

Where they hang out

In the late summer and autumn, take time to look for colonies of hibernating snails. They often accumulate in huge numbers behind dense climber growth, under loose slabs, piles of pots, or even under loose tree bark.

Snails hibernate in clusters, so hunting can be efficient.

An array of defences

The barriers that work best seem to vary from garden to garden, some of the favourites are copper (copper rings, copper tape, and copper-impregnated fabric), cocoa shells, pine needles, and crushed shells.

Taste for alcohol

Beer is the traditional lure, but interestingly slugs and snails seem to show little appetite for most alcohol-free drinks – perhaps they just do not have the same smell!

Empty and top up your traps regularly – they soon fill up!

Setting traps

Trapping slugs is an age-old technique and well worth trying. Make sure that the beaker in which you put the lure is plunged into the soil, but that the rim protrudes 1–2cm (½–¾in) above the soil surface. This should prevent useful creatures, such as ground beetles, from ending up in the trap.

Cereal killer

Stale milk works well as a slug bait, and if you sprinkle a small quantity of porridge oats or muesli into the liquid you choose, it appears to make it even more appealing.

Parasites

The biological control for slugs works very well, especially against keeled slugs, but the soil does need to be kept moist so that the nematodes can move around freely. Since snails live above the soil level, they are not affected by the bio-control.

Adult weevils attack leaves, while larvae feed on roots.

Vine weevils

Chemicals are available to control vine weevil. There is also an effective biological control in the form of a nematode, which generally proves most effective when used as a drench in mid-spring or from late summer to early autumn. The soil needs to be fairly warm and moist.

Competent climbers

Vine weevils cannot fly, but they are extremely good climbers and can scale all but a totally smooth surface. A sticky barrier of non-setting glue or petroleum jelly often proves to be a great defence. To protect plants on greenhouse staging, try standing the legs of the staging in bowls kept topped up with water – vine weevils don't like to swim either.

After dark

Most vine weevil activity happens at night, so if you want to check that these really are the pests that are responsible for the leaf notching on your plants, go on an evening walk around the garden with a torch.

Do not disturb?

Vine weevils are extremely good at "playing dead" when disturbed – do not be fooled by this.

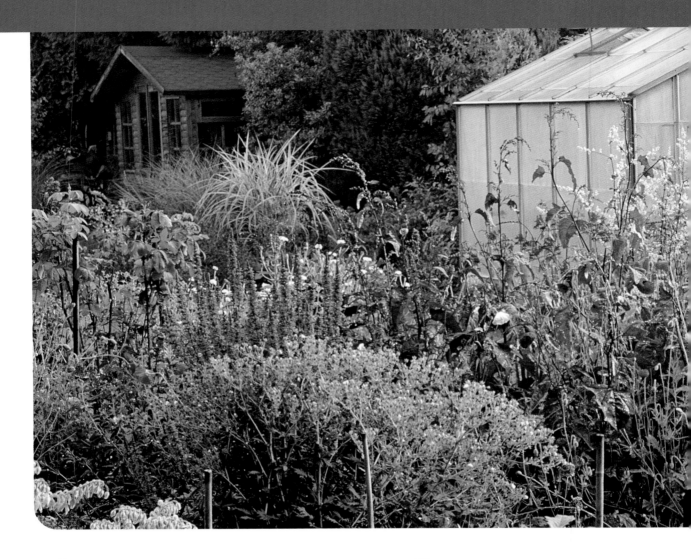

Greener gardening

There are few gardening fashions and trends that I would recommend following. I'm a great believer that your garden is your bit of free-from-constraints space, and that you need to do what you want to do, not what someone else tells you to do. However, the issue of caring for our environment sweeps aside this rule.

Love your garden and there is a good chance you will also have more than a passing concern for the planet and everything that lives on it. But that is not to say that you want to be a fully

fledged organic gardener who sticks to a strict code of conduct. You may simply want to be a bit greener and enjoy what I call commonsense gardening. Either way you will be reducing your adverse impact on the garden and the environment as a whole, while continuing to enjoy gardening.

Going green
With the current interest in greener gardening, it is so easy to go green. If you have ever wanted

to use environmentally friendly methods in the garden, don't be put off by the thought that you'll be turning your pleasurable hobby into a weighty milestone – greener gardening really is no harder than conventional gardening – perhaps it requires a little more thought, but to an extent the more organically maintained garden may be better equipped to look after itself. And then, of course, you'll also be able to enjoy the knowledge that you have done your bit in a worthwhile yet very easy way.

This chapter shows you how to:

❀ Save water in the garden.

❀ Recycle household water outside.

❀ Use water sparingly.

❀ Adopt greener methods.

❀ Master organic techniques.

❀ Use biological controls and traps.

❀ Create a composting system for your kitchen and garden waste.

Creating a water-wise garden

Whether you are subject to seasonal watering restrictions, have a water meter and are worried about the cost of watering, or simply want to want to irrigate your plants less, water is a resource that we should all conserve, whatever the weather.

All soils are helped by organic matter.

Dig in organic matter

Bulky organic matter, such as well-rotted manure, garden compost, leaf mould or used proprietary compost from seasonal containers, will always help to reduce water use by increasing the soil's ability to retain moisture. This is especially useful on light, sandy soils because these tend to drain very rapidly and also have little organic matter in them.

Clay soils

If you have a heavy soil that gets rather too wet when it rains, it will still suffer if water is not readily available. During very dry weather, clay soil will shrink and form cracks, often damaging plant roots in the process. The cracks are often quite deep, and can increase moisture loss from deeper levels in the soil.

Dense clay hardens in dry weather.

Improving soil texture

As well as improving the soil in a whole bed or border, it is worth incorporating extra organic matter into individual planting holes and pits, and making these as large as possible.

Weed regularly

Weeds take a significant quantity of moisture from the soil, so regular weeding is a good idea. If the soil has developed a slight cap or crust (this is especially likely on heavier soils), this helps to keep moisture in to some extent, so try to keep the surface of the soil intact when weeding, if at all possible. Light hoeing or hand-pulling generally creates a lot less disturbance than forking.

The ideal time to weed is after rain when the ground is soft.

Dealing with large weeds in dry conditions

If conditions are really dry and some larger weeds have appeared, then try cutting the weeds off at the base, leaving just a stump, causing no soil disturbance at all – it takes a bit of extra time, but you can then remove the weeds properly later on, when conditions are a bit better.

Weed waste

When weeding in hot weather, always allow the severed bits of annual weeds that have not set seed to remain on the soil surface. They soon frazzle up in the heat, and then form a lightweight mulch which helps to conserve the moisture in the soil.

Mulching magic

Mulching is one of the best ways to reduce moisture loss from the soil surface by evaporation. To have most effect, only apply mulch to a soil that has been thoroughly wetted. To be really effective, an organic mulch should be 5–7.5cm (2–3in) deep, kept clear of the plants' stems, and applied so that it covers the plants' root area.

Water does not evaporate easily through loose mulch.

Using black plastic

Black plastic can be used as a mulch, and certainly seals moisture in effectively, but is not something I would recommend. It also prevents water from getting into the soil from above, and reduces the ability of oxygen to get into the soil or carbon dioxide to leave. As a result, it often adversely effects the populations of the various soil organisms.

The diversity of mulch

All too often mulching is associated with flowerbeds and borders, but it is also a really useful way to reduce moisture loss from vegetable plots, fruit canes and bushes, and even containers.

Lightweight hurdles are quickly installed and filter the wind well.

Create shelter

Both sun and wind have a dehydrating effect on plants, and also directly on the soil. Creating a bit more shade and erecting some form of windbreak will have a significant effect on water usage, especially on a particularly sunny or very windy site.

Plant adaptation

Research suggests that you can succeed in training a plant to survive on less water. Water only one half of the root system at a time, with the minimum amount necessary to prevent wilting: many plants seem able to adapt to surviving on less water – try it out.

Recycling water

If you do not already have a water butt, go out and buy one. If you already have one or two, consider getting a third. Apart from rain, each day a phenomenal amount of "grey water" is produced from a house, much of which could safely be used on plants.

Stands or legs are essential for butts.

Setting up

A full water butt is extremely heavy, so make sure that a new water butt is put on a very firm, level base and that it is not leaning against anything it shouldn't. Check the height of its stand carefully when you set it up – you need to be able to easily place and remove a watering can beneath the tap on the butt, and ideally have a level area on which you stand the can so that you can leave it to fill while you turn your back and get on with another quick job.

Filling your can

If it is not possible to position the butt adequately high off the ground for easy watering can filling, then use a short off-cut of garden hose attached to the end of the tap to allow you to fill the can a short distance from the butt.

Use a flexible hose for filling a watering can.

Stretching the pipe

Getting a piece of hose properly and firmly fixed to the tap can be a tricky job. Take a mug of boiling water out to the water butt, and plunge one end of the hose pipe into the water for about 30 seconds – but take care not to scald yourself. This softens the pipe and makes it much easier to stretch it over the tap. It then rapidly contracts to make a watertight fit.

Very hot water is needed for a tight fit.

Install a pump

If you have water butts quite far from the main areas needing the water, it is really useful to have a butt pump. This gives enough pressure for you to use a garden hose directly from the water butt. You can also siphon water into a container closer to the area that needs water.

Collect grey water

Water butts connected to roofs will only fill up when it rains, and that may well mean they are empty when it has not rained for a while, just when you need water most. Make sure you have at least one butt connected to the downpipe from the house so you can collect suitable "grey" water from the bath, hand basins, and the shower. The final rinse water from a washing machine may also be used, but water from earlier rinses, dishwashers, or any chemically softened source may contain contaminants.

Water with bath water

Try siphoning or pumping water directly out of the bath through a window and onto your garden if you do not have a suitable water butt connection.

Keeping the water in the butt clear

Fixing a piece of medium-gauge mesh over the end of the downpipe from a roof will help to dramatically reduce the quantity of larger contaminants, such as leaves, insects and twigs, getting into the butt. Make sure you remove the mesh regularly because it will soon clog up, especially during autumn and winter.

Use oil to avoid mosquitoes

If mosquito larvae start to appear in the water butt during warm weather, make sure the lid of the butt is firmly in position; this should help to reduce the number of eggs that can be laid in the water. A tiny quantity of plant oil, such as sunflower or olive oil, poured onto the surface of the water will form a very thin oily layer and should kill off the larvae before they hatch. Use as little as possible, and make sure you do not bail water out of the butt or else you will take the oil too. When the time comes to drain the butt, tip out the last bit (containing the oil) rather than letting it get into the tap.

Oil is a safe way to kill mosquito larvae, effectively by smothering.

Annual clear-out

From time to time you will need to empty out and thoroughly clean a water butt, otherwise algae will build up to such a level that you will be watering them onto your plants. Use a broom and some soapy water to reach the deeper areas at the base of the butt.

Water quality

Water collected in a butt may have picked up some bacterial or fungal contaminants on its journey from the roof to the watering can. Just in case, it is best to use stored water on more mature plants and those growing in open ground, not pots.

Fit more butts than downpipes

Fitting a good-sized water butt to a downpipe from the guttering on a house, shed, garage, conservatory, or greenhouse will give a great supply of water after rain. The amount collected after a heavy downpour can be considerable, so a single butt is likely to be filled to capacity quickly. Use connector pipes to link the first butt to an additional butt, and you can double the amount you collect.

Using water carefully

Whatever the size or style of your garden, you will need some water to maintain it, but water is a precious resource so you should try to avoid wasting it. Careful use of water does not mean your garden need suffer.

It's all about timing

Water evaporates rapidly if it hits a warm surface or is applied during hot, bright weather. In the warmer months, water your garden either in early evening once the soil has cooled (so that plant roots can take up the moisture before the conditions heat up the following day), or very early in the morning before the soil warms up (allowing the water to reach the roots before temperatures rise again).

How often?

It's better to water thoroughly but less frequently than to apply a little water more often. A good drenching soaks down to the plant roots, where it is needed, but a light sprinkling may only moisten the soil surface, not reaching roots and evaporating before the plant can benefit. If the upper soil is repeatedly soaked while the soil around the roots stays dry, the plant may start to produce roots near the surface, which are much more easily damaged.

Create a basin

If you create a slight dip or basin in the soil around the base of a plant, when you apply water it will run towards the plant and not away from it. Ideally do this at planting. Provided you take care not to damage the roots or risk them growing too close to the soil surface, you can create a shallow, yet efficient, basin around an established plant.

Water the plant base

Plants may be damaged by water on their leaves or petals, especially during hot weather, and many infections thrive on wet surfaces; wetting leaves also wastes water. Aim the end of the watering can or the hose directly at the base of the plants, beneath the foliage: you will avoid all the problems and the plants will enjoy all the benefits.

Water the roots, not the foliage for best results.

A pipe or even a deep pot helps you to get water to the roots.

Watering roots efficiently

A length of pipe close to the roots of a plant, with one end protruding above the surface, allows you to pour water down directly to the roots. After watering, cover the hole so that it cannot act as an escape route for soil moisture.

Avoiding run-off

If the soil has become very dry, there is a tendency for the water to run off the soil surface when it is finally wetted, by rain or by you. It is then lost to an area of the garden where is it not needed, or worse still, to a paved or similar area. You can prevent a lot of this run-off by simply wetting the soil surface slightly before wetting it thoroughly. Whether rain looks imminent after a dry spell, or you plan to do some watering, half an hour or so beforehand, gently wet the soil and far more water will then get through to where it is needed.

Efficient hosing

If your hose doesn't have a nozzle or gun – perhaps when hosing from a water butt – make a few sharp kinks in the hose if you have to do something else briefly while watering. Bending the hose double near the end and poking the kink into the mesh of a bit of chicken wire usually stops the flow – not as efficient as turning the tap off, but far better than leaving it.

Lawns and watering

❀ Don't panic if your lawn turns brown: most lawns are more tolerant of drought than it might appear. They usually recover completely under all but under extreme conditions.

❀ The tougher the lawn grasses are, the better they are at surviving drought, so try to avoid very fine and smart lawns.

❀ If a very dry lawn is suddenly watered or rained on, it is inclined to shed most of the water and little will reach the roots. Spike the surface with a garden fork before watering and a lot more water will get into the soil.

❀ If you allow your lawn to grow a little longer when there is a drought, the world won't fall apart. Far from it, the lawn will actually resist the adverse effects of drought better when not cut too short or too frequently.

❀ Letting the clippings remain on the surface of the lawn after mowing (provided they are not too long) will help during a drought, because they will act rather like a mulch and help to retain soil moisture.

Hosepipe nozzles

Invest in a nozzle or gun for the end of your hose, rather than watering with your thumb over the end. Make sure it either produces a range of sizes of droplet, and will cut off the water supply when not in use so that if you have to leave it for a moment it won't keep using water.

Sprinklers

Sprinklers may be an extremely easy way to water your garden, but they can also be extremely wasteful. If you are going to use one, either set an alarm to remind you to move it around frequently, or fit a timing device to the tap.

A lawn with longish grass survives dry spells better than a fine, close one.

Greener gardening methods

Greener gardening is not just about you altering some of your gardening methods and habits, but also about helping the garden to look after itself and, at the same time, make life easier for you.

Use native plants

It makes sense to shop locally as far as possible. Buying plants that have been grown locally, rather than imported from the other side of the world, is often not as difficult as you might think. Increasingly nurseries and garden centres are making it easier to see which plants are at least grown in this country.

Help plants to help themselves

Keeping your soil in good health, with plenty of natural nutrients from organic sources and a fair helping of naturally occurring soil micro-organisms, helps to keep plants robust. This makes them better able to cope with pests or infections, and if they do get damaged, plants that are basically healthy and vigorous are better equipped to produce plenty of replacement growth.

Work with nature

Try to resist the temptation to grow plants that will always struggle in the conditions you have to offer. They will be more prone to pest and pathogen attack, and hard to keep healthy.

Make room

Check your planting distances and stick to them. Plants that are crowded are likely to suffer competition, and many infections and pests thrive in overcrowded schemes.

This border will have looked sparse at first.

Move fast

Regular checks on plants allow you to catch problems early, do what it takes to stop them spreading, and often without there even being any need of any sort of remedy. If you find a problem, act promptly.

If you act fast you will beat pests more easily.

Green pruning

Secateurs can be a useful tool for green gardening. If you promptly prune out any problems such as cankers, they are easier to control, and if you routinely prune woody plants to keep them open-centred, they enjoy better air circulation and are less prone to problems.

Plant debris in your garden

Some advocates of greener gardening say that it is good to leave plenty of plant material around the garden to act as refuges for beneficial insects, while others say that these refuges will attract problems; I say use common sense. Only leave seemingly healthy twigs or foliage around the garden, and don't be too tidy – but if there is too much debris, yes, it can act as a perfect slug and snail hotel.

Fallen leaves can mulch earth, but may kill grass.

Choosing pots and planters

Try to go for non-plastic materials, or pots and planters made from recycled plastic. There is an increasing number of good-looking wooden, ceramic, and woven-stem planters available.

Larger pots can be expensive: be creative and try re-using other containers.

Recycle plant pots

Always save, clean, and then re-use plant pots and trays that you get from the garden centre. Cleaned out properly, there is no reason why they cannot be used again and again. If you find you build up an excessive quantity of them, then offer them to local fund-raising groups or schools who may need lots of pots for raising large numbers of plants.

Environmentally friendly wood

If you are buying wooden planters or furniture, fences or trellis, make sure that the wood is environmentally acceptable – various certification schemes exist, such as FSC, which means you can have wood and a clear conscience.

A plant isn't fussy about the origins of its pot: all it needs are drainage holes and a decent depth.

Use recycled materials

Wherever possible, try to use recycled materials in your garden – food containers for raising seedlings, plastic bottles as compost scoops or mini-cloches, clear plastic fruit punnets as miniature propagator tops, etc. Try to repair or refurbish garden furniture to keep it going that little bit longer.

Organic techniques

Whether you decide to become, or indeed already are, an organic gardener, there are plenty of techniques that are well worth using… and if the idea of being an organic gardener does not appeal, read on as you will still find the tips useful.

Rotate plants

Crop rotation makes great sense in the vegetable garden or plot (*see* page 119). Generally, ornamental plants are grown for more than one year, and some are pretty well permanent and cannot be rotated, but most of us grow at least some bulbs and corms, such as tulips or gladioli, that we lift, or use seasonal bedding plants. Try to make sure you put any one type of plant in a different spot each year. This makes it less likely that pests and pathogens, especially those that live in or on the soil, will build up to damaging levels. It also helps to reduce any nutrient imbalances that could occur if the same or closely related plants were grown on the same spot for many years in succession.

Grow resistant varieties

It is becoming increasingly easy to track down varieties of your favourite plants that show good resistance to certain problems. Check seed and plant catalogues each year because availability varies, and try to choose at least some of your plants on the basis of pest or disease resistance. Vegetable seed suppliers are especially helpful when it comes to making it clear which varieties are resistant to what, and are particularly useful for organic or green gardeners.

Planting and sowing times

Sometimes you can avoid a problem by taking care when you sow or plant. For example, early potatoes are much less likely to succumb to slugs, wire worm, or blight because they are generally out of the ground before these become most damaging. Similarly, later sowings of carrots rarely succumb to carrot fly.

Creating barriers

One of the best ways to prevent pest attack is to create a barrier to that pest, perhaps of netting, fleece, or very fine mesh, so it simply cannot get to the plant to lay eggs on it or eat it.

Barriers are excellent protection against certain insects, but some crops need insect pollination.

Position barriers early

If you are using barriers, they may not need to be in place at all times, but it is always best to get them in position a bit early. Seasonal variations can mean that pests or pathogens appear earlier than you expect them, or than the books suggest.

Repeat applications

Many organic sprays are less inclined to remain active for long once applied – this is obviously part of their appeal. Remember that this may mean that more frequent applications are necessary than if you were using a chemical spray.

To spray or not to spray

I prefer to avoid using any garden chemicals but some, such as those based on derris and copper, are regarded as acceptable for use by organic gardeners.

Although some of the sprays allowed by organic standards are highly toxic, they biodegrade quickly.

Many garden insecticide sprays will damage all insects; this includes the organic sprays.

Spraying time

Non-selective sprays can damage beneficial insects including bees and other pollinators. Always apply the treatment as directly as you can, and make sure that you spray at dusk or later, once most of the pollinating insects are no longer on the flowers.

Timing your pest control

The timing of any control measure is important, so make sure you are doing what is necessary at the right time. A spray may be organic, but it may have little if any effect if applied too early or too late, and in some instances may even cause harm.

Minimize damage

Green or organic gardening should mean that you have little need to use any sort of pest-control agent. If you do, those such as the sprays based on fatty acids or plant oils have a much lower impact both on harmless creatures and on the environment as a whole.

Biological controls and traps

These are perfect for the green gardener. Buying packets of mites or insects to release into your greenhouse might seem crazy, but these are predators or parasites of the pests that trouble you, and they act like guided missiles. Traps are also useful in the garden.

Check the instructions before applying.

Follow the instructions

When using biological controls it is just as important that you read and follow carefully the instructions as it is with chemicals. They may be green solutions, but they will not perform as they should if used incorrectly.

Sticky traps

Sticky traps can catch flying pests in large numbers. The colour yellow attracts insects, and some traps also carry a pheromone attractant.

Timing of controls

If you decide to use biological controls, bear in mind that being living creatures they need to be purchased and used promptly, so order them as soon as you see the first signs of the pest infestation starting up. Order them too early and before the pest arrives, and they will not survive, order them when the pest has already done a lot of damage and is in huge numbers, and you are giving them too much of an uphill battle.

Sticky traps help to control whitefly and thrips.

Controls in the greenhouse

Most biological controls available are for use against greenhouse pests. The protected greenhouse or conservatory environment means problems are quick to spiral out of control, but also allows you to use predators or parasites that need protected, warm conditions to thrive and sort out your pests.

Don't combine with pesticides

Biological-control predators and parasites are likely to be damaged by most pesticides. You should not use chemical controls at the same time, or for at least the last few weeks before introducing the biological controls. Some chemical pesticides have a much longer residual effect than others, so check with your biological control supplier.

Keep an eye on the overnight temperature.

Ideal temperatures

Most biological controls are temperature sensitive and need a minimum temperature of about 20°C (68°F) to perform well. Generally this is not too hard to achieve because the pests they control tend to become a problem only when temperatures are fairly warm.

Controls don't need control

Biological controls available to gardeners are very specific in their action. This means that there is no need to worry about, say, the parasitic wasp that has been introduced to control a pest such as whitefly. The wasp is only interested in whitefly: it will not attack anything else.

Range of controls

There is an ever-increasing range of biological controls available. They include controls for glasshouse whitefly, red spider mite, mealybug, aphids, some scale insects, thrips, vine weevil, slugs, chafers, and leatherjackets.

Preventing escape

Biological controls are generally pretty well-behaved and stay around the pest-infested area. There's therefore no need to worry about them walking off or flying out through the greenhouse vents. The one exception is the mealybug predator, *Cryptolaemus*, the adult beetle stage of which can fly off. Simply cover the plants on to which you have released it with fleece for a few days, to get it used to its new home.

An Australian ladybird (here the larvae) controls mealybugs.

The biological control mite used to control red spider mite is orange-red.

Sticky barriers

Grease bands are traditionally used around the trunks of fruit trees to prevent wintermoth caterpillars climbing them. They can also be put around pots to protect the plants in them; this will stop ants moving aphids onto the plants.

Composting your kitchen and garden waste

Compost bins or heaps are invaluable. By all means recycle some of your green waste via your local refuse collection service or tip, but if you want to do the best thing for your garden and the wider world, avoid transporting it, and compost at home.

Compost bin set-up

❀ Two or more separate bins means that one can be emptied while the other is being filled. It is much simpler and easier to make good compost this way.

❀ The bigger the bin the better: a capacity of 1 cubic metre (yard) is ideal.

Add animal manure

Compost activators help to add extra nitrogen to the composting material, so increasing the rate and extent to which it is broken down. Adding some fairly fresh animal manure (such as horse, cow, pig, or sheep) will have the desired effect.

Use a good mix of soft and woody matter.

Bacteria, fungi, and soil organisms cause decay.

This may take months to achieve, but it is worth it.

Use organic manure

If you want to be truly green, consider the origins of the manure you use in your garden, and avoid anything that is not from organic farms. You can of course cut back on transport of this too, and use material from a pet rabbit's hutch, or from local chickens or geese.

Keep adding, keep turning

Add fresh plant matter, dry woody materials, and scrunched up paper in roughly even quantities regularly. Turn the heap often with a border fork and add water if it looks dry.

Composting grass clippings

If you have a lot of grass clipping from your lawn, it is generally impossible to add them all to the compost in one go (unless of course you have a huge composting system). Add what you can and save a bag or two for later, or consider making a separate bin for grass clippings. You can help this to compost down with the use of an activator formulated especially for use on grass clippings – ordinary activators are not suitable.

Heap maintenance

Organic matter will not break down readily if the heap becomes either too wet or too dry. Aim to keep it just moist, and if possible use a bit of old carpet or a blanket to keep the heap a bit warmer during the winter and between turning it.

Too much grass added to a mixed heap in one go can turn slimy.

The bacteria that start the composting process like to be warm and moist, but not too wet.

Layer compost material

It is best to add material to the heap in layers. Never use too much of any one type of material in one go and, ideally, alternate layers of drier material with moister, greener ingredients. You may get away without turning!

What to compost, what not

If you want to include old jumpers, fabric or carpet in your composting system, make sure that they contain no artificial fibres, just cotton, linen, other plant-based materials, and wool. Chop up this type of material thoroughly before adding it to the heap, and ensure that you have plenty of fresh, moist garden ingredients to hand. Avoid using meat scraps in your compost heap. They will attract vermin.

Lighting & design

You may not have thought about using lighting in your garden, but it can make a real difference. There are four main reasons why you might want to consider adding light to a garden: security, practicality, safety, and decoration.

If you have bright security lights that switch on when the sensor detects movement, always make sure that there is an override on the PIR switch; this allows you to switch them off when you want to sit out in the garden after dark and use other, more subtle lighting methods.

Lighting your garden

The range of garden lighting is far greater today than ever before, with everything from small solar-powered lights to elaborate systems that require professional installation. Generally, softer lighting is perfect for that outdoor room effect, and stronger, more directional lighting works better for producing dramatic, artistic effects. It is worth looking at catalogues from a few garden lighting specialists and checking out some night-lit gardens before you start.

Design inspiration

You can also enhance your garden by modifying its design. You may have had the same garden design for years or you may be working with a new garden. Whatever your raw materials, you do not have to completely overhaul the design. Whether you want to build a new arch to make use of the verticals or install a few new plants to make your beds look bigger – in this chapter you will find small tweaks you can apply that will make the world of difference.

This chapter shows you how to:

❀ Light your garden in an attractive yet practical way.

❀ Get inspiration and ideas for changing your garden's design and layout.

❀ Change the look of your garden by working on the vertical with arches, supported climbers, and trees.

❀ Transform your plot with optical illusions and tricks of the eye.

Lighting the garden

Not every garden or gardener benefits from, or aspires to, garden lighting but it is worth looking into. When used skilfully it can do great things for gardens from the tiniest backyard to the most elaborate country estate.

Small fittings with LED bulbs are ideal for lighting decks, and are widely available in kit form.

Low glow

To make steps safer you can either install specially designed lights into the tread of the steps when they are constructed, or position attractive low-level, low-voltage lights either side of the flight of steps.

Practical lighting

Use lighting to make it easier and safer to access the far end of your garden, or to illuminate your terrace or patio for that late-evening glass of wine or barbecue.

Simple solutions

If you want a very quick and low-cost lighting solution in your garden, simply suspend a light from a sturdy tree branch, from which it can cast delicate shadows on the ground or plants beneath. Your light could be as simple as a tea-light in a clear glass container, or a storm lantern, or a self-contained solar-powered light.

Special effects

Lighting can create beautiful and dramatic effects that you can enjoy both when outside and from inside the house. Try out different lighting positions with a powerful torch to cast shadows, highlight the textured bark of an old tree, or make the most of a wonderful branch system.

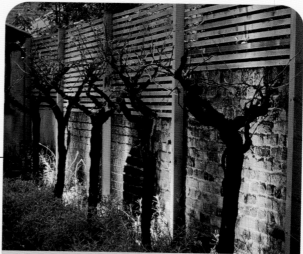

Ground-level lights behind the trees throw them into silhouette against the textured wall.

For maximum impact, spotlight only one or two objects.

Highlight textures

A beam of light positioned close to the ground so that it shines up the trunk of a tree or wall will illuminate the textures. The effect this produces looks particularly good on trees with peeling, patchy, or patterned bark, such as many of the eucalyptus or *Prunus* trees, or snakebark maples (*Acer*).

Think theatrically

A spotlight or two will make a great statement lighting up a favourite planter, urn, statue, or plant. Position the light at the side or from the base of the feature and you should create some really dramatic shadows. Be careful with brighter lights – several carefully positioned lights always produce a more attractive effect than just one or two extremely bright ones.

Ambient lighting

On a terrace, patio, or barbecue area, provide subtle lighting using globe lights, or perhaps even a few strings of outdoor white fairy lights draped around a nearby wall, arbour, arch, or pergola, or through the branches of an adjacent tree. You'll be able to see what you're doing or what you're eating, and it'll be a lot safer too.

Low voltage is safest

There are many attractive low-voltage and easy-to-install kits available that you can set up and position yourself. It goes without saying that when dealing with electricity you need to take great care: only use equipment sold specifically for outdoor use, and follow any installation and safety advice closely. For a more elaborate lighting system, it is best to employ a specialist garden lighting firm to install it.

Underwater lighting provides glow without glare.

Lighting water

Lights can produce fantastic effects in ponds, fountains, or other water features, adding a truly magical air to your evenings in the garden. You will need special underwater lights, but that extra expense is well worthwhile.

There are many solar light designs, but low-level path lights are perhaps the most useful.

Eternal sunshine

The range of solar-powered garden lights is constantly increasing and there are several different sorts available. Some you can float in a pond, others are suspended or simply pushed into the ground close to paths and steps, or amongst your plants, and some have larger, separate solar collectors for more power. All of them absorb energy from the sunlight during the day and then illuminate your garden at night – not the brightest of lights, but good for subtle effects.

Charging up

Most solar lights last longer and perform better if you run them down completely and then allow them to receive a full charge from the sun (or even artificial light), usually for 16 hours or so, but check the instructions for precise details. If you do this before the first use, and occasionally after, the life of the battery is greater.

Solar lights stand alone

Solar-powered garden lighting is well worth considering. It has particular appeal because the lights need no specialist installation work and there are effectively no running costs.

Switch to the professionals

For installation of any lighting other than a complete low-voltage kit, you will need to employ a registered contractor or notify the building authorities.

Catching the rays

Most solar garden lights have obvious solar panels on them, ensure that they are able to produce as much light as possible. Always position the light so that the panel is in full sun for as much of the day as possible.

Be a good neighbour

❀ Don't fill your garden with constant bright lights that blind your neighbours and the wildlife: only switch the lights on when you need them, or use PIR switches.

❀ To avoid light pollution, choose lights that shine down, and don't leave dramatic uplighting on all night.

❀ If you want dusk-to-dawn security lights, use low-energy bulbs or low-voltage systems and aim the lights down. Save brighter lights for PIR switching.

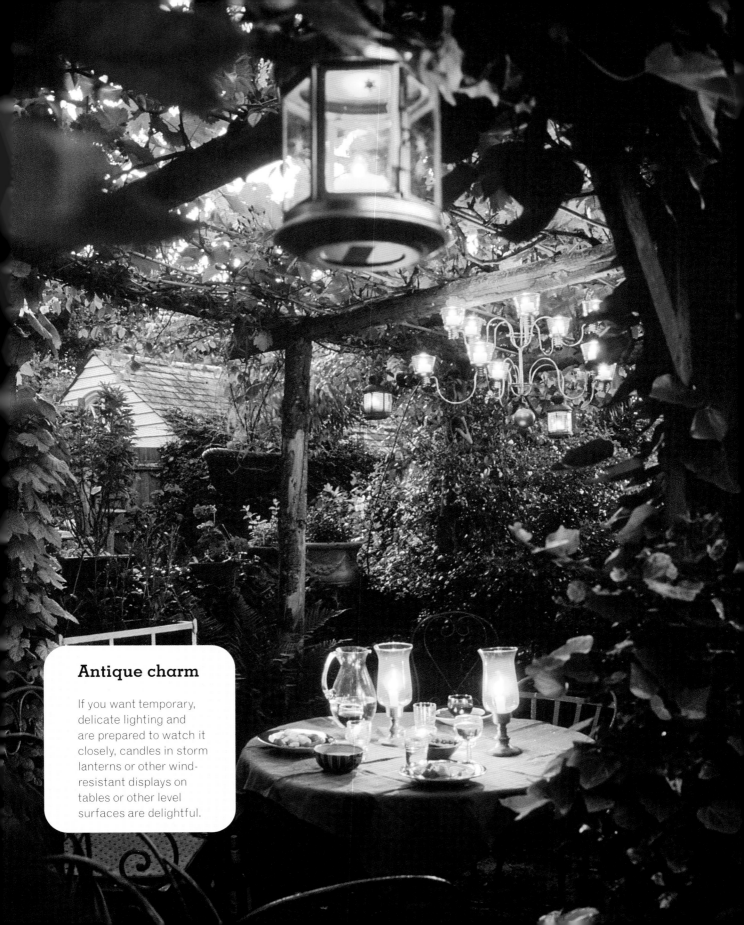

Antique charm

If you want temporary, delicate lighting and are prepared to watch it closely, candles in storm lanterns or other wind-resistant displays on tables or other level surfaces are delightful.

Design inspiration

The garden of your dreams is very much a personal thing and how you want it to look is up to you, but especially if you're starting from scratch, here are some design ideas and effects that are well worth considering.

Plan your priorities

Whether you are faced with the totally blank canvas of a completely unplanted patch of soil, or you just want to make a few changes and improvements, it is worth sitting down with a bit of paper – ideally larger rather than smaller – and making a list of exactly what you are trying to achieve or improve. On the rest of the paper, sketch out the rough shape of the garden and do some designing. Use smaller pieces of marked paper to represent any movable features.

Small change, big effect

You can make a garden appear quite different by simply altering the size or shape (or both) of the lawn. If you remove an area of turf carefully, it is quite possible to re-use it in another part of the lawn, and this also means you will not need to go to the trouble of trying to match in newly bought turf with the old.

Not set in stone

Altering the size or shape of a terrace or patio also dramatically alters a garden. The slabs can always be re-used, perhaps to turn a boring, static square into a more interesting shape. You can even move a patio entirely.

Enclosing your garden

If some parts of your garden are unappealing because of an ugly view or because a neighbour's windows overlook them, leaving no privacy, try altering your boundaries.

❀ Consider installing a higher boundary fence or growing a taller hedge. There may be restrictions that limit the height of the boundary, so it is advisable to check with your local planning department, just in case.

❀ If you already have a perfectly good boundary but it is simply too low, it is worth considering adding trellis to the top of it. Trellis panels are relatively inexpensive and are easily added on top of an existing fence.

Trellis panels taller than your fence refresh the design while adding height.

If a shed is on a boundary, perhaps a little negotiation could see it wreathed in climbers.

Hiding small eyesores

If there is an unsightly view that is only visible from one area or an object that is relatively small, such as a neighbour's garage, shed, or climbing frame, then you may be able to block it out using some additional planting. You can use trees to either totally block out an eyesore, or perhaps to break up the view of the eyesore so that it feels less intrusive.

Disguising necessary evils

Arches, pergolas, and screens planted with attractive climbers will add interest to your garden, and can also be used to obscure eyesores beyond or within your own plot.

Use visual aids

When planning where to put up any fence, trellis, arbour, or pergola, take a post or even a bamboo cane the same height as the proposed installation and position it in the intended place. This will make it much easier to get an accurate picture of whether your idea will actually work.

Look from all angles

Always check that what you do or don't want to see in the garden is visible or hidden from all the necessary angles and heights. Stand and look from various different positions in the garden, and from several windows in your house, even the upstairs if necessary.

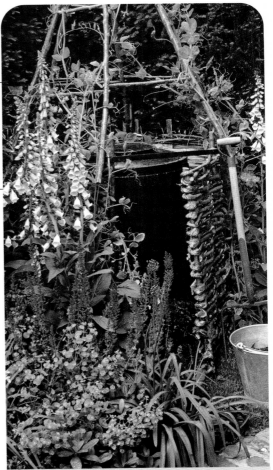

Train plants over items like compost bins – as long as you still get access.

Research problem gardens

If your garden is one of those so-called "problem" types, perhaps suffering the effects of being coastal, windy, dry, or very damp, go and look at gardens open to the public that have similar problems to see how they solve them. It is worth taking a look over neighbouring gardens too, and always remember to take a note-book and pen.

List the pros and cons

When overhauling a garden, methodically list all the things you like about it, and everything that's less appealing. You may find all you want to keep is one fantastic tree – or that really all your problems are caused by one overgrown tree that is casting excess shade and taking all the goodness from the soil. Remember that the appearance and impact of some features will change with the changing seasons.

Coastal gardens suffer wind and salt, but their mild climate gives new opportunities.

Consider sun and shade

Plot the areas of sun and shade, and of light shade and deep shade, at key times of day throughout the year. Not just at noon, or your seating area may be dark and cool when you want an evening drink. Remember, if you go out to work, you can spend seven evenings in the garden each week, but only two lunchtimes.

Don't rush in

In a new garden, you should ideally wait at least a full year before overhauling it so that you can see what comes up – many great secrets are often revealed. Just clear obvious weeds to ensure that those potentially wonderful hidden plants are able to appear in their full glory.

Get the style right

Look at your house and any other existing, immovable features when thinking about your design – classic lawns and flowerbeds look good with most styles, but a strongly Mediterranean style with lots of mosaics inspired by a holiday visit may look really strange around a mellow stone cottage.

Do some climate research

Really research your local climate if you are in a new area or thinking of a totally new planting. Find a local weather station on the web and look at the seasonal averages of temperature, sunshine, and rainfall to find out just how hardy the plants need to be. These are much better than zone maps in books, which usually don't have that level of detail.

Reaching new heights

A garden that is just on one level may seem a bit flat and unexciting, so it is always worth trying to add some height to your plot. The site may be level, but you can create interesting effects by introducing vertical structures and plantings.

A structure's appeal increases as plants grow over it.

Instant height

Erecting an arch or arbour can totally transform a garden, especially once planted up. It need not be huge if space is short; anything will help.

Trees increase the volume of plant material, and are valuable to wildlife.

A quick and inexpensive way to raise your sights.

Simple supports

In a tiny plot, a wigwam of canes clothed in annual climbers, such as sweet peas (*Lathyrus*), can produce the desired effect and need not cost much – just a handful of canes and some sweet pea seeds.

Living structure

A specimen tree can have a huge effect, acting as a focal point while adding height at the same time. Choose something with real impact and ideally with more than one season of interest – offering, say, autumn colour and good-looking bark, or spring blossom followed by fruits later in the year.

249

Tricks to transform your plot

The garden you have in front of you may seem to have certain unavoidable – and perhaps some unappealing – features, but with thought, planning, and some careful planting, you can often make it look quite different.

Trick the eye

If the garden is not as long as you'd like it to be, you can transform how long it seems with some careful planning. Create a path that tapers, gradually becoming narrower as it gets further from the house. You can then exaggerate the effect even further by planting up the sides of the path with shrubs or trees that are progressively shorter the further they are from the house. Add the final deceptive touch by planting up two containers, each of the same design and with the same types of plants in it, but one much smaller than the other. By installing the smaller one in the distance, and the larger one in foreground, the illusion is complete.

Creative cutting

If your short garden already has a hedge in it, try creating a clear but gentle slope on top of it, trimming the hedge so that you take more off the height at the far end, and less off the end close to the house.

Stealing beauty

A small garden can be made to seem larger if you allow it to make use of any views that surround it. If you are lucky enough to have a garden that overlooks fields, hills, or woodland for example, then make sure that you can see these wonderful views from within the garden itself, not just from the upstairs windows.

Distant glimpses or vistas can blur your boundaries.

Window on the world

A frame emphasizes any view.

If you feel you need higher fences for wind protection, you can still enjoy distant views. Create a circular aperture, often known as a moon-gate, in a hedge or a wall, or simply make sure that part of your fence overlooking the view is quite low.

Reflected glory

A carefully installed mirror, positioned at the end of a walkway or alcove, will reflect back a view of your garden, making it appear as if the garden extends much further into the distance. To make the mirror most effective, allow plants growing near or next to it, to encroach over the edges slightly.

Dividing the view

Sometimes dividing a garden into separate "rooms" or areas, ideally each with a different feel or atmosphere, will help to make a garden seem larger. This works especially well if you ensure that you cannot see all areas of the garden from any single location.

Blurring the boundaries

Rather than making solid screens within a garden, use living boundaries, perhaps consisting of loosely planted hedging or a line of bamboos, so that you can see through them to some extent, without getting a complete or too-clear view of the other "rooms".

Bamboo makes an excellent semi-transparent screen.

Sweet peas provide an eye-catching and beautifully scented divider.

Pale but significant

By including plenty of plants with pale or pastel-coloured foliage or flowers, you help to increase the apparent size of a bed or border.

Climbing coverage

Trellis panels planted with climbers make good internal dividers. Use lightweight climbers such as jasmine and sweet peas (*Lathyrus*).

An elegant combination of foxgloves and daisies.

Plants with big impact

If a flowerbed or border is smaller than you would like, try growing plants that have particularly striking foliage colours or shapes towards the front of the border – the back will then seem to recede.

Repeating plants or featuring striking colours at the front makes a bed feel bigger.

Index

Acknowledgments

The publishers would like to thank to all who have contributed to this book.

Special thanks to Pippa Greenwood for her time, energy, and enthusiasm.

All photographs have been taken by Torie Chugg for Octopus Publishing Group with the exception of the following.

Key: b bottom, c centre, l left, r right, t top

Alamy: Angela Jordan 47t, blickwinkel 237cr, Brian Hoffman 56b, Carole Hewer 237t, Garden World Images Ltd 4 cl, 60b, 144bc, 220r, Holmes Garden Photos 148, Natural Visions 99c, Nordicphotos 231, WoodyStock 215cr

Andrew Lawson: 46tl, 251cl, Chilcombe House, Dorset 110, Design: Carol Klein/Glebe Cottage 28, Design: Rosemary Verey/Barnsley House 87, Manoir aux Quat' Saisons 25t, Torie Chugg 216b

Clive Nichols: 83b, Denmans, Sussex 249cr, Design: Cartier/RHS Chelsea Flower Show 1998 247b, Design: Claire Mee 242b, Design: Claire Warnock & Rachel Watts 233tr, Design: Jacquie Gordon/RHS Chelsea Flower Show 1999 249cl, Design: Joe Swift 240, Design: R Golby/RHS Chelsea Flower Show 1995 232r, Design: Ruth Chivers 55, Garden & Security Lighting 242t, Greenhurst Garden, Sussex 76t, Launa Slatter, Oxon 52cr, Pettifers, Oxon 15cr, The Nichols Garden, Reading 243t, The Old School House, Essex 53b

Construction Photography: 168r

Derek St Romaine: 63b, 97, Mr & Mrs Hickman, Thames Ditton, UK 106l

DK Images: Dave King 236r, Mark Winwood 48cr, Peter Anderson 146cr, Steve Hamilton 143b,188, 199t

FLPA: A & L Detrick 19cl, Angela Hampton 227t, J van Arkel/Foto Natura 151b, Nigel Cattlin 99l, 135t, 217 b, 223c, 237bl, Wayne Hutchinson 236l

Gap Photos: Amanda Darcy 62b, 112b, Andrea Jones 31tl, Brian North 222l, Clive Nichols 142t, Clive Nichols/Pettifers, Oxon 64, Elke Borkowski 37cr, 38tl, 243b, FhF Greenmedia 86bl, 93t, 115b, 129b, 137l, Friedrich Strauss 51b, 52t, 66bl, 76c, Geoff Kidd 221cl, Howard Rice 81b, 88l, J S Sira/Design: Conran 131cl, Janet Johnson 89t, 127r, 186b, Jerry Harpur 161, Jerry Harpur/Design: Stephen Anderton 44, John Glover 33c, 37cl, 83t, 149cr, 226r, 245, John Glover/Design: Barbara Hunt 30l, John Glover/Design: Marnie Hall 227b, Jonathan Buckley 41r, 203b, Jonathan Buckley/Design: Carol & Malcolm Skinner 92l, Jonathan Buckley/Design: Simon Hopkinson, Hollington Herb Nursery 249bc, Juliette Wade 136l, 144tl, 144cr, Leigh Clapp 113c, Leigh Clapp/Spurfold Garden, Surrey 147cr, M Howes 89b, 160r, 175cl, 187b, 195c, 230r, Mark Bolton 24t, 75t, 145t, Mark Bolton/Design: Kate Frey/RHS Chelsea Flower Show 2005 150br, Mark Bolton/Sir Michael & Lady Angus 127l, Paul Debois 58b, Rice/Buckland 40tl, 54c, 138r, 204l, Richard Bloom 88cr, Richard Bloom/Keith Lewis's Garden, Surrey 224, Richard Bloom/The Elisabeth C. Miller Botanical Garden, Seattle 176r, Sarah Cuttle 147b, Suzie Gibbons/Design: Kathy Taylor 246, Visions 235l, Zara Napier 108b, 239r

Photolibrary/Garden Picture Library: Alec Scaresbrook 49, 149tl, Anne Green Armytage 16cl, Bill Beatty 217t, Botanica 84bl, 113t, Christopher Gallager 114l, David Cavagnaro 118l, Eric Crichton/RHS Chelsea Flower Show 1994 17cl, Flora Press 48bl, Francois de Heel 129t, 151tr, Friedrich Strauss 41l, 48br, 60t, Georgia Glynn Smith 180t, Howard Rice 54bl, 115b, 139r, 143t, Jacqui Hurst 136r, James Guilliam 126r, Jane Legate 96l, 155cl, John Beedle 77, John Glover/Design: Sarah Raven/RHS Chelsea Flower Show 1998 140, John Swithinbank 211cl, Juliette Wade 95b, 239l, Linda Burgess 49br, Lynne Brotchie 78, Mike Howes 125, 131tr, Marie O'Hara 101b, 150t, Mark Bolton 164l, 248, Mark Bolton/Design: Stephen Hall/RHS Chelsea Flower Show 2005 156, Mark Winwood 165tr, 167, 178t, Mayer Le Scanff 115t, Rice/Buckland 210bl, Ron Evans 33t, Rosalind Wickham 61br, Steve Hamilton 105br, Susie Mccaffrey 137r, Zara McCalmont 39cl

Garden World Images: 7t, 22bl, A Graham 109r, Botanic Images Inc. 82bl, C Fairweather 166l, D Bevan 56t, 68t, F Davis 59l, 151cl, J Dracup 96c, 128r, 185tl, J Swithinbank 40b, 46bl, 82t, 124, L Cole 126l, 222r, M Fry 166cr, N Astley 114b, N Bell 145b, P Smith 146cl, T McGlinchey 47r, 49r, 57b, 93b, 95cr, 142bl, 154l, 159t, 159b, 160l, 162r, 163l, 163r, 166tr, 170c, T Cooper 155t, T Sims 76b, 100r

istockphoto.com: Stacey McRae 82br

Mel Watson: 85

Modeste Herwig: 61t

Neil Soderstrom: 31cr, 43br, 73tr, 73cr, 77cl, 181r, 205t, 210t

Octopus Publishing Group Limited: Lee Beel 185bl & cr

Photoshot/Photos Horticultural: 61bl, 80t, 81t, 84cr, 119r, 134t, 179, 181b, M Howes 200

Science Photo Library: Brian Gadsby 184cl

Shutterstock: 75b, 202cl, 14, A & S Aakjaer 100l, Alan Egginton 175tr, Aleksandar-Pal Sakala 51t, Anna Dickie 52cl, Brandon Blinkenberg 182l, Chrislofoto 22br, 27t, Christina Richards 74r, 117tr, deetone 9, Eugene Bochkarev 54t, Fotosav 117b, Graca Victoria 22t, Ilya D Gridnev 66r, Jeff Banke 73l, Jeff Gynane 19tr, Jerry Horbert 250l, Joanna Zopoth-Liliejko 219tr, Kanwarjit Singh Boparai 202tl, Lars Magnin 2, Malle 15cl, 42l, Mark Bolton 63t, N Joy Neish 62t, Niserin 104l, Norma Cornes 34, Phil Morley 219cl, ppl 162l, Richard a McGuirk 105tr, rossco 10, Sally Wallis 120, Sharon D 17br, Sharon Kennedy 150bl, Sony Ho 26bl, Stephen Finn 101tl, Steve Lovegrove 112t, Steve Simzer 101tr, The Supe87 244, Thomas & Amelia Takacs 23cl, V J Matthew 32tr, Vasyl Helevachuk 211b, Vera Bogaerts 50l, 107, Zaporozhchenko Yury 74l

The Garden Collection: Andrew Lawson 251cr, Derek Harris 106r, Derek St Romaine 172, Gary Rogers/Design: Alex Daley & Alice Devaney. RHS Tatton Park 2005 165c, Jane Sebire 165b, Jonathan Buckley/Design: Alison Hoghton & David Chase 90, Jonathan Buckley/Design: Anthony Goff, Spencer Road, London 164cr, Jonathan Buckley/Design: C Lloyd, Great Dixter 33bl, Jonathan Buckley/Design: Roger Oates 212, Jonathan Buckley/Design: Stephen Firth & Brinsbury Students 26tl, Liz Eddison 19br, 96br, 158r, Liz Eddison/Design: C Beardshaw/RHS Chelsea Flower Show 2002 153, Liz Eddison/Design: Kate Rayner, RHS Tatton Park 2001 12, Liz Eddison/Design: Kay Yamada/RHS Chelsea Flower Show 2003 247t, Liz Eddison/Design: Luc Larmor/International Festival of Gardens, Chaumont-Sur-Loire 2005 251tr, Liz Eddison/Design: Thomas Hoblyn/RHS Tatton Park Show 2006 170t, Marie O'Hara 154cr, 174cl, Nicola Stocken Tomkins 35, 119b, 178b, 250r, 251bl, Torie Chugg/Design: Sue Hitchens 59r

Thompson & Morgan: 135br

Torie Chugg: 86r, 174r, 176l, 182br, 183l, 184r, 186t

Author acknowledgments:

Pippa Greenwood would like to thank Chris and his staff at Hilliers Garden Centre, Liss, where many of the photographs were taken, all at Mitchell Beazley for their wide-ranging input, and her family and friends for their inspiration, patience, and props borrowed.